China Since 1949

China Since 1949

Second edition

Linda Benson

Routledge
Taylor & Francis Group

LONDON AND NEW YORK

First published 2002 by Pearson Education Limited
Second edition 2011

Published 2013 by Routledge
2 Park Square, Milton Park, Abingdon, Oxon OX14 4RN
711 Third Avenue, New York, NY 10017, USA

Routledge is an imprint of the Taylor & Francis Group, an informa business

ISBN 978-1-4082-3769-4 (pbk)

British Library Cataloguing in Publication Data
A CIP catalogue record for this book can be obtained from the British Library

Library of Congress Cataloging-in-Publication Data
Benson, Linda.
    China since 1949 / Linda Benson. – 2nd ed.
       p. cm.
    Includes bibliographical references and index.
    ISBN 978-1-4082-3769-4 (pbk.)
1. China—History—1949–   I. Title.
    DS777.55.B416 2011
    951.05–dc22
                          2010045105

Set in 10/13.5pt Berkeley Book by 35
Printed and bound in the United States of America by
Edwards Brothers Malloy on sustainably sourced paper

Introduction to the series

History is narrative constructed by historians from traces left by the past. Historical enquiry is often driven by contemporary issues and, in consequence, historical narratives are constantly reconsidered, reconstructed and reshaped. The fact that different historians have different perspectives on issues means that there is also often controversy and no universally agreed version of past events. *Seminar Studies in History* was designed to bridge the gap between current research and debate, and the broad, popular general surveys that often date rapidly.

The volumes in the series are written by historians who are not only familiar with the latest research and current debates concerning their topic, but who have themselves contributed to our understanding of the subject. The books are intended to provide the reader with a clear introduction to a major topic in history. They provide both a narrative of events and a critical analysis of contemporary interpretations. They include the kinds of tools generally omitted from specialist monographs: a chronology of events, a glossary of terms and brief biographies of 'who's who'. They also include bibliographical essays in order to guide students to the literature on various aspects of the subject. Students and teachers alike will find that the selection of documents will stimulate discussion and offer insight into the raw materials used by historians in their attempt to understand the past.

Clive Emsley and Gordon Martel
Series Editors

Contents

Publisher's acknowledgements

We are grateful to the following for permission to reproduce copyright material:

Documents

Document 1 from *Women, the Family and Peasant Revolution in China*, University of Chicago Press (Kay Ann Johnson 1983) pp. 235–9; Document 8 reprinted with the permission of the Free Press, a Division of Simon & Schuster, Inc., from CHINESE CIVILIZATION: A Sourcebook, Second Edition, Revised & Expanded by Patricia Buckley Ebrey. Copyright © 1993 by Patricia Buckley Ebrey. Copyright © 1981 by the Free Press. All rights reserved; Document 10 from CHINA READER, VOL. 4 by Nancy Milton and Franz Schurmann, David Milton, copyright © 1974 by David Milton, Nancy Milton & Franz Schurmann. Used by permission of Vintage Books, a division of Random House, Inc.; Document 13 from BRINGING DOWN THE GREAT WALL by Fang Lizhi, translated by J. Williams, copyright © 1991 by Fang Lizhi. Used by permission of Alfred A. Knopf, a division of Random House, Inc.; Document 15 from Selling the Burden, *Far Eastern Economic Review,* 18/2/1999, pp. 15–16 (Susan V Lawrence), © Dow Jones and Company, Inc.; Document 19 from The New Superpower: China's Emerging Middle Class, *Adweek*, pp. 1–3, 5 (Noreen O'Leary). Adweek article used with permission of e5 Global Media, LLC; Document 23 from Part Traditionalist, Part Naturalist, Part Dissident by Dorothy Spears, *The New York Times*, © 21/02/2010, p. 32. The New York Times All rights reserved. Used by permission and protected by the Copyright Laws of the United States. The printing, copying, redistribution, or retransmission of the Material without express written permission is prohibited; Document 25 from Nationalist Fervor Runs Amok, *Globe and Mail*, 24/10/2004 (Geoffrey York); Document 29 from Diplomacy of the Dollar, *Far Eastern Economic Review*, 10/5/2001, pp. 16–17 (Bruce Gilley and Murray Hiebert) © Dow Jones and Company, Inc.; Document 32 from Blueprints for War or Peace in Future China-Taiwan Relations: Two Important Documents, *Asian Affairs: An American Review*, 31:3, 154–155, 156–162 (Chai Winberg 2004), © Taylor & Francis.

Picture credits

The publisher would like to thank the following for their kind permission to reproduce their photographs:

Plate 2 © Corbis/Swim Ink; Plate 3 © Getty Images/Agence France Presse/Archive Photos; Plate 4 © Getty Images/Keystone/Hulton Archive; Plate 5 © Corbis/XinHua/Xinhua Press; Plate 6 © Press Association Images/Gouhier-Hahn-Nebinger/ABACA; Plate 8 © Press Association Images/John Giles/PA Archive; Plate 10 © Robert Harding World Imagery/Jochen Schlenker.

All other images are the author's own.

In some instances we have been unable to trace the owners of copyright material, and we would appreciate any information that would enable us to do so.

Author's acknowledgements

It is a pleasure to acknowledge and thank the many colleagues and friends who have helped me over the years to understand the dramatic changes that have taken place in China since 1949. Although too numerous to mention individually their collective wisdom and scholarly endeavours remain a source of inspiration. Special thanks are due to the series editor, Gordon Martel, whose patience as I revised my 'final' drafts was much appreciated, and to Colin Mackerras who suggested that I write the book in the first place. To all of those at Pearson Education who worked on the final editing and production of the book, I also extend my sincere thanks.

Many of my students in introductory and advanced courses on China played a part greater than they may ever know in helping to frame some of the discussion in the text. Former students who have gone on to work, travel and study in China have also contributed by letting me share, via e-mail, in their personal discovery of an Asia much changed from my own first experiences there.

I also gratefully acknowledge the loving support of my family; my parents, Ben and Margaret Benson; my sister Nancy; my brother Douglas, and sister-in-law Dorothy Wu Ching-song. I take special pride in my nieces, Julia and Jessica, and my nephew, Eric, all of whom share Asian roots.

My husband, David Maines, provides me with daily doses of support and inspiration. He has also brought into my life his own wonderful family, including our grandchildren, Ellen and David. We not only take pride in them and our nieces and nephews, but also – whether we deserve to or not – in all the young people and their parents who have populated our lives and, from time to time, our house: Lizzy, Hanah, Matthew, Luke, Jesse, Kamran, Qian, Karima, Omar, Abbas and Faith. This new generation of scholars, adventurers and entrepreneurs will, hopefully, share a world in which young people in China and the United States are free to shape their own new routes to international friendship and understanding.

A note on romanization and pronunciation of Chinese words

Chinese terms, names and places in this book are romanized according to the *pinyin* system which has generally replaced the earlier form (Wade–Giles). Therefore, the older spellings of *Peking*, *Chiang Kai-shek* and *Mao Tse-tung* appear in these pages as Beijing, Jiang Jieshi and Mao Zedong.

For English speakers, the new form has the advantage of being easier to read and pronounce because the sound of most consonants and vowels is close to the corresponding English letter, with some exceptions, listed below.

c = a combination of z and s
q = ch
x = sh
zh = j as in Joe

Chronology

1949

10 January   Final battle between the Chinese Communist Party (CCP) and the Nationalists ends in victory for the CCP

September   Chinese People's Political Consultative Conference (CPPCC) convenes in Beijing to pass the Common Program

1 October   Mao declares the establishment of the People's Republic of China (PRC); 1 October becomes China's National Day

1950

February   Mao and Stalin sign the Treaty of Alliance and Friendship

April   New Marriage Law is announced

June   North Korea invades South Korea

Land reform begins in rural China

October   UN troops drive into North Korea toward the Chinese border

Chinese troops enter Tibet

November   North Korean and Chinese troops force UN troops back into southern Korea

1951

April   Douglas MacArthur is recalled from Korea; ceasefire discussions result in an agreement but fighting continues

The 17-Point Agreement between Tibet and China is signed

1953

January   China's First Five Year Plan begins

February   Plans to begin the first mutual aid teams are announced

July   Truce is signed between North and South Korea

1954

September   China's first constitution is promulgated

1955

November   Membership in Agricultural Producers Cooperatives reaches 41% of peasant-farmers

1956

September   Eighth National People's Congress meets for the first time in 11 years; total CCP membership reaches 10.7 million

December   Membership of peasant-farmers in Agricultural Producers Cooperatives reaches 96%

1957

April–May   The '100 Flowers' Campaign, to encourage discussion of policies and implementation since 1949, begins

June–August   The Anti-Rightist Campaign is launched against those critical of the CCP in the '100 Flowers' Campaign

1958

May   The Great Leap Forward is formally adopted; communes form in rural areas of China

1959

March   Tibetan revolt; Dalai Lama flees Tibet; both sides abrogate the 17-Point Agreement

April   Liu Shaoqi replaces Mao as China's head of state

June   Khrushchev withdraws Soviet support and criticizes Mao's plans for the Great Leap Forward, deepening the split between the two Communist states and leading to the withdrawal of Soviet advisers

July   CCP leadership meets at Lushan to discuss the Great Leap policies; Mao's criticism of Peng Dehuai leads to the latter being ousted from all positions of power

The 'three bitter years' begin as shortages in rural and urban China become apparent

1962

May	Extreme deprivation leads over 100,000 Kazaks and Uighurs to flee Xinjiang for the USSR
August	Mao calls for 'rectification' to rebuild the CCP and launches what becomes known as the Socialist Education Campaign

1966

February	Mao's wife, Jiang Qing, becomes cultural adviser to the military and forms a political alliance with Lin Biao
July	Mao swims in the Yangzi River in his first public appearance in many months
August	Mao calls for a 'cultural revolution' and launches the Great Proletarian Cultural Revolution
	Thousands of young Red Guards visit Beijing to glimpse Mao
October	Attacks in the Chinese press against unnamed 'capitalist roaders'
	Wallposters denounce cadres accused of being against the revolution; violence in China escalates

1967

August	Beginning in August and lasting through to July 1968, revolutionary committees are formed to replace regular governments at all levels
	Violence continues

1969

April	The CCP Central Committee declares the Cultural Revolution to be a great success; Liu Shaoqi is officially dismissed from all posts and expelled from the CCP; Lin Biao is declared Mao's successor
June–August	Fighting erupts between Soviet and Chinese troops on China's northwestern and northeastern borders

1971

July	Henry Kissinger visits Beijing to arrange President Nixon's visit to China
October	The UN votes to recognize the People's Republic of China as the only government of China; the UN seat held by the Taiwan-based Republic of China and a place on the Security Council are both transferred to the People's Republic of China
12–13 September	The '571 Affair' in which Lin Biao, Minister of Defence, is reportedly to have led a coup attempt against Mao, shocks the Chinese public

1972

February   American President Richard Nixon visits China and signs the Shanghai Communiqué

1975

July   Jiang Jieshi dies; his son, Jiang Jingguo assumes the presidency of the Republic of China, Taiwan

1976

8 January   Death of Zhou Enlai

July   Death of Zhu De

26 July   Tangshan earthquake, south of Beijing, kills over 240,000 people

9 September   Death of Mao Zedong

6 October   Hua Guofeng announces the arrest of Mao's widow and her three closest supporters, collectively known as the 'Gang of Four'

1978   The new constitution is announced

December   Posters critical of Deng Xiaoping appear on Democracy Wall in central Beijing

1979

1 January   The United States recognizes the Beijing government as the official government of China and withdraws recognition from Taiwan

28 January   Deng Xiaoping visits the United States

29 March   Wei Jingsheng is arrested

October   Wei is sentenced to 15 years' imprisonment

1980

7 September   Hua Guofeng is removed from office; Zhao Ziyang becomes Premier

September   New Marriage Law requires the use of contraception; the limiting of family size to one child officially begins

November   Trial begins of the Gang of Four

1981

25 January   Formal verdict condemns the Gang of Four

April   Hu Yaobang succeds Hua Guofeng as CCP Chairman

1984

July Britain and China reach a settlement on the return of Hong Kong to China; final document is signed on 19 December 1984

1985

September The start of student demonstrations calling for government reforms on university campuses in major Chinese cities; demonstrations erupt periodically until June 1989

1988

February Jiang Jingguo, President of Taiwan, dies, and is succeeded by his Vice-President, Li Denghui

25 March Li Peng is named Premier of China by the National People's Congress Organic Law of Villagers Committees put into effect

1989

15 April Hu Yaobang dies; students honour him by gathering in Tiananmen Square, thus beginning 'Beijing Spring'

22 April Demonstrations expand; some 100,000 people gather in Tiananmen Square

26 April Students in Beijing are denounced as conspirators in an editorial in the *People's Daily*

15 May Mikhail Gorbachev arrives in Beijing

18 May Students meet in televised exchange with CCP leaders

20 May Martial law is imposed in Beijing

24 May Zhao Ziyang is dismissed as Secretary-General of the CCP; he is officially removed from all official positions the following month

4 June Tiananmen Square massacre as People's Liberation Army troops clear demonstrators from the centre of Beijing

23 June Jiang Zemin, mayor of Shanghai, is officially named Secretary-General of the CCP, replacing Zhao Ziyang

1991 Collapse of the USSR; independence of Central Asian republics is declared

1994

December Construction begins on the Three Gorges Dam project, on the western reaches of the Yangzi River; estimated cost US$30 billion and estimated construction time of 14 years to build the world's largest hydroelectric dam

1997

19 February   Deng Xiaoping dies

1 July   Hong Kong is returned to Chinese control

October   Jiang Zemin visits the United States

1998   Zhu Rongji becomes Premier, with responsibility to deepen the economic reforms begun by Deng Xiaoping

State Environment Protection Administration is established

1999

April   10,000 members of the spiritual movement, *Falungong*, or Wheel of the Law, hold a silent demonstration in Beijing

10 May   Protestors, angry over the accidental bombing of the Chinese embassy in Belgrade, stone the American embassy in Beijing

22 July   *Falungong* movement is banned

December   Macao, Portuguese controlled since 1557, is returned to China

Number of Chinese users of the internet reaches 17 million

China announces the 'Go West' campaign to expand development in western China

2000

February   America grants China permanent normal trade relations, paving the way for China to enter the World Trade Organization (WTO)

March   China issues warnings over the possible victory of the Democratic Progressive Party (DPP) in the Taiwan elections

Chen Shuibian, of the DPP, wins election to the presidency of Taiwan, marking the first time the Nationalist Party loses control of that office since 1949

June   Kim Dae Jung of South Korea meets with Kim Jong Il of North Korea in the first ever such meeting between North and South

November   George W. Bush elected President of the United States

2001   Revisions to the Marriage Law announced, clarifying property rights in marriage and divorce

September 11   Terrorist attack destroys New York's World Trade Centre; second attack occurs on the US Pentagon building, Washington, DC

October	President Bush visits China which agrees to support the 'War on Terror'
	Beijing wins the right to host the 2008 Summer Olympics
	United States begins military action in Afghanistan
	Collision between Chinese fighter jet and US surveillance plane over the South China Sea
	The Shanghai Five reorganized as the Shanghai Cooperative Organization, with China, Russia, Kazakhstan, Kyrgyzstan, Tajikistan and Uzbekistan as members
December	China officially admitted to the WTO
	Chinese President Jiang Zemin announces his policy of the 'Three Represents' which opens the door for entrepreneurs to join the CCP

2002

September	China ratifies the Kyoto Protocol on limiting greenhouse gases
November	The National Party Congress officially adopts Jiang Zemin's notion of the 'Three Represents' which removed barriers to admitting entrepreneurs, intellectuals and scientists to the CCP

2003	China inaugurates the New Rural Cooperative Medical System
January	SARS epidemic in China, Taiwan and Hong Kong
January–December	74,000 incidents of unrest occurs across China, driven by complaints over corruption, unfair taxation and poverty
March	Hu Jintao becomes President of China
	United States begins war with Iraq
	China launches first successful manned space flight

2004

November	China signs a trade agreement with 10 Southeast Asian countries
	George W. Bush re-elected President of the United States

2005

April	Anti-Japanese demonstrations in China turn violent as protestors decry depictions of Japan's Second World War record in China in Japanese textbooks
Summer	Demonstrations by farmers occur throughout the spring and summer over land rights issues and charges of corruption by local officials

October	China launches a second successful manned space flight
December	China repeals the agricultural tax, effective 1 January 2006

2006

May	Structure of the Three Gorges Dam completed
July	The government orders popular website and chat forum Century China to shut down
	New railway from Beijing to Lhasa completed
August	China experiences a major drought, the worst in 50 years, affecting 18 million people
October	National People's Congress approves statement on building a 'harmonious society'
November	The China–Africa Cooperation Forum (CACF) meets in Beijing; China promises further aid in loans to assist African development
December	An on-going crackdown on corruption nets its fourth high-ranking official for the year, as the government uncovers further instances of bribery and embezzlement

2007 Number of internet users reaches 137 million or 10% of China's population

February	President Hu tours eight African nations
October	Chinese National Space Administration launches first moon orbiter
July	China's food and drug agency announces execution of its former chief executive for taking bribes, following scandals over food quality

2008 China's GDP reaches US$4.3 trillion

January	Worst snowfall in decades hits China, stranding thousands of travellers
March	Violent clashes in Tibet; the region is closed, but images of violence spread worldwide via camera phones and internet
	Ma Yingjiu wins Taiwan presidency defeating Chen Shuibian
	China holds the 10th National Women's Conference
May	An estimated 80,000 perish in the powerful Sichuan earthquake, with 375,000 injured and thousands homeless
June	China and Taiwan agree to set up offices in each other's territory following the first formal bilateral talks since 1999
July	Russia and China sign a treaty resolving long-standing border disputes
8 August	The Beijing Olympics opens to both Chinese and world athletes

September	Chinese astronaut Zhai Zhigang successfully completes China's first spacewalk
November	China announces a massive economic stimulus package of 4 trillion *yuan* (US$586 billion)
	Barack Obama elected president of United States
2009	China becomes the world's largest automotive market, surpassing the United States
	Chinese trade surplus with the United States reaches US$368 billion
	China poised to surpass Japan as the world's second largest economy
March	Nine of the world's top 50 companies, as measured by market capitalization, are Chinese, up from only 1 in 2000
July	Urumqi, capital of the Xinjiang-Uighur Autonomous Region erupts in the worst ethnic violence since reforms began; 197 people killed and over 1,600 injured
September	Taiwan's former President, Chen Shui-bian, sentenced to life in prison for financial malfeasance while in office
1 October	China celebrates the 60th anniversary of the 1949 revolution
November	The number of billionaires in China rises from 2 in 2000 to 100
December	Chinese foreign currency reserves reach US$2.4 trillion, an increase of over 1250% since 2000
	Human rights activist Liu Xiaobo sentenced to eleven years in prison
2010	
January	Google announces possible withdrawal from China over government censorship
	China announces a rise of 17.7% in exports
March	China becomes the world's largest maker of wind turbines and solar panels
May–October	Shanghai hosts the World's Fair/World Expo
July	Google license is renewed and limited internet service via Google resumes
October	Liu Xiaobo awarded the Nobel Peace Prize

Who's who

Chen Shuibian (b. 1950): Born in Taiwan, Chen led Taiwan's opposition party, the DPP, to victory in the 2000 and 2004 presidential elections. After serving his second term, Chen was convicted of criminal malfeasance and, along with his wife, sentenced to life in prison in 2009.

Chiang Ch'ing-kuo See *Jiang Jingguo*.

Chiang Kai-shek See *Jiang Jieshi*.

Cui Jian (b. 1961): Beijing-born musician, songwriter and vocalist. He was among the most popular young musicians to perform in Tiananmen Square during Beijing Spring of 1989. Since then, he has continued to perform both in China and on world tours.

Dalai Lama The highest-ranking religious figure within the Tibetan Buddhist religion. In addition to being a spiritual leader, most Tibetans regard the Dalai Lama as the rightful temporal leader of Tibet as well. The current Dalai Lama, the 14th man to hold this title, lives in India where he has headed a Tibetan government in exile since 1959.

Deng Xiaoping (1904–97): Known as China's 'paramount' leader, Deng joined the Communist movement in his teens and dedicated his life to the Communist cause in China. A survivor of the Long March, he held a number of positions in the Party and the military, rising to Secretary-General of the Party before being vilified in the Cultural Revolution. By 1978, he had emerged as one of the top leaders once more and, with help from his key supporters, launched widespread reforms. His legacy of a more open China, stronger economy and improved lives for millions of Chinese was marred by the Tiananmen Square Massacre of 1989 and growing corruption as the country shifted toward a market-driven economy.

Deng Yingzhao (1904–92): Government official and activist, known for championing women's rights, particularly through the Chinese Women's

Federation. The wife of Zhou Enlai, Deng held positions in the Party in her own right after 1976.

Fang Lizhi (b. 1936): Astrophysicist at China University of Science and Technology (CUST), and currently a university professor in the United States. Fang was among China's leading scientists when he began to speak out against Chinese government policies in the 1980s. His outspoken criticism led to his being blamed for the student demonstrations of 1989, after which he was forced to leave China.

Hu Jintao (b. 1943): President of China, 2003 to the present; became Secretary General of the CCP in 2002 and Chairman of the Central Military Commission in 2004. Hu rose through the Chinese Communist Youth League and held top CCP posts in Guizhou and Tibet. In the 1990s, he was brought to Beijing where he served as President of the Central Party School and member of the Politburo. Widely considered as the probable successor to President Jiang Zemin, his election was announced in 2003.

Hu Yaobang (1915–89): Former Secretary-General of the CCP in the 1980s. Hu was among the men chosen by Deng Xiaoping to inaugurate reforms in government and the CCP. However, in 1987 his support for student activists calling for greater democracy led to his dismissal from his post. His death, from natural causes, in April 1989 touched off the student demonstrations that marked the beginning of Beijing Spring.

Hua Guofeng (1921–2007): Hua rose from relative obscurity to become Premier of China following the death of Mao in 1976. He was soon eased out of his top position by Deng Xiaoping and replaced by Deng's own hand-picked men.

Jiang Jieshi (1887–1975): President of China (1928–49) and on Taiwan from 1950 until his death in 1975. Jiang rose to power after the death of Dr Sun Zhongshan in 1925 through his military leadership of the Northern Expedition. Adamantly anti-Communist, Jiang pursued the CCP despite the growing Japanese threat. He belatedly began preparations to defend China in 1937 but the Japanese invasion forced him to retreat inland, to Chongqing in Sichuan province, where he and the Nationalists managed to hold on until the end of the Second World War. Despite considerable US aid after the war, Jiang lost to the CCP and retreated to Taiwan where he continued to lead the Nationalist Party until his death, one year before that of his nemesis, Mao Zedong.

Jiang Jingguo (1909–88): Son of Jiang Jieshi by Jiang's first wife, the younger Jiang received his education in the USSR and married a Russian. In the 1940s, he held posts in the Nationalist-led government; after the move to

Taiwan, he became head of the Nationalist secret police before assuming the presidency after his father's death in 1975. Like his father, he died in office, in 1988.

Jiang Qing (1914–91): Third wife of Mao Zedong and major political figure in the Cultural Revolution. Jiang Qing began her career as a film actress; she married Mao in 1938. In 1966 she emerged from relative obscurity to take a major role in the Cultural Revolution. After Mao's death, she was widely blamed for the excesses of the Cultural Revolution and, following a show-trial in 1980–1, was sentenced to death; the sentence was later commuted to life imprisonment. She died in a prison hospital, reportedly by her own hand, in 1991.

Jiang Zemin (b. 1926): President of China, 1993–2003; Secretary General of the CCP, 1990–2002; Chairman of the Central Military Commission, 1989–2004. An engineer by training, Jiang's political career began in the 1950s, eventually leading to his position as mayor of Shanghai in 1986. In June of 1989 Jiang was abruptly re-assigned to Beijing where Deng Xiaoping supported his elevation to the top positions in the country. Following Deng's death in 1997, Jiang continued to dominate the government and the Party. He gradually relinquished control to his successor, Hu Jintao, beginning in 2002.

Li Denghui (Lee Teng-hui) (b. 1929): President of China on Taiwan (1988–2000). US-educated Li was a native of Taiwan and thus the first native to hold the top political office on the island. He continued many of the policies he inherited from the Jiang family but also made some significant changes, including the lifting of restrictions on travel to China for Taiwan passport-holders and recognition of the DPP, which previously was denied the legal right to exist despite its large following.

Li Peng (b. 1928): Premier, 1988–1998; Chairman, National People's Congress 1998–2003. An adopted son of Zhou Enlai, Li was educated in the USSR as an engineer in the 1950s. He quickly rose within the CCP, holding a number of positions in the government and the Party prior to serving as Premier and Chairman of the NPC. Blamed by some for the deaths at Tiananmen Square in 1989, others regard him as a modernizer, especially for his leadership in promoting the Three Gorges Dam project.

Lin Biao (1907–71): General in the People's Liberation Army (PLA) and Minister of Defence under Mao. Lin was a military hero of the Civil War and rose to become Defence Minister in the 1960s when he was also named as Mao's successor. A leader of the Cultural Revolution, he prepared the 'Little Red Book' of Mao's quotes used by thousands of PLA soldiers and Red

Guards. Lin was accused of plotting against Mao in the '571 Affair' and the official CCP account asserts that he died in 1971 when his aeroplane was shot down over Mongolia as he fled China after the failed coup attempt.

Liu Binyan (1925–2005): Dissident journalist and author. Liu worked as a journalist for the CCP newspaper, the *People's Daily*. Appalled by increasing corruption in the Party after 1980, he wrote a series of exposé articles for which he was finally expelled from the CCP. He chose to leave China and worked as a human rights activist and writer in the United States.

Liu Shaoqi (1898–1969): Chairman (President) of China, 1959–1968. Liu was educated in the USSR and was considered a leading CCP theoretician. During the Great Leap Forward, he was named Chairman of the PRC (the title 'president' being suspended at that time) and through a series of cautious reforms, began to rebuild China's economy. Condemned as a 'capitalist roader' during the Cultural Revolution, he died in prison. In 1980 he was posthumously rehabilitated by Deng Xiaoping.

Liu Xiaobo (b. 1955): Professor and dissident author. A participant in the 1989 Tiananmen Square movement, Liu remained in China and was periodically detained by the authorities. He was arrested in 2008 and sentenced to 11 years in prison. In 2010 he was awarded the Nobel Peace Prize for his long-standing advocacy of human rights in China.

Ma Yingjiu (b. 1950): Also spelled Ma Ying-jeou. Elected in 2008 as the 12th President of Taiwan; member of the Nationalist Party; his election eased relations with the PRC.

Mao Zedong (1893–1976): Chairman of the CCP and leader of China's Communist revolution. Born in rural Hunan province, Mao received a university degree and, upon moving to Beijing, was introduced to the ideas of Marx by founders of the CCP, Chen Duxiu and Li Dazhao. Mao led the Jiangxi Soviet government in 1931 and rose to prominence during the Long March when the CCP finally repudiated USSR leadership. He rebuilt the Party and its military units at Yanan during the Second World War, and led the CCP to victory in 1949. As Chairman of the CCP, Mao's accomplishments and failures have left a mixed assessment of his role after 1949, but he nonetheless is the single most important figure in the history of modern China.

Peng Dehuai (1898–1974): PLA general and Minister of Defense in the 1950s. Peng gained prominence for his leadership during the Korean War, but his reputation was not adequate to protect him from Mao's denunciation of him in 1959, when Peng's negative appraisal of the Great Leap Forward was circulated to the Party elite. He lost his positions of power in 1959 and was never readmitted to the highest echelons of the CCP leadership.

Peng Zhen (1902–97): Former mayor of Beijing and member of the CCP Central Committee and Politburo. Purged in the Cultural Revolution, Peng returned to a position of influence under Deng Xiaoping in the 1980s.

Qin Shi Huang Di (r. 221–210 BCE): Founder of the Qin dynasty, he was the first ruler to use the title of emperor and is, therefore, often referred to as the First Emperor of China. His vast tomb, unearthed near Xian in the 1970s, attests to the military foundations of his empire as it contains thousands of clay (*terracotta*) warriors, a major resource for the study of the Qin period.

Sun Zhongshan (1866–1925): Also known as Sun Yat-sen and Sun Yixian. Considered the Father of the Republic by both the Nationalist and Communist Parties, Sun served as President briefly in early 1912. The Nationalist Party grew from his earlier political organizations. He died before he was able to lead the Northern Expedition which he hoped would unify China.

Wang Guangmei (1922–2006): American-born wife of Liu Shaoqi, Wang was detained in solitary confinement between 1967 and 1979, accused, like her husband, of opposing the Maoist revolution.

Wei Jingsheng (b. 1950): Accused of opposing the Chinese government, Wei was sentenced to 15 years in prison in 1979. He served most of his sentence in solitary confinement. After his release, he once more spoke out against government policies and was rearrested. In 1998 he was released on medical grounds and currently lives in the United States.

Wen Jiabao (b. 1942): Premier of China, 2003–present. Educated as a geologist in Beijing, Wen worked in Gansu province during the Cultural Revolution until reassigned to Beijing in 1982 where he worked with reformers Hu Yaobang and Zhao Ziyang. In 1989 he risked his career by going with Zhao to Tiananmen Square to speak with students. He subsequently allied with Jiang Zemin who retained him in his government. When Hu became President, Wen was elevated to the position of Premier.

Yuan Shikai (1859–1916): A Qing dynasty general who brokered the abdication of the child-emperor, Puyi, in 1911–12, paving the way for the new republic. Yuan used his position as head of the military to gain first the premiership of the new republic and then the presidency. His repressive government was unpopular. He died in 1916, the same year in which he planned to make himself Emperor of China.

Zhao Ziyang (1919–2005): Premier of China, 1980–1989. Zho began his political career holding offices in Guangzhou. He was hand-picked by Deng Xiaoping to serve as Premier in 1980 and to reform the commune system.

Zhao's introduction of the contract responsibility system brought rapid expansion of agricultural expansion, and helped to launch China's economic revival after years of Maoist rule. Zhao was abruptly removed from office in 1989 after voicing support for China's students, and remained under house arrest until his death at age 85.

Zhou Enlai (1898–1976): One of the most important and respected leaders of the twentieth century, Zhou joined the Communist movement while a student in Europe and returned to support the CCP in the 1920s. Zhou held a number of high positions prior to 1949, and after the success of the revolution he served as China's Premier and as chief architect of China's foreign policy. Despite his ambiguous role in the Cultural Revolution, he is remembered as a force for moderation and reason during the Maoist period.

Zhu De (1886–1976): General of the PLA. Zhu was Mao's close colleague and supporter from 1928 onwards and was largely responsible for handling military organization. General Zhu remained a loyal follower throughout his lifetime, preceding Mao in death by just a few months.

Zhu Rongji (b. 1929): Premier of China, 1998–2003. Born in Mao's home province of Hunan, Zhu joined the CCP in 1949 and graduated from Qinghua University in 1951. He held a number of positions in the State Planning Commission and other national-level governmental posts before becoming Shanghai's mayor in 1988, replacing Jiang Zemin with whom he had worked closely. In 1990, he was moved to Beijing and held a number of positions before being named Prime Minister in 1998 by President Jiang Zemin. His major task was to deepen China's economic reforms while maintaining political stability.

Glossary

Agrarian Reform Law of 1950: Law authorizing the redistribution of land in China, as a result of which approximately half of the farmland was redistributed, mainly by confiscating the landholdings of wealthy landlords and allotting these to poorer families.

Agricultural Producers Cooperatives: Begun in 1955, these organizations called upon the peasant-farmers of China to pool all their resources and their land in order to increase production which was, in the CCP's view, impeded by the existence of small, individual plots of land. These in turn led to the formation of the communes in 1958.

Anti-Rightist Campaign: A political campaign launched in the summer of 1957 to identify and remove from positions of power members of the CCP who were not adequately 'left' or pro-Communist in their thinking. Many Party stalwarts were sent for re-education in remote rural areas, despite years of dedicated service to the CCP cause.

Baidu: Literally meaning '100 degrees', Baidu is China's premier Chinese-language internet search engine and is the world's largest in terms of the number of users. Its founder, Robin Yanhong Li, is one of China's new multibillionaires.

Beijing Spring: The period of April, May and early June of 1989 when student-led demonstrations in the capital city of Beijing appeared to be pushing the CCP toward greater democratization. The 'Spring' ended on 4 June 1989, with the PLA clearing Tiananmen Square by force and, in the process, killing an unknown number of people.

Big Character Posters: See *Dazibao*.

Buddhism: A universal, world religion based on the teachings of the historical Buddha of the sixth century BCE in the area of present-day Nepal. The basic tenets focus on escape from the pain and suffering which marks all human life and ending the cycle of repeated birth and death by following moral precepts and, ultimately, attaining a state of enlightenment.

Cadre: A supporter of the Communist cause engaged in work on behalf of the movement. Cadre may also indicate a member of the Communist Party in China. The Chinese language equivalent is *ganbu*.

Capitalist roader: Epithet used during the Cultural Revolution against those in positions of authority deviating from the Maoist line. Among those so accused in 1966 were Liu Shaoqi and Deng Xiaoping.

CCP: Acronym for the Chinese Communist Party. Founded in July 1921 by a small group of intellectuals and students in Shanghai, the CCP grew slowly at first, but gained a large following during the Second World War, enabling it to defeat the Nationalist Party of Jiang Jieshi in 1949.

Central Committee of the Chinese Communist Party: This elite group, which has varied in size from 100 to 300, includes all top leaders of the CCP and is the source of Party policy. Membership on the Central Committee is limited to the highest-ranked members of the CCP.

Civil War: After the Second World War, efforts at mediation between the two leading parties in China failed, and from 1946 to 1949 China experienced a Civil War which ended in CCP victory in 1949.

Comintern: The Communist International, founded in the USSR by Lenin to spread Communism throughout the world. A number of Comintern agents worked with the Communist and Nationalist Parties prior to the CCP victory in 1949.

Common Program: Adopted in 1949, this was the basis for China's government until it was replaced with the first constitution in 1954.

Commune: First formed in the summer of 1958 as a part of the Great Leap Forward, communes incorporated all peasant-farmers and workers into large work organizations intended to become self-sustaining economic and social units. Subdivided into brigades and teams, the communes were reduced in size in the early 1960s, but overall they proved inefficient and were dismantled in 1980–3.

Communism: A political philosophy that views the ideal society as one in which all property is held in common, class divisions disappear and the state apparatus is no longer required; a Utopian form of economic and social organization.

Confucius: A sixth-century BCE Chinese sage who stressed the need for harmony and balance in human affairs and whose teachings provided a moral, ethical code of behaviour that endured for centuries in China.

Constitution of 1982: China had three previous constitutions adopted in 1954, 1975 and 1978, respectively. The 1982 constitution reflected the early reforms that took hold after 1978 and its four amendments expanded and confirmed new rights, such as the right to have and to inherit private property.

Contract responsibility system: Adopted in the early 1980s as part of the reform era, this system allowed peasant-farmers to lease land and plant crops of their choice. Because of its success in increasing agricultural output, it replaced the commune system.

Conurbation: Densely populated urban area that includes a major city, its outlying suburbs and small towns.

CPPCC: Acronym for the Chinese People's Political Consultative Conference which first convened in 1949 to pass the Common Program. The Program served as the legal basis for the new government and named Mao as China's head of state. The CPPCC continues to meet as an advisory body to the government of China.

CR: Acronym for the Cultural Revolution. The full name of this movement is the Great Proletarian Cultural Revolution. It was launched by Chairman Mao in 1966 and ended in 1976, the year that Mao died.

CUST: Acronym for China University of Science and Technology, a major technological university in the central Chinese province of Anhui.

Cultural Revolution: See *Great Proletarian Cultural Revolution*.

Dalai Lama: The highest-ranking religious leader in Tibetan Buddhism. Having fled China in 1959, the fourteenth Dalai Lama established a Tibetan government in exile at his refuge in Dharmsala, India.

Danwei: Chinese term for work unit. In the Maoist era, every worker belonged to a *danwei* which not only paid his or her salary, but also provided health care, housing, child care and other services.

Daoism (or Taoism): An ancient school of thought in China derived from the observation of nature and the belief in dual forces of *yin* and *yang*, respectively, represented by the moon and the sun, the negative and the positive, and the dark and the light. Daoism is one of the *san jiao*, or Three Teachings, of China; the other two are Buddhism and Confucianism.

Dazibao: Chinese term for 'Big Character Poster'. A poster containing opinions and/or political slogans pasted on to walls in public places. The right of Chinese citizens to put up these posters was granted in the Chinese constitution of 1978, but the leadership revoked this and other forms of public expression in 1980 as part of efforts to curtail the democracy movement.

Democracy Wall: Located in central Beijing on Changan Boulevard in 1978, this wall was covered with Big Character Posters in the early years of the democracy movement in China. After 1980, the wall was off limits to such posters, and although an alternative site was established for this particular form of public expression, its inconvenient location precluded its becoming an important site for democracy activists.

DPP: Acronym for Taiwan's Democratic Progressive Party which, in 2000, gained the Taiwan government presidency; President Chen was the first individual outside the Nationalist Party to hold this top office. He lost the 2008 election to Nationalist Party candidate Ma Yingjiu.

Encirclement and Annihilation Campaigns: Five campaigns undertaken between 1931 and 1934 by the Nationalist Party under Jiang Jieshi (Chiang Kai-shek) intended to destroy the CCP. Only the last, conducted with German military advice, was able to dislodge the CCP, which began its Long March in October 1934 to escape the Nationalist campaigns.

Ethnic minorities: See National minorities.

Fabi: Chinese term for 'legal currency'. The term was replaced with *renminbi*, or people's currency, when the CCP came to power in 1949.

Falungong: Also known as *Falun Dafa*, variously translated as the Law of the Wheel or Buddhist Law. A late twentieth-century spiritual movement based on the ancient teaching of *qigong*, a system of breathing exercises and physical movements, and on a mixture of Buddhist and Daoist beliefs. Banned in 1999, followers continued to defy the government by the public practice of their rituals. Arrests and detentions continued and drew international criticism of China's religious policies.

Feminization of agriculture: The predominance of female labour in agricultural work which became low-paid and low-status labour. Young men sought better pay and status in town or city enterprises, leaving women to work the family's leased land during the reform era.

Fifth modernization: Democracy. Students called for the addition of this fifth item to the official 'Four modernizations' of the early Deng era, demanding that the government not only modernize industry and agriculture, but also the government itself.

571 Affair: Shorthand for a plot against Mao by his Minister of Defence, Lin Biao, in September 1971. Lin's attempt at assassination failed, and his commandeered Air Force jet was reportedly shot down over Mongolia. A full account of the incident has yet to be written.

Floating population: As part of the reform era, restrictions on travel and movement in China loosened, allowing many rural workers to 'float' or move in search of employment. An estimated 120 million people were part of this mobile group at the end of the twentieth century.

Four Big Rights: In the 1978 Chinese constitution, the Chinese people were given the rights of *daming*, *dafang*, *dabianlun* and *dazibao*, which meant, respectively, the right to speak out freely, air views fully, hold great debates and write Big Character Posters. These were all revoked in 1980 as part of government efforts to curtail the emergent democracy movement.

'Four Olds': Denounced during the Cultural Revolution, the four 'old' practices that the CR tried to eradicate were old habits, customs, culture and thought. As part of this onslaught on the past, young Red Guards destroyed temples, religious sites, books and Western goods such as pianos and clothing.

Four Pests Campaign: A 1950s campaign of the CCP to eliminate common pests throughout China, including rats, mosquitoes, flies and sparrows.

Ganbu: See *Cadre*.

Gang of Four: Consisting of Chairman Mao's wife, Jiang Qing, and her three key supporters in the Cultural Revolution, this 'gang' was blamed for the excesses of the Cultural Revolution. In a show trial, Jiang Qing was sentenced to death for her actions; the sentence was commuted to life in prison.

GDP: Acronym for gross domestic product. A figure produced by deducting the value of income earned on investments made by a country's citizens abroad from a country's total GNP; usually based on annual figures.

Geomancy: A form of divination that sought to improve future prospects or fortune by placing buildings or tombs in places considered to be auspicious; in Daoism, *feng shui*, which translates literally as wind-water, is a form of geomancy.

GMD: Acronym for Guomindang (also romanized as Kuomintang and abbreviated as KMT), or the Nationalist Party. Originally founded by Dr Sun Zhongshan, the Party was dominated in the 1930s by Jiang Jishi and, following the Civil War, its leaders retreated to Taiwan where it remains an important political force.

GNP: Acronym for gross national product. The total value of a nation's annual output of goods and services.

Great Leap Forward: An economic movement launched by Mao in 1958 to make China the equal of Britain in 15 years. It led to widespread famine and the deaths of millions. As part of the Great Leap, the communes became the basic unit of socialist production and remained as such until the system was dismantled in the early 1980s.

Great Proletarian Cultural Revolution: A political movement launched by Chairman Mao Zedong in 1966 which became a violent assault on those considered disloyal to Mao and the Communist movement. Although the most extreme phase ended in 1969, the aftermath continued to affect the lives of millions until Mao's death in 1976. See also *Red Guards*.

Guomindang: See *GMD*.

Han dynasty: From 206 BCE to 220 CE, this important dynasty laid the foundations for the imperial Chinese state. Because of its importance, the name 'Han' is also an ethnonym used to distinguish 'Han Chinese' from ethnic minorities such as the Tibetans or Mongolians in China.

Hong Kong: As a result of the treaty settlements after the Opium War of 1839–42, Hong Kong island, off the south China coast, was ceded in perpetuity to Britain. The original town on the island was called Victoria, in honour of Queen Victoria, but as the population increased and additional land was leased from China, the whole enclave came to be known as Hong Kong. Returned to China in 1997, the area is now a special administrative region of China.

Hui: Chinese who follow Islam. Some Hui people trace their roots to the arrival of traders from the Arab world during the Tang dynasty (618–906 CE). This 'foreign' origin is cited as a reason for the Hui being classified as an ethnic minority group, although their language and most of their cultural practices are the same as those of the Han Chinese population.

Iron rice bowl: A term used to designate a permanent position, literally an unbreakable 'bowl' that guaranteed basic livelihood or 'rice'.

IUD: Intrauterine device. A contraceptive device inserted by a physician to prevent pregnancy. This is the most commonly used method of birth control in China.

Jiangxi Soviet: Founded in 1931 in the border area of Jiangxi and Fujian, this was an area controlled by a 'Soviet' or governing council led by Mao Zedong. A number of 'Soviets' emerged in rural China after 1927 when the CCP moved underground, and the Jiangxi Soviet was the largest of these. It was abandoned in 1934 as a result of Nationalist attacks.

Korean War: Conflict that began with the invasion of South Korea by North Korean Communist forces in June 1950 and ended with a UN-brokered truce in 1953, leaving Korea divided at the same border as when fighting began.

Kuomintang: See *GMD*.

Landlord: A man who held larger than average amounts of land and hired farm labourers to work it, or rented his land to others. In the 1950s, landlords and their families became the target of various campaigns and landlord status disadvantaged any individuals so labelled for over three decades.

'Little Red Book': Officially entitled *The Quotations of Chairman Mao*, this pocket-sized book, usually with bright red plastic covers, was carried by members of the Chinese military and by the young members of the Red Guards in the 1960s; after Mao's death in 1976, the books disappeared, re-emerging in the 1990s as tourist souvenirs.

Long March: The journey of the CCP in retreat from the Jiangxi Soviet base after repeated attacks by the GMD, from October 1934 to December 1935. High attrition rates reduced the marchers from nearly 100,000 to 8,000 by the time they arrived at Yanan, in northern China.

Lop Nor: A lake, now a dry lake-bed, in eastern Xinjiang; the area is the site of China's nuclear-testing programme.

Lushan: A mountain retreat for CCP leaders and the site of the 1959 Lushan Conference at which Mao denounced his long-time colleague, Peng Dehuai, for criticizing the Great Leap Forward. Following the meeting, Mao stepped down as President of China, although he retained the title of Chairman of the CCP and head of the Chinese military.

Macao: A former Portuguese colony in south China, at the mouth of the Pearl River, near Hong Kong. Macao was returned to Chinese control in 1999 and became a special administrative region.

Manchuria: The ancestral lands of the Manchu people who established China's last dynasty, the Qing (1644–1912). In the 1930s, Japan occupied this area of northeastern China, and proclaimed it a new state, 'Manchukuo', under the last emperor of the Qing, Puyi, who served as a figurehead. The area reverted to Chinese control after 1945. After 1949, it was reorganized by the new Chinese government into the provinces of Heilongjiang, Jilin and Liaoning.

Mao Zedong Thought: Also, Maoism. The political thought of Mao Zedong, including his interpretation of Marxism and Leninism, and derived from his various writings on socialism, capitalism and Communism.

Marriage Law of 1950: One of the first laws passed by the new CCP-led government of China, this made men and women legally equal, set minimum ages for marriage, and outlawed concubinage, among other practices. Its most controversial clause granted women the right to sue for divorce.

Marriage Law of 1980: This revision of the original 1950 law raised the minimum age for marriage and also required all married couples to practise birth control, among other provisions.

Marriage Law revisions of 2001: While retaining clauses from the earlier versions, the 2001 law had new clauses on division of marital property, prenuptial agreements and penalties for a spouse who caused a marriage to fail.

May Fourth Movement: This political and intellectual movement began on 4 May 1919, as a protest against the Treaty of Versailles. As one of the allies in the First World War, China had hoped to benefit from the settlement, mainly in the form of treaty revisions with the European powers, but, instead, America and the European states granted Japan the former German concessions in China rather than returning them to Chinese control. The student-led protests of 4 May in major cities throughout China led to a new intellectual awakening and the rise of Chinese nationalism. As a result of the protests, the Chinese government did not sign the treaty.

Mutual aid teams: These small groups of villagers were organized in the early 1950s to formalize the practice of sharing tools and draught animals among villagers in order to facilitate agricultural production. Based on the success of the teams, the CCP quickly moved to a higher stage of shared ownership and production which was much less popular.

National minority (shaoshu minzu): Refers to ethnic groups with official recognition and legal status as minorities. Although some 400 groups requested this designation in the 1950s, only 55 groups are recognized as such, entitling them to participate in the regional autonomy system that was designed to ensure minorities a voice in local government.

National Party Congress: The body which chooses the top CCP leadership and, theoretically, the source of the CCP's legitimacy. The first Congress was held in 1921, at the time of the Party's formation, and Congresses met irregularly through the Maoist period. The 17th NPC was held in October 2007 and the 18th is scheduled for 2012.

National People's Congress: In theory, this body is the highest legislative authoritative body in the People's Republic of China, but in practice the Congress convenes for only one to two weeks, making it impossible for its nearly 3,000 members to provide oversight of government policy or its implementation. The 11th Congress convened in March of 2009.

Nationalism: A political philosophy based on the idea that separate peoples have unique and distinctive traits; it often includes the notion that each people should have a separate and independent state.

Northern Expedition: A military campaign, from 1926 to 1928, undertaken by Jiang Jieshi (Chiang Kai-shek) to defeat the warlords and to unify China. Its success brought Jiang to the presidency of China, which he retained from 1928 to 1949, except for brief, strategic 'retirements' from which he always re-emerged stronger politically.

'*Old Feudal*': A term used to describe anyone still adhering to old ideas after the Communist revolution of 1949.

One-child policy: China's policy limiting each couple to only one child. Rewards and punishments to enforce this policy were determined at the provincial level, and in the early years of implementation some punishments were very severe, drawing international criticism. In practice, couples could secure permission for a second child, particularly when the first child was female, and most ethnic minorities were exempt.

'*100 Flowers' Campaign*: Initiated in 1957 by Chairman Mao, this campaign called upon the people to offer criticism of policies and cadre behaviour; the programme was ended abruptly in early June 1957.

Opium Wars: The first war, primarily limited to coastal China in 1839–42, ended in the Treaty of Nanjing between Great Britain and China. The second war, 1856–8, involved France and Great Britain and ended in the Treaty of Tianjin. China's losses gave Western states greater privileges in China and began a period referred to as 'semi-colonialism' by the present government.

Organic Law of Villagers Committees: Passed in 1988, this law was intended to give local villages more say in the running of village governments and more autonomy for village officials. Through village-level elections, competition for local offices increased and gave villagers the opportunity to vote corrupt or incompetent officials out of office.

Patriarchy: Male dominance in society and in the family, reinforced in China by traditional Confucian values.

PLA: People's Liberation Army; the official name of China's armed forces.

PNTR: Permanent normal trade relations; granted to China by the United States in 2000, paving the way for China's entry into the WTO.

Politburo: Contraction for Political Bureau, members of which are chosen from the numerically larger Standing Committee of the Central Committee of the CCP. This group, almost exclusively male, is the most powerful group in China.

Qigong: Ancient form of breathing exercises mixed with physical movements to enhance health and prolong life.

Qin dynasty (221–208 BCE): A relatively short dynasty which followed legalist principles in imposing a harsh rule of law over northern China. It provided a basis for the Han dynasty which followed it.

Qing: The last dynasty of China (1644–1912); founded by Manchus from northeastern China with assistance from their allies, the Mongols, and from Ming-dynasty (1368–1644) generals who defected to the Manchus in 1644.

Qur'an (or Koran): The sacred book of Islam, containing the teachings of the Prophet Mohammed, dating from the seventh century CE.

Rape of Nanjing: The assault on the civilian population of Nanjing by the Japanese army in December 1937. An estimated 100,000 non-combatants died, and countless women were raped in a three-week period.

Red Guards: Young people who participated in the Cultural Revolution, at the invitation and instigation of Chairman Mao, beginning in 1966. Initially drawn from the ranks of cadres' families, the movement expanded to include thousands of teenagers who viewed themselves as saving the revolution and purifying China of all counter-revolutionary tendencies. They were ordered to disband and return to their homes in 1969, after causing havoc throughout China.

Reform era: Dated from Deng Xiaoping's rise to power beginning in 1978 and continuing in the first decades of the twenty-first century.

Regional autonomy system: Established to give minority groups a voice, 'autonomous' governments were formed at the lower levels first, culminating in the formation of five autonomous regions; each level included representatives of all minorities living in the area. Although special powers were given to these units, in practice CCP domination ensured conformity with national government policy and allowed little deviation from Beijing-mandated policies.

Republic of China: The current name used by the government authorities on Taiwan, an island off China's eastern coast, which has remained separate from the Chinese mainland since 1949.

Responsibility system: See *Contract responsibility system*.

17-Point Agreement: The agreement signed in 1951 between representatives of the Tibetan leader, the Dalai Lama, and the new Chinese government. Both sides eventually repudiated the agreement which was in effect from 1951 until the spring of 1959.

SEZ (Special Economic Zone): Instituted by Deng Xiaoping to jumpstart the Chinese economy in the reform era, these zones offered foreign investors generous terms in the form of tax relief and low costs. The most successful was Shenzhen, a rapidly growing city just across the border from Hong Kong.

Shanghai Communiqué: An agreement signed between the United States and China in 1972, declaring their mutual intention to open talks and explore the possibility of resuming official diplomatic relations.

Shenzhen: Former village just across the border from Hong Kong, Shenzhen was made an SEZ in 1980; in the next two decades, its population grew to 4 million, including a large, well-trained workforce employed by international corporations manufacturing a wide range of goods.

Sino-Soviet split: This famous rift in Chinese–Soviet relations occurred in 1958 when Mao, angered at the Soviet leadership's attitude toward China, broke off relations. Soviet advisers then working in China were recalled, and relations between the two Communist powers remained cold until the 1989 visit of Mikhail Gorbachev to China, in the midst of student demonstrations.

Siying: Chinese term for private enterprises.

Social gospel: The Christian Protestant movement to include education and medical services as part of its evangelical efforts in China prior to 1949.

Socialist Education Campaign: This political campaign to instill proper socialist values in the Chinese population was ordered by Chairman Mao in 1962, but the outcome fell short of his expectations, leading him to launch the Cultural Revolution in 1966.

'Speak Bitterness' meetings: As part of the land redistribution process overseen by the CCP in 1950–3, villagers were encouraged to tell of their past abuse at the hands of local landlords, and these gatherings were thus an opportunity to speak of the 'bitter' past. The public denunciations drew peasants into the revolutionary process and often ended in the villagers sentencing the landlord to death.

State Environment Protection Administration: Created in 1998 to address increasing environmental pollution problems, the SEPA is to enforce laws and policies dealing with environmental protection.

'Strike Hard' Campaign: A police campaign which began in the mid-1990s intended to crack down on crime throughout China. The increased presence of policemen on the streets and in highly populated areas such as markets and parks was noticeable, but complaints of less public crimes, such as bribery and the embezzling of public funds, continued.

Taijiquan (t'ai ch'i): An ancient form of flowing physical exercise practised by many Chinese for general health and well-being.

Taiwan: Island off the eastern coast of China, home to the Republic of China.

Takla Makan Desert: Located in the southern area of Xinjiang, the Takla Makan is one of the world's most arid places; it contains enormous natural gas and oil deposits, and is therefore marked for exploitation in the early twenty-first century.

Taoism: See *Daoism*.

Three Bitter Years: The years of 1959–61 are referred to as bitter years because of prolonged famine and food shortages throughout China, as a result of both man-made and natural disasters. During this time, an estimated 30 million Chinese people died.

Three Gorges Dam: A major hydroelectric project which is the world's single largest dam. Located in Sichuan province on the upper reaches of the Yangzi River, the resultant reservoir flooded acres of farmland and submerged historic sites and entire villages, requiring the relocation of millions of people. The dam supplies electricity to western China where demand is enormous. The full cost of the dam in human and environmental terms has yet to be fully determined.

Three Obediences: In traditional patriarchal China, a woman was taught to be obedient to her father during her childhood, to her husband when married and to her son when she was widowed. These 'three obediences' meant that a woman would always be subservient to a male relative.

Tiananmen Square Massacre: On 4 June 1989, the CCP leadership ordered the military to clear Tiananmen Square, an open area in the centre of Beijing, where hundreds of students and their supporters continued their two-month-long demonstration. The term 'massacre' refers to the use of overwhelming military force against unarmed civilians, an unknown number of whom died.

Treaty of Alliance and Friendship: This treaty between China and the USSR was signed in 1950; it provided for Soviet loans to China and the assignment of Soviet technicians to assist in China's modernization. The treaty was abrogated in 1958.

Treaty of Versailles: This treaty was the settlement which followed the First World War, in which China played a minor part on the side of the European allies. Chinese expectations for generous treatment were dashed when former German concessions were granted to Japan rather than being returned to China. Following massive protests, China did not ratify the treaty.

Uighurs: Also spelled Uygur, Uyghur. A Turkic Muslim people, the majority of whom live in the Xinjiang-Uighur Autonomous Region in northwestern China.

USSR: Acronym for the Union of Soviet Socialist Republics. Founded in 1917 after the Bolshevik revolution ousted the tsar and took control of the former Russian empire, the USSR collapsed in 1991. Although the new Russian state lost many of its Central Asian republics, it retained control of Siberia and, therefore, continues to share a border with northeastern China.

Vietnam War: Initially a local conflict between the Communist forces of North Vietnam and the US-backed Nguyen government of the South, the confrontation escalated with increased US involvement in the 1960s. The United States withdrew its troops in 1975, and in 1976 Vietnam was united under Ho Chi-min's Communist Party.

Wan xi shao: Chinese slogan translated as 'later, fewer, further between', which was used with the new family planning regulations to remind women that the government recommended having children later, having fewer in number, and spacing births by waiting four–five years between children.

Warlord: Men who ruled areas of China through the exercise of military force. Between 1916 and 1928, the central government was unable to govern China effectively because warlords dominated large areas of China. Although some lost power during the Northern Expedition of 1926–8, in the north and west of China warlords continued to dominate provincial governments into the 1940s.

World Bank: Formed at the end of the Second World War to finance the rebuilding of war-torn states and the development of former colonies, the Work Bank loans money to its member-states for projects all over the globe. China became a major borrower in the 1990s.

WTO: Acronym for the World Trade Organization. The WTO is a global agency that sets trade regulations and requires all members to conform to global standards for trade and commerce.

Xiahai: Chinese term which literally translates as 'into the sea', but which came to mean leaving government positions to 'jump' into the new economy of the 1990s.

Xiamen: Chinese coastal city in Fujian province designated an SEZ as part of the reform-era efforts to attract foreign investors to China.

Xinjiang-Uighur Autonomous Region: China's largest minority region, Xinjiang is home to Muslim peoples such as the Uighur, Kazak, Tajik and Kyrgyz. Han migration into the region since 1949 has drastically changed the ethnic composition: from 5% of the population in 1949, Han now account for an estimated 40%.

Yuan: A general Chinese term for money. Officially, the currency today is called *renminbi*, or the people's money.

Zhongnanhai: The private, guarded compound in Beijing which houses China's top leaders. It is located on Changan Boulevard, just to the west of the former imperial palace of the Qing Dynasty.

Zunyi Conference: In January 1935, a meeting was held at Zunyi, a city in Guizhou province, by the leadership of the CCP resulting in the repudiation of Moscow-trained advisers and the decision to follow Mao, whose rise to the leadership of the CCP dates from this period.

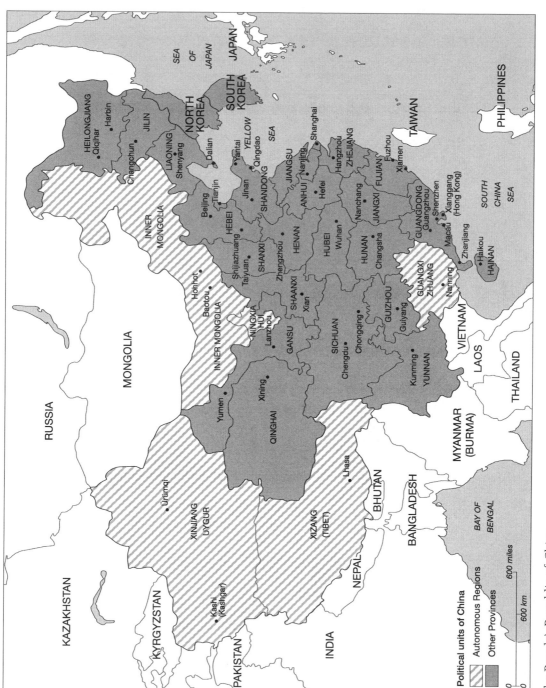

The People's Republic of China

Part 1

CHINA'S PAST

1

General introduction

China's spectacular rise to global prominence is one of the most remarkable stories of our time. In the first half of the twentieth century, millions of rural and urban Chinese lived in poverty, struggling to survive in a country that was continually torn by war and domestic upheaval. But, since that time, China has undergone a dramatic transformation. It has embraced the technological advances of recent decades and provided new opportunities for millions of Chinese to improve their lives. A new, growing middle class has signalled the emergence of a Chinese society where access to good education and health care as well as a higher standard of living is becoming the norm, rather than the exception. While problems have accompanied this economic transformation, China has become the world's second largest economy, and, as a result, China's future holds unprecedented prosperity for 1.3 billion Chinese.

The route to China's success has been as tortuously uneven as it has been rapid. China's history since 1900 – the first 50 years of which are summarized in Part Two, below – has been punctuated by natural and man-made disasters, arrogant leadership, disastrous policy decisions and incomprehensible disregard for the welfare of millions. The early years under Communist leadership brought important changes, but only since 1978 has the ruling Communist Party found more workable solutions to the challenges that have plagued the government and people for the past 200 years.

This account of modern China since 1949 seeks to provide the student and general reader with a brief survey of the major events that mark the transition of China from a poor developing country to a global trading power with political and economic clout throughout the world. Although the story of the Chinese Communist Party (hereafter **CCP**) is a central part of modern China's history, and thus is one component of the present work, this book also records the impact of CCP policies on ordinary people's lives. It shows how the majority of the population managed to accommodate some of the most

CCP: Acronym for the Chinese Communist Party. Founded in July 1921 by a small group of intellectuals and students in Shanghai, the CCP grew slowly at first, but gained a large following during the Second World War, enabling it to defeat the Nationalist Party in 1949.

extreme phases of the CCP's radical political agenda through 1976 and then turns to the impact of recent reforms on all groups and classes. In particular, it follows some of the most important changes for women and minorities since 1949. Although members of both categories would agree that the changes have been significant, overall much remains to be done before either group attains equal opportunity to pursue education and employment.

Periodization for this book departs from the standard treatment in most texts on modern China. The initial attempts of the CCP to legitimize its rule in China and its early, highly ambitious policies are outlined in Chapter 3, which covers the period from 1949 to 1957. When these policies failed to bring about the kind of revolutionary society that the new leaders envisioned, the revolution entered a much more radical stage. The most extreme leftist period was between 1958 and 1969 when China was thrown into turmoil, as the ageing leadership sought to hasten the transformation of its country into a socialist paradise. Unfortunately, economic plans and political campaigns proved disastrous. Instead of moving China forward, the economy slowed, and the modest gains of the early years were threatened. Politically generated violence in the 1960s **Cultural Revolution (CR)** left its mark on the economic system as well as on thousands of Party faithful who found themselves excoriated and ousted from their positions of influence. Ordinary citizens were at the mercy of young **Red Guard** units who marauded through the countryside. Although these policies and campaigns ended by the early 1970s, the radical policies of the revolution did not end until the 1976 death of **Mao Zedong**, Chairman of the CCP and founder of the People's Republic of China (hereafter PRC). Therefore, the period from 1958 to 1976 is treated here as a whole, and allows discussion of the radical Marxist agenda to be the focus of Chapter 4.

With the death of Mao and the discrediting of Maoist attempts at continuing revolution, the next generation of Communist leaders began the rebuilding of China, enabling its rapid shift toward a modern economy open to foreign investment and to experimentation with cultural and political forms, all of which had been anathema to the old guard under Mao. This new period of change was led by the ageing **Deng Xiaoping** who, unlike Mao, chose to place other, younger and better-educated members of the Party at the helm of China's **'reform era'**. Chapter 5 traces the start of this economic transformation and its impact on different sectors of the population to 1989. It includes a reassessment of the **Tiananmen Square Massacre** of 4 June 1989. Despite a temporary setback to the reform movement in 1989, the process of economic reorganization continued in the 1990s, an assessment of which is the focus of Chapter 6. Chapter 7 provides a discussion of the new kinds of problems that emerged as reform deepened in the 1990s, including

CR: Acronym for the Cultural Revolution. The full name of this movement is the Great Proletarian Cultural Revolution. It was launched by Chairman Mao in 1966 and ended in 1976, the year that Mao died.

Red Guards: Young people who participated in the Cultural Revolution, at the invitation and instigation of Chairman Mao, beginning in 1966. They were ordered to disband and return to their homes in 1969, after causing havoc throughout China.

Mao Zedong (1893–1976): Chairman of the CCP and leader of China's Communist revolution. Born in rural Hunan province, Mao was introduced to the ideas of Marx by founders of the CCP, Chen Duxiu and Li Dazhao. Mao rose to prominence during the Long March. After WWII he led the CCP to victory.

Deng Xiaoping (1904–97): Once known as China's 'paramount' leader, Deng joined the Communist movement in his teens. In 1978, he emerged as one of the top leaders and, launched widespread reforms. His legacy of a more open China, stronger economy and improved lives for millions of Chinese was marred by the Tiananmen Square Massacre of 1989.

the nearly unchecked environmental degradation that ensued as demand for energy expanded, growing levels of corruption as officials gave into temptations arising from a wealthier economy, and social inequalities related to China's rapid transformation.

Chapter 8 introduces the rise of new social classes in China since 2000, and explores the impact of China's tremendous economic growth on women, the family and minorities. It also examines changes in education and, especially, in health care as China sought to replace the old socialist system of health care with a new one funded in part by the government and partly by the people themselves. New efforts to improve China's degraded environment are a positive development, driven by citizen activists as well as by new government regulations. An overview of fresh and innovative developments in the arts, entertainment and popular culture showcases Chinese creativity, and a discussion of technology and communication examines both the positive impact of the internet on social networks, for example, and the government's efforts to rein in open discussion in China's cyberspace.

Chapter 9 provides an overview of the current Chinese government, the CCP and the military, especially the major changes that have occurred since 2000. It also offers an account of China's economic rise, the government's 'economic stimulus plan' to ward off the impact of world recession on the Chinese economy, and, briefly, the probability of China being able to sustain the economic growth rates of the first decade of the twenty-first century.

Chapter 10 focuses on the state of China's relations with the world. It begins with a discussion of China and the major world powers, the United States and the European Union (EU), and then explores China's new relationships with Latin American and African nations, some of which are led by individuals who are viewed as exploitative and tyrannical. China's relations with its immediate neighbours, with India, Southeast Asian and Central Asian states, and with countries to the north and northeast are surveyed as a way to examine China's enormous impact on the Asian region. The special connection between Taiwan and China and the easing of relations across the Taiwan straits are addressed at the end of the chapter.

Throughout the text, the impact of the Communist leadership's policies on specific populations, such as women and national minorities, is used to examine the ramifications of policy implementation and to illustrate the fact that much of CCP policy prior to 1976 was more reaction to events as they developed rather than careful planning to address issues systematically. Poorly thought out, and even more poorly executed, policy choices led to the suffering and death of millions, an unintended but nonetheless devastating consequence. These are contrasted, in the concluding chapter, with the astonishing transformation that occurred under Deng Xiaoping and his successors

Reform era: Dated from Deng Xiaoping's rise to power beginning in 1978 and continuing in the first decades of the twenty-first century.

Tiananmen Square Massacre: On 4 June 1989, the CCP leadership ordered the military to clear Tiananmen Square, where hundreds of students and their supporters continued their two-month-long demonstration. The term 'massacre' refers to the use of overwhelming military force against unarmed civilians, an unknown number of whom died.

who have created both a new society and an economic powerhouse, while managing to maintain the CCP's hold over political power.

THEMES IN RECENT CHINESE HISTORY

China's history under the leadership of the Communist Party is marked by dramatic policy shifts that affected the lives of millions of people. These changes, which originated at the top, did not follow courses anticipated by the Party, nor were the results what the Party leadership intended. As history attests, revolutions rarely lead to the kind of society that the revolutionary leadership planned, and China's history since 1949 shows that China is no exception.

The last 60 years reveal continuing tensions within the new political system and within Chinese society. Among the most important of these are:

- Tradition and revolution;
- Rural and urban development;
- Central and regional authority;
- Communism and modernization.

Patriarchy: Male dominance in society and in the family, reinforced in China by traditional Confucian values.

One-child policy: China's policy limiting each couple to only one child, which drew international criticism. In practice, couples could secure permission for a second child, particularly when the first child was female, and most ethnic minorities were exempt.

Geomancy: A form of divination that sought to improve future prospects or fortune by locating buildings or tombs in places considered to be auspicious; in Daoism, *feng shui*, which translates literally as wind-water, is a form of geomancy.

Tradition and revolution

The tension between traditional Chinese culture and the new revolutionary society that the government fostered after 1949 remains a part of Chinese life. Chinese society has clearly changed in dramatic and measurable ways, yet patterns of the past remain. One example is in **patriarchal attitudes** which have yet to make a full retreat. Male children remain valued above females, as evinced in the 1990–2000 demographics which indicate a lopsided male–female ratio. Thus, while the **one-child policy** (see discussion in Chapter 5) has had a great impact in China by reducing family size, the preference for male children has been little changed. The status of women is another area in which patriarchal attitudes persist. Although the various constitutions adopted in China since 1954 accorded women full equality with men, as a group women lag behind men in earnings, education levels and employment opportunities. Furthermore, traditional folk practices such as **geomancy**, or *feng shui*, and the belief in kitchen gods re-emerged in some rural areas after the death of Mao, attesting to the strength of such old beliefs despite years of CCP efforts to eradicate them. As China continues to change, patterns of the past will nonetheless continue to colour the society that emerges.

Rural and urban development

From the 1800s onwards, China's wealth was concentrated in its large urban centres, particularly those located along its coast and river valleys. After 1900, as modern industrial production expanded, urban areas grew in importance, deepening the economic disparity between rural and urban China. Despite CCP efforts to equalize rural–urban income, significant differences in living standards remained during the Maoist period (1949–76), although income levels of rural and urban China under Mao were more equal than at any time in modern history. Government-imposed limits on mobility meant less pressure on the cities as the poorly educated rural population – some 70% of China's total – remained in the countryside. However, after Mao's death, the standard of living rose more quickly in the cities. As the reforms progressed in the 1990s, urban residents enjoyed a per capita income double that of rural areas. By 2000, the gap between rural and urban had risen further, with urban income nearing four times that of rural residents. Eased restrictions on travel and, to some extent, on residency requirements led increasing numbers of poor men and women to China's cities. Many took whatever work was available and moved from town to town as necessary. This **'floating population'** (see discussion in Chapter 7) was dramatic evidence of the income disparity that emerged during the reforms. Despite government efforts to reverse this trend, the rural–urban divide continued to expand in the twenty-first century.

Floating population: As part of the reform era, restrictions on travel and movement in China loosened, allowing many rural workers to 'float' or move in search of employment. An estimated 120 million people were part of this mobile group at the end of the twentieth century.

Central and regional authority

The great differences between rural and urban China also relate to different agendas of regional and central authorities. Initially, the CCP kept power centralized at Beijing and strengthened that central authority through many of its policies under Mao. Provincial governments conformed to central directives during the Maoist period as the Party imposed agricultural reforms and then moved quickly to the **commune** system. Under the reforms of the Deng government, however, more leeway was given to provincial and regional officials, particularly with regard to investment and economic development. Areas in advantageous geographical positions quickly benefited from the changes. The result was that the aggressive and wealthier provinces of the coast grew rich while those in the poorer hinterland fell further behind, causing the rural–urban income gap to widen. As the economy decentralized, control also decreased in some areas of policy, although the government kept a tight rein on banking and currency. Greater economic freedom has led to more provincial and regional ability to deviate from CCP-mandated policies in some spheres, but the central government has

Commune: First formed in the summer of 1958 as a part of the Great Leap Forward, communes incorporated all peasant-farmers and workers into large work organizations. Overall they proved inefficient and were dismantled in 1980–3.

maintained its ability to intervene effectively at any level if needed. Regional power or discontent has yet to challenge the power of the Chinese state, as action in Tibet (2008) and in Xinjiang (2009) has shown. The CCP continues to focus on modernization and economic development as the primary means to maintain stability and forestall any efforts at challenging its political power or legal authority.

Communism and modernization

Communism: A political philosophy that views the ideal society as one in which all property is held in common, class divisions disappear and the state apparatus is no longer required; a Utopian form of economic and social organization.

USSR: Acronym for the Union of Soviet Socialist Republics. Founded in 1917 after the Bolshevik revolution, the USSR collapsed in 1991. Although the new Russian state lost many of its Central Asian republics, it retained control of Siberia and, therefore, continues to share a border with northeastern China.

From the beginning, the PRC's goal was to bring both **Communism** and modernization to China. Maoist economic plans, initially borrowed from the **USSR**, sought to make China a strong, modern state, and that required an aggressive modernization agenda. However, as described in the next chapters of this book, Maoist modernization made only halting progress and at times appeared to move backwards, not forwards. From 1958 to 1976, revolution took precedence over modernization, as Mao enjoined China's people to be 'more Red [Communist] than expert'. A new period began under Mao's successor, Deng Xiaoping. After 1978, modernization became the single most important goal of the regenerated CCP. This shift away from the Maoist vision constitutes the most dramatic historical moment in China's history since 1949. Long delayed, China's modernization at last moved into high gear, and these new successes gave new life to the CCP in an age when few Communist-led states have managed to survive.

In the year 2000, as the PRC entered its second half-century, the original CCP goals of a strong nation with a modernized yet essentially socialist economy were recast to stress modernization bolstered by nationalism. The success of the reform period has placed China among the world's top economies, although its per capita income places it in a lower-middle income status when measured internationally. At the end of the first decade of the twenty-first century, the majority of the Chinese people appeared satisfied with the new opportunities the economy offered, even as old problems continued and new ones emerged.

Do economic freedoms and a capitalist economic system portend the collapse of the CCP? At the turn of the twenty-first century, the CCP clearly retained a firm hold over the administrative apparatus. The Party's new appeal to nationalism (see discussion below) and a widespread reluctance to take a chance on political reforms that might slow economic growth suggest that it will be some time before the CCP relinquishes its authority. Much will depend on the government's ability to overcome the problems that accompany its continuing reforms, as discussed in later chapters.

These tensions remain key elements in China today and provide the framework for examining the policies that have reshaped contemporary Chinese society in ways that the revolutionary old guard of the pre-1949 days certainly could not have anticipated as they struggled for uncertain victory.

TERMS AND CONCEPTS

Modern China has been marked by the growth of Chinese nationalism which, in 1900, was a nascent force in the movement toward revolution. In the 1990s, an appeal to nationalism marked CCP efforts to unite China's citizens under Communist leadership, replacing the Marxist rhetoric of previous decades and indicating a maturation of Chinese nationalism. Because nationalism has had such a great impact on China, it is important to clarify its meaning as used in the text, along with other important forces, such as Marxism, socialism and Communism, all of which are discussed briefly in this section.

'**Nationalism**' emerged in nineteenth-century Europe as an outgrowth of competitive nation-states and referred to pride in the history and culture of one's nation, a term that was in turn defined as a group of people with common language, territory, history and culture, separated from other neighbouring peoples by virtue of a unique set of characteristics. The fact that most European peoples were historically a mixture of peoples, languages and cultures was no obstacle to governments intent on fostering nationalism, which was accomplished through the fora of print media and state-sponsored education. Nationalist slogans impressed upon citizens the importance of their particular heritage and their distinctiveness, and served to unite the people of each nation-state in ways not previously possible.

> **Nationalism:** A political philosophy based on the idea that separate peoples have unique and distinctive traits; it often includes the notion that each people should have a separate and independent state.

A corollary useful to ambitious states was that a nation was entitled to its 'traditional' lands. As most boundaries in Europe were established through war at one time or another, disputes over what land belonged to which nation were intensified by the doctrine of nationalism which, in its most extreme form, justified war to regain land and reach a nation's 'natural boundaries'.

The notion of nationalism was exported to the developing world of the twentieth century. In China, this European notion was embraced by the Father of the Revolution, **Dr Sun Zhongshan**, who believed that a lack of nationalism held the Chinese people back; he urged the widespread adoption of nationalism through his 'Three Principles', which were to guide the country into the republican era. Several of the events described below

> **Sun Zhongshan** (1866–1925): Also known as Sun Yat-sen and Sun Yixian. Considered the Father of the Republic by both the Nationalist and Communist Parties, Sun served as President briefly in early 1912. The Nationalist Party grew from his earlier political organizations.

indicate the spread of this new concept in early twentieth-century China. China's Communist Party came to power in part because of its embrace of modern Chinese nationalism, which remains an important component of the Communist movement in China today.

Socialism and Communism were two additional Western imports that had enormous impact on modern China. Based on the teaching of Karl Marx (1818–88), Marxism, socialism and Communism all called for an egalitarian economic and social system. Under socialism, the 'means of production', such as factories and agricultural land, would be owned and operated by the people themselves, who would share equally in the profits. Homes and personal property would remain privately owned. Under Communism, a Utopian ideal, no private ownership would be needed as all social and economic differences would be erased, along with authority of any kind. Although Marx viewed Communism as the inevitable culmination of human social organization, he also wrote of revolution as the means by which the working class would gain the power to remould society into a Communist paradise. In that ultimate state, the need for government apparatus itself would disappear, thus guaranteeing total equality and freedom for all.

Both socialism and Communism emerged during the Industrial Revolution, which gave rise to a wealthy class of capitalists whose great fortunes derived from the low wages and mass-production techniques of the age. Long working hours in terrible conditions of noise and dirt brought only subsistence to workers while generating huge profits for factory owners. The enormous gap between rich and poor led Marx to examine the historical evolution of the phenomenon and ultimately to the call for worldwide revolution to free the workers from their miserable lives. For some intellectuals and political activists, the term 'capitalist' personified the evils of the age. The activities of socialist and Communist organizers deepened social divisions and radicalized the struggle between the growing urban labour force and the wealthy factory owners.

The exploitative conditions facing workers in China at the turn of the twentieth century mirrored the conditions of European workers. But because many factories in China were foreign-owned – by Europeans and Japanese – early union organizing also tended to be nationalistic. Because much of the early union movement was led by members of the CCP, nationalism became an intrinsic part of Chinese Communism. Although the Nationalist Party, first under Dr Sun and then under **Jiang Jieshi**, attempted to use nationalism to boost support for its programmes, it would be the Communist Party that co-opted nationalism for its own cause, first in its union organizing and then by waging effective guerrilla warfare against Japan during the Second World War. The founding of the PRC was presented as a victory of the Chinese nation, and successive PRC policies repeatedly called upon the people to

Jiang Jieshi (1887–1975): President of China (1928–49) and on Taiwan from 1950 until his death in 1975. Jiang rose to power after the death of Dr Sun Zhongshan in 1925 through his military leadership of the Northern Expedition.

sacrifice for the good of the country. Although nationalistic appeals remained an aspect of the Party's rhetoric, internal politics pushed nationalism to one side as the CCP focused on domestic problems. However, in the 1990s the CCP returned to a strongly nationalistic stance which was used to bolster flagging support for the Party, once more linking Communism and nationalism in the service of the ruling Party. As an emerging economic power, China found nationalism a useful tool as it competed for trading advantages and greater international power. As demonstrated in the following pages, the forces of revolution, nationalism, socialism and Communism continue to shape an increasingly wealthy and powerful modern China.

2

Geographical and historical background

GEOGRAPHY

China covers over 9.5 million square kilometres (3.7 million square miles), making it approximately the size of the continental United States. Unlike the United States, which has a population of 300 million, China's population in 2010 exceeded 1.3 billion, the largest population in the world under a single government. Exacerbating the impact of such a large number of people is the fact that the majority live on less than 40% of China's territory. The reason for this lies in China's extremely varied topography. Large expanses of the land are covered with deserts such as the Gobi and the Takla Makan, or high mountains, such as those of the Tibetan plateau. Historically, these areas were only part of the Chinese empire for short periods of time; their inclusion as a part of today's China is a direct result of the expansion of the last dynasty which was able to conquer and hold the regions now known as Inner Mongolia, Xinjiang, Tibet and Qinghai (see Map). To distinguish these newer additions from the core of traditional Chinese territory, the term 'China proper' is used to refer to provinces that have been part of China for over 2,000 years.

The major river systems of China proper include the Huang He (Yellow River) in the north, the Chang Jiang (also called the Yangzi) in central China and the Xi Jiang (West River) in the south. All three rivers flow west to east, allowing for relatively easy transport from the hinterland to the coast. These river systems sustain millions of Chinese, who have cultivated fields watered by these rivers for hundreds of years. Agriculture in the north supplies wheat and other hard grains, while the area from the Chang Jiang south grows rice and tea, products long associated with Chinese civilization.

Given China's varied topography, the country has abundant natural resources. Coal, oil, natural gas and many kinds of ore are found across the country, and some of these deposits – oil in particular – are only now being systematically tapped. Cotton and silk have been produced for over 4,000 years by the Chinese and continue to be important exports. Modern manufacturing draws on this abundance of natural resources.

Another great asset is the population itself. Innovative, inventive and creative, the Chinese have made invaluable contributions to the world's people, including the invention of paper, the compass, the water-mill, printing, paper currency and gunpowder. In the arts and literature, China's people have left a remarkable record of creative achievement and, after emerging from the relative isolation imposed during the Maoist era, are again contributing to the world's cultural life through film, literature and the fine arts.

HISTORICAL OVERVIEW

China's long-recorded history stretches back over 4,000 years. Its imperial system of government emerged from a series of small kingdoms based in the area of the Huang He in north China. In 221 BCE, the ruler **Qin Shi Huang Di** unified the small states and gave his name to the new dynasty, the **Qin**, from which we derive the name China. He was the first ruler to use the title emperor which remained in use in China until 1912.

Although the Qin dynasty was brief (it ended not long after Qin Shi Huang Di's death in 210 BCE), successive dynasties built on Qin successes. The Han ruling family, which followed the Qin, retained the Qin administrative system but re-established the influence of **Confucian** ideals that stressed education and responsibility among government officials. The Han (206 BCE–220 CE) proved a successful and long-lived dynasty, gradually expanding the boundaries of the Chinese empire toward the south.

Over the centuries that followed, the imperial system held together remarkably well, welding the population together through a strong, centralized administration and a shared value system, based in Confucian teachings. While China was periodically torn by the upheavals that attended the rise and fall of the 25 major dynasties, or ruling houses that have governed China, the reconstituted imperial state would re-emerge, building on the institutions and practices of the past but also adding new contributions to China's varied historical record.

By the time of the last of these dynasties, the **Qing** (1644–1912), China controlled more territory than at any time in its past. It not only controlled China proper and the lands of Tibet and the far northwest, it also held sway over the neighbouring states of Korea, Mongolia and Vietnam. The Manchu elite of the Qing ruled a multiethnic empire comprised of many peoples and cultures, and to their credit they held their far-flung empire together with skill into the nineteenth century.

Qin Shi Huang Di Founder of the Qin dynasty, and First Emperor of China. His vast tomb, unearthed near Xian in the 1970s, attests to the military foundations of his empire as it contains thousands of clay (*terracotta*) warriors, a major resource for the study of the Qin period.

Qin dynasty (221–208 BCE): A relatively short dynasty which followed legalist principles in imposing a harsh rule of law over northern China.

Confucius: A sixth-century BCE Chinese sage who stressed the need for harmony and balance in human affairs and whose teachings provided a moral, ethical code of behaviour that endured for centuries in China.

Han dynasty: From 206 BCE to 220 CE, this important dynasty laid the foundations for the imperial Chinese state.

Qing: The last dynasty of China (1644–1912); founded by Manchus from northeastern China with assistance from their allies, the Mongols, and from Ming-dynasty (1368–1644) generals who defected to the Manchus in 1644.

Opium Wars: The first war, in 1839–42, ended in the Treaty of Nanjing between Great Britain and China. The second war, 1856–8, involved France and Great Britain and ended in the Treaty of Tianjin. China's losses gave Western states greater privileges in China and began a period referred to as 'semi-colonialism' by the present government.

Yuan Shikai (1859–1916): A Qing-dynasty general who used his position as head of the military to gain first the premiership of the new republic and then the presidency. He died in 1916, the same year in which he planned to make himself Emperor of China.

Warlords: Men who ruled areas of China through the exercise of military force between 1916 and 1928. In the north and west of China warlords continued to dominate provincial governments into the 1940s.

Treaty of Versailles: This treaty was the settlement which followed the First World War, in which China played a minor part on the side of the European allies. Chinese expectations for generous treatment were dashed when former German concessions were granted to Japan rather than being returned to China.

Around 1800, however, the dynasty began a slow, inexorable decline. Pressure to open its borders to traders from England and other European states led to military confrontation in the two **Opium Wars** of the middle of the nineteenth century. In both, China was the loser. It was forced to grant not only trading privileges and legal importation of British India-grown opium, but also to cede parts of its territory to European powers, opening the age of Western imperialism in East Asia. Furthermore, internal rebellion nearly toppled the dynasty between 1850 and 1864, and although the Qing defeated the rebels, they were unable to forestall the continuing decline of their military and political power. Reluctantly, the Qing rulers embarked on limited reforms in the early twentieth century, but these were too little too late. By 1911, reformers and revolutionaries looked for more radical and more rapid reform than the Manchus wished to offer. On 10 October 1911, an insurrection began at Wuhan, in central China, and quickly spread across China. When top Qing military commanders refused Qing orders to suppress the movement, the fate of the dynasty was sealed.

The new republican government which replaced the dynasty was led by Dr Sun Zhongshan, a southerner who had been educated in what was then British Hawaii. A medical doctor by training and a Christian as a result of his British education, Dr Sun dedicated his life to the idea of a republican government in his homeland. However, within the first months of his provisional presidency, divisions surfaced between the revolutionaries, leading to a transfer of power to **General Yuan Shikai**, a former Qing-dynasty general who had belatedly joined the revolutionary forces in 1911. Yuan's government proved oppressive and the republic that emerged was far from the ideal of Sun and other leaders whose hopes were frustrated by Yuan's reactionary government. Yuan's death in 1916 momentarily opened the way for a more democratic system, but although the central government at Beijing continued to proclaim its authority, power quickly devolved to regional military leaders, popularly referred to as **warlords**. These men constituted the *de facto* government of China as they vied for the opportunity to assume control of the central government.

During the period of warlord power (1916–28), young Chinese began to search for a political system that could address the division and instability in China and tackle the seemingly unsolvable domestic problems of rural poverty and economic decline. The weak government of the new republic had entered the First World War in the hope of resolving issues related to the old treaty system which was still in force, but the **Treaty of Versailles** which ended the war simply affirmed European colonial possessions and privileges in China. Worse, in the view of many Chinese, was the fact that the treaty allowed Japan to assume the former privileges of defeated Germany, thereby giving Japan a stronger foothold in China. In May 1919, young intellectuals in China's urban centres rose in protest over the possibility that the government would accept these humiliating terms. On 4 May, thousands of students and professors took to the street of Beijing and other major cities in protest. This outpouring of nationalistic fervour was symbolic of China's struggle to find a political form. The eventual success of the demonstrators in forcing the central government to repudiate the treaty signalled the emergence of a political role for students which would be echoed in successive decades.

It was during this period of intellectual upheaval that the Chinese Communist Party was founded in 1921. Few among the 50 or so founding members could have envisioned that their Party would come to dominate China in less than 30 years. The new Party was the creation of China's new generation of activist students and professors, who looked to revolutionary political philosophies of the West to resolve China's long-standing social inequities. Guided at first by members of the USSR's newly organized **Comintern**, the young CCP joined forces with the Nationalist Party, which was still under the leadership of Dr Sun, in 1923. This short-lived alliance dissolved soon after Sun's death in 1925 as the ambitious Jiang Jieshi assumed control of the military arm of the Nationalist movement.

As the Nationalist commander-in-chief, Jiang began a highly successful campaign, the **Northern Expedition**, to defeat the warlords in 1926, just a year after the death of Dr Sun; by 1927 he and his army effectively controlled China south of the Yangzi River and in the spring of that year took the city of Shanghai, with the aid of Communist Party allies. However, Jiang distrusted CCP intentions and in a sudden coup attempted to eliminate CCP members of the movement. Although some CCP members escaped Shanghai's 'White Terror' of 12 April 1927, hundreds ultimately died as Jiang ordered a bloody eradication campaign which continued through the summer (Mackerras, 1998: 44–5). The leaders of Sun's Nationalist Party relieved Jiang of his command, but without his leadership the Northern Expedition foundered. In the winter of 1928, Jiang was recalled; in return for his continuing the military struggle, he was made provisional President of the republic. By the summer of 1928, Jiang had either defeated or co-opted the remaining warlords and central China was reunified under his control. The CCP was now a banned organization, as were the union movements that had thrived under Communist leadership.

The defeat of the warlords and the reunification of much of the country did not resolve major issues facing China – a weak economy, great rural poverty, and widespread corruption and crime. Policies to address these and other issues were slow to evolve; new laws aimed at more equitable land-holding and limits on land rents, for example, were not enforced, leaving millions to struggle at subsistence level. Much of Jiang's energies focused instead on the CCP which, although now underground, had made headway

Comintern: The Communist International, founded in the USSR by Lenin to spread Communism throughout the world. A number of Comintern agents worked with the Communist and Nationalist Parties prior to the CCP victory in 1949.

Northern Expedition: A military campaign, from 1926 to 1928, undertaken by Jiang Jieshi (Chiang Kai-shek) to defeat the warlords and to unify China. Its success brought Jiang the presidency of China.

Manchuria: The ancestral lands of the Manchu people who established China's last dynasty, the Qing (1644–1912). In the 1930s, Japan occupied this area of northeastern China, and proclaimed it a new state, 'Manchukuo', under the last emperor of the Qing, Puyi, who served as a figurehead.

Jiangxi Soviet: Founded in 1931 in the border area of Jiangxi and Fujian, this was an area controlled by a 'Soviet' or governing council led by Mao Zedong.

Encirclement and Annihilation Campaigns: Five campaigns undertaken between 1931 and 1934 by the Nationalist Party under Jiang Jieshi (Chiang Kai-shek) intended to destroy the CCP.

Long March: The journey of the CCP in retreat from the Jiangxi Soviet base after repeated attacks by the GMD, from October 1934 to December 1935. High attrition rates reduced the marchers from nearly 100,000 to 8,000 by the time they arrived at Yanan, in northern China.

Zunyi Conference: In January 1935, a meeting was held at Zunyi, a city in Guizhou province, by the leadership of the CCP resulting in the repudiation of Moscow-trained advisers and the decision to follow Mao, whose rise to the leadership of the CCP dates from this period.

among impoverished peasant-farmers. Large CCP bases emerged in south and central China, and Jiang's military campaigns against these bases became his top priority. As a result, he left northeastern China, or **Manchuria**, open to Japanese attack, which came in 1931. To deal with this threat, Jiang signed a truce with Japan, enabling him to continue his campaigns against the Communists but costing him the Manchurian region, one of China's most industrially advanced areas.

Between 1927 and 1934, the CCP remained under the guidance of the Comintern. The official policy or 'line' at that time was to continue with efforts toward revolution among the urban proletariat. This policy was increasingly untenable, however, and gradually the top Soviet-trained leaders and their Soviet advisers moved to the safety of the rural Communist bases. Among the largest of these was the **Jiangxi Soviet**, in southeastern China's most remote and poverty-stricken counties. Here, a young leader named Mao Zedong had risen to prominence. In 1931, he was named President of the Soviet, although he was not then the head of the Communist Party. His government relied on the efforts of peasants, not urban workers or intellectuals, for Mao had already determined that the peasant-farmer, not the urban industrial worker, should be the basis of China's Communist revolution.

During the fifth of Jiang's '**Encirclement and Annihilation Campaigns**' against the Communists, Jiang's army threatened to overrun Mao's Jiangxi base. The leaders voted to retreat, and in the fall of 1934 they began what came to be known as the '**Long March**' which lasted until the end of 1935. Criss-crossing western China on a year's trek that covered over 6,000 miles, this retreat took an enormous toll: 90% of the 100,000 people who began the march died or deserted as the CCP took beating after beating. At a pivotal meeting in January 1935, held at the town of Zunyi, the CCP rejected the leadership of the Soviet-trained members of the Party who were blamed for the disaster. The **Zunyi Conference** marked the beginning of Mao's rise to leadership of the movement, which he firmly assumed by 1936.

Although badly mauled in the Nationalist onslaught, battered units of CCP began to gather at a new base, in the poor inland province of Shaanxi, west of the Yellow River. Here they rebuilt their movement on the eve of the Second World War. Land reform and other policies rewarded local peasant supporters and the area under Communist control began to grow.

The full-scale invasion of China by Japan in 1937 forced Jiang and his government to face the Japanese who had used their base in Manchuria to expand into counties just north of the Great Wall and in Inner Mongolia. The early stages of the Japanese invasion began on 7 July 1937, near Beijing; soon a second front opened at Shanghai. Japanese military successes quickly mounted and by the end of the summer the major cities north of the Yellow

River were in Japanese hands. By December 1937, the Japanese had successfully taken Shanghai and attacked Jiang's capital of Nanjing, which became the site of Japanese war atrocities. For over three weeks, the Japanese took revenge for Chinese resistance by brutalizing the civilian population of the city. An estimated 100,000 died in what came to be called the '**Rape of Nanjing**'. Jiang and his government moved inland, to the Yangzi River city of Chongqing, where Jiang sought to hold on.

By the end of 1938, Japan occupied the major cities of eastern China and controlled the seaboard. Trapped far inland, without benefit of the production or finances of the wealthy industrial east, the Nationalist government resorted to oppressive taxation soon followed by forced military conscription. These twin evils were a nightmare for those under Nationalist control and garnered increasing ill-will for the Jiang government among all sectors of the population.

After 1941, with the entry of the United States into the war, American military aid finally began to reach the wartime capital. But only with the defeat of Japan by the Allies in 1945 was Jiang able to regain control of his country.

The end of the Second World War did not bring peace. Instead, the well-disciplined CCP and its military built on their war reputation and skillfully used propaganda to contrast its accomplishments with those of the Nationalists. They were inadvertently assisted by the poor performance of the Nationalist government in the months immediately following the Allied victory. The Nationalists' resumption of control in eastern China was marked by extreme instances of corruption as rapacious Nationalist officials amassed personal fortunes at the expense of Chinese who had endured Japanese rule or suffered the deprivations of refugee life for eight long years.

Animosity between the CCP and Nationalists also re-emerged despite American efforts at mediation. Instead of reconstruction, in 1946 China entered upon a short, brutal **Civil War** (1946–9) with each Party investing its future in the military struggle. With major contributions of American military and financial assistance, Jiang and his well-equipped army outnumbered the Communist **People's Liberation Army (PLA)** by two to one. The Nationalists gained a series of quick victories and it appeared that Jiang would emerge the winner, as many observers predicted. But poor military leadership and low morale among Nationalist troops contributed to a series of devastating defeats in Manchuria in 1947–8. In a final battle of massed troops north of the Yangzi River, the PLA proved victorious. Jiang pulled back, finally retreating to a last redoubt on the island of **Taiwan**. There, some 2 million evacuated troops prepared for a final onslaught which never came. Instead, in the summer of 1949, the Chinese Communist Party sought to consolidate its control over the mainland, leaving aside the British colony of

Rape of Nanjing: The assault on the civilian population of Nanjing by the Japanese army in December 1937.

Civil War: After the Second World War, efforts at mediation between the two leading Parties in China failed, and from 1946 to 1949 China experienced a Civil War which ended in CCP victory in 1949.

PLA: People's Liberation Army; the official name of China's armed forces.

Taiwan: Island off the eastern coast of China, on which the Republic of China is based.

Hong Kong: As a result of the treaty settlements after the Opium War of 1839–42, Hong Kong island, off the south China coast, was ceded in perpetuity to Britain. Returned to China in 1997, the area is now a special administrative region of China.

Macao: A former Portuguese colony in south China, at the mouth of the Pearl River, near Hong Kong. Macao was returned to Chinese control in 1999 and became a special administrative region.

Hong Kong, the Portuguese colony of **Macao**, and the defeated men of the Nationalist Party on Taiwan.

As the country's new leader, Mao declared the establishment of the People's Republic of China in Beijing on 1 October 1949, from a podium erected in front of Tiananmen, the Gate of Heavenly Peace. 'China has stood up', Chairman Mao declared, thus inaugurating a new era in Chinese history.

Part 2

CHINA UNDER THE COMMUNIST PARTY

3

China's new revolutionary road, 1949–57

For the majority of China's 500 million people the 1949 Communist victory over the Nationalist forces of Jiang Jieshi was cause for celebration. Long years of war that had divided the country and brought misery and poverty to millions ended, and although there was uncertainty about the shape that the new government would take, there was reason for hope as China began a period of reconstruction. Peasants and workers who had supported the revolutionaries anticipated the beginning of a new era and the CCP moved quickly to institute changes that would reward the people's support.

The problems facing the new government were enormous. In addition to alleviating the great misery inflicted by years of warfare, the government needed to address widespread malnutrition and public health issues. Much of China's infrastructure was shattered by years of war: public and private buildings were destroyed or damaged, and roads, railways and bridges were in ruins, making it difficult to reach many remote rural areas. The economy was reduced to a bartering system, as the old Nationalist currency, the *fabi*, was valueless. In the middle of the twentieth century, China had an estimated gross national product (**GNP**) per capita that was only one-third to half that of England in the late seventeenth century, and agricultural output still accounted for about half of the country's total GNP (Uhalley, 1988: 82–3). Further, thousands of surrendered Nationalist military units posed a potential challenge to CCP control, as did the thousands of former Nationalist supporters still in China, unable to flee to Hong Kong or Taiwan. The challenges posed by these problems would be daunting for any government; the new People's Republic faced them head-on and the immediate results were impressive, particularly given the enormity of the tasks undertaken.

Fabi: Chinese term for 'legal currency'. The term was replaced with *renminbi*, or people's currency, when the CCP came to power in 1949.

GNP: Acronym for gross national product. The total value of a nation's annual output of goods and services.

THE CCP LEADERSHIP

Leading the efforts to address these issues and rebuild the country was Mao Zedong. At the age of 55, Mao held the titles of Chairman of the Chinese Communist Party, President of China and chief military commander. As the CCP was now the most powerful force in China, the title Chairman (of the Party) came to represent Mao's supreme status. Yet Mao was little known outside China. Only a handful of Westerners had ever met him or other top Party leaders; many Chinese had heard only vague stories about the revolutionary hero who now held the future of their country in his hands.

Who was he? As eminent historian of modern China Jonathan Spence writes, 'Mao's beginnings were commonplace, his education episodic, his talents unexceptional; yet he possessed a relentless energy and a ruthless self-confidence that led him to become one of the world's most powerful rulers' (Spence, 1999: xi). Born in the central Chinese province of Hunan in 1893, Mao was the eldest son of a prosperous farmer. Unlike the vast majority of his contemporaries, Mao received a college education. Upon his graduation in 1918, he moved to Beijing and met China's leading Marxists at Beijing University. When the CCP was founded in 1921, Mao was one of the youngest members. The direction of his life was fixed thereafter in the cause of Communist victory. He supported himself by writing but, upon his father's death, he also had a private income to finance his endeavours. When the CCP was attacked in 1927, as recounted above, Mao began his life as an underground revolutionary which continued until the Party's victory in 1949.

Mao's personal life mirrored his political and military struggles. His first wife, Yang Kaihui, was executed by the Nationalist government in 1931. He divorced his second wife and fellow revolutionary, He Zizhen, to marry a young film actress, **Jiang Qing**, in the late 1930s. Of the ten children born to him as a result of these marriages, only four survived to adulthood and none would gain the stature of their larger-than-life father.

Like Mao, most of the leading figures in the CCP spent their adult lives in the service of the Communist revolution and all boasted special ties to China's top leader. One of the most invaluable men at the top of the Party structure was **Zhou Enlai** (1898–1976), who became China's Premier and head of the State Council (see description of the state and Party structure, below). Zhou's background was more international and cosmopolitan than Mao's because Zhou studied in Europe as a young man and spoke both French and English. As a result, he brought a broader understanding of international politics and, particularly, of European thinking to the upper echelons of the Party, balancing Mao's China-centred perspective. He had originally joined the Communist movement in Europe and upon his return

Jiang Qing (1914–91): Third wife of Mao Zedong and major political figure in the Cultural Revolution. In 1966 she emerged from relative obscurity to take a major role in the Cultural Revolution.

Zhou Enlai (1898–1976): One of the most important and respected leaders of the twentieth century, Zhou held a number of high positions prior to 1949, and after the success of the revolution he served as China's Premier and as chief architect of China's foreign policy.

to China in 1924 he joined the young Chinese Communist movement based in Shanghai. He barely escaped the 1927 'White Terror' and, like others in the CCP, chose to join Mao at the new base in rural Jiangxi. When Mao rose to the top of the CCP in 1935, Zhou became one of his closest allies. Throughout his long career, he held top posts in both the Party and the government.

During the years of struggle leading to the CCP's victory, the most prominent military figure was **Zhu De** (1886–1976). Zhu's warlord army origins did not prevent Zhou Enlai from sponsoring him for membership in the CCP. Zhu's arrival at Mao's Jiangxi base in 1928 marked the beginning of a strong alliance between Zhu and Mao which carried the two men through the long war years to victory in 1949. Zhu remained a strong supporter of Mao and held to the principle that the military should always serve the Party, not dominate it.

Another important leader was **Liu Shaoqi** (1898–1969) who, like Mao, was also from Hunan province in central China. Liu worked as a labour-union organizer for the CCP in the 1920s and gained a reputation for both administrative work and theoretical writings. A hero of the Second World War, Liu emerged in 1949 as the number two man in the CCP hierarchy. For a brief period, he was also designated as Mao's heir.

Although somewhat lower on the ladder in 1949, Deng Xiaoping (1904–97) was also among the CCP leaders who joined the movement in his late teens. Educated partly in Europe when he was still in his teens, Deng's youthful experience was closer to that of Zhou Enlai, whom Deng first met while working and studying in Europe. Like Zhou, he returned to join the Chinese movement in 1926 and, following the 1927 purge, joined Mao's Jiangxi forces. Deng survived the Long March, and after the victory in 1949 he was assigned to various regional positions before being brought to Beijing in 1952 as a Deputy Premier under Zhou. His political abilities led to his appointment as Secretary-General of the CCP in 1956, a post that gave him great power and close proximity to the ruling inner circle of the Party. Although Deng was to suffer in the political campaigning initiated by Mao in 1966, he was the ultimate survivor, and emerged as the 'paramount leader' of China in 1978, after Mao's death.

In the early years of the PRC, these men shared a strong personal bond. As a group, they were pragmatic, dedicated and battle-hardened revolutionaries. Unfortunately, years of experience as professional revolutionaries did not guarantee successful transition to careers that required bureaucratic decision-making and policy formulation in widely diverse areas, such as economic planning, education, medical care, engineering and technology. Many of the CCP's early errors in attempting too much, too fast may in part be blamed on this old revolutionary guard which forged ahead with little

Zhu De (1886–1976): General of the PLA. Zhu was Mao's close colleague and supporter from 1928 onwards and was largely responsible for handling military organization. He remained a loyal follower throughout his lifetime.

Liu Shaoqi (1898–1969): Former President of China. Liu was educated in the USSR and served the CCP mainly as a theoretician. Following the disaster of the Great Leap Forward, he became President of China and through a series of cautious reforms, rebuilt the economy in the early 1960s.

research or caution, embarking on widespread reform without fully compre-hending the possible outcomes of their decisions. Regional and county lead-ers also found their new responsibilities a challenge as the range of decisions for which they were responsible became increasingly complex. **Cadres** were responsible for everything from initial land reform to lecturing the village population on the new Marriage Law [**Doc. 1, pp. 130–1**]. Their limited understanding of these policies was another reason why many of the early efforts to motivate and reform conditions in the rural areas, for example, went more slowly than anticipated and resulted in changes that were not always equitable or effective. It is not surprising, therefore, that many mis-takes were made in major policy decisions at the top and in the local level operations of the CCP.

Overall, trained and skilled individuals who were needed to rebuild the country were in short supply in 1949. Less than 1% of the population held college degrees. Many of those with education and/or experience in govern-ment positions were former employees of the Nationalist Party and were therefore viewed with suspicion. Nonetheless, many former Nationalist officials were retained out of necessity because of the need for educated men and women in positions of responsibility. Likewise, demobilized soldiers were utilized for public works projects as a way of keeping them under the watchful eyes of the new government and its supporters.

THE PARTY, THE GOVERNMENT AND THE MILITARY

The new government emerged in stages. The first constitution was not ready until 1954, a fact that reflected the unexpectedly rapid collapse of Jiang's military in the Civil War. Lacking a formal document as the legal basis of the new state, the CCP organized the **Chinese People's Political Consultative Conference (CPPCC)**, a body that convened in Beijing during September 1949. The 662 delegates to the conference reflected the CCP's intention to be inclusive and therefore included representatives of not only the CCP, which dominated the proceedings, but also a few left-wing members of the Nationalist Party or **Guomindang (GMD)** and some representatives of pre-Second World War groups such as the People's Salvation Association. This body passed the Organic Law of the People's Central Government of the People's Republic of China and the **Common Program** which served as the provisional legal basis of the new state. In general, the Common Program constituted a plan for gradual change while defending China against 'imperialism, feudalism and bureaucratic capitalism' (Selden, 1979). The

Cadre: A supporter of the Communist cause engaged in work on behalf of the movement. Cadre may also indicate a member of the Com-munist Party in China. The Chinese language equivalent is *ganbu*.

CPPCC: Acronym for the Chinese People's Political Consultative Conference which first convened in 1949 to pass the Common Program. The CPPCC continues to meet as an advisory body to the government of China.

GMD: Acronym for Guomindang (also romanized as Kuomintang and abbre-viated as KMT); same as the Nationalist Party. Originally founded by Dr Sun Zhongshan, the Party retreated to Taiwan where it remains an important political force.

Common Program: Adopted in 1949, this was the basis for China's government until it was replaced with the first constitution in 1954.

conference named Mao as the new head of state and chose the membership of the government council which operated as the central authority in China until the constitution took effect.

Real power, however, lay with the CCP. Mao stood at the top of a vast pyramid that, at its base, included the rank-and-file members of the Party, numbering some 4.5 million in 1949. The Party organization paralleled the civil government, with committees and Party officials at every level, from the village to the central government. Party members held government posts as well so that the Party was tightly interwoven with the civil government at all levels in the person of dual office-holders. As the CCP's hold strengthened, the two systems became indistinguishable.

A shortage of Party members led to active recruiting in the 1950s. As a result, the Party membership grew to 10 million in 1955. Many of this generation of Party members had rudimentary education at best, but their loyalty to the Party was a more important prerequisite than education. The term *ganbu*, often translated as cadre, referred to both Party and non-Party supporters of the CCP, particularly in the 1950s. In later periods, a cadre was invariably a Party member.

An ambitious cadre could hope to be made head of a local organization in his or her village; smaller numbers achieved posts at the county level and a yet more select group held provincial Party positions. Closer to the seat of power were those with national-level posts which constituted the top of the pyramid. In theory, all of these positions were filled by Party elections, but there was, in fact, the most choice at the local level where people usually knew the candidates. For higher posts, the CCP chose candidates who usually stood unopposed.

The top Party leaders were confirmed in their positions by the **National Party Congress (NPC)**, the first of which was held in 1921, the year of the Party's formation. Because of the Second World War, the Party Congress in 1945 was only the Seventh; the Eighth was not convened until 1956. The NPC also elected members of the **Central Committee of the CCP**, which constituted the top Party elite and numbered from 100 to 300 members. The Central Committee was the real seat of power as its meetings, or plenums, continued year-round whereas the NPC itself met at irregular intervals for only two weeks. More select than the Central Committee was its core group, the Political Bureau, usually abbreviated to **Politburo**, which included the top 12–24 men in China. A final tier was the Standing Committee of the Politburo, which was virtually in permanent session and which thus constituted the ultimate power-holders in the country. In the 1950s, Mao dominated this select group.

Mao also dominated the military which, in the 1950s, remained under his close comrade-in-arms, Zhu De. Party supremacy over the military was

National Party Congress: The body which chooses the top CCP leadership and, theoretically, the source of the CCP's legitimacy. The First Congress was held in 1921, at the time of the Party's formation, and Congresses met irregularly through the Maoist period. The 17th NPC was held in October 2007 and the 18th is scheduled for 2012.

Central Committee of the Chinese Communist Party: This elite group, which has varied in size from 100 to 300, includes all top leaders of the CCP and is the source of Party policy.

Politburo: Contraction for Political Bureau, members of which are chosen from the numerically larger Standing Committee of the Central Committee of the CCP. This group, almost exclusively male, is the most powerful group in China.

confirmed by the new government: the civil government included a group called the Central Military Commission, which, technically, was responsible to the National People's Congress. A parallel organization, the Military Affairs Commission, was accountable to the CCP's Central Committee. This dual governmental and Party oversight of the armed forces meant that no military challenge to Mao or the Party emerged in the first two decades of CCP rule.

In terms of its internal organization, the branches of the Chinese military, their division into hierarchal units of command, and their ranks from private to general are the same as those of any modern military. However, as the power behind the Party, the People's Liberation Army was not, and is not, politically neutral. Members of the armed forces are trained in Communist political theory and every unit has a political officer assigned to it. On several occasions, the PLA was used to support political agendas, as detailed in later chapters, and in this important way it differs considerably from the military establishment in Western states.

In the 1950s, the military had a crucial role in establishing CCP power, particularly in the border regions. Tibet, Xinjiang and Qinghai had become virtually self-governing prior to 1949. The arrival of the PLA in these areas marked the beginning of the reintegration of these areas with the rest of China for the first time in the twentieth century. Between 1950 and 1953, the suppression of 'bandits', a euphemism for any opposition to the CCP as well as for actual criminals, was assigned to the PLA, which gained effective control of the border areas during the first four years of the PRC.

INTERNATIONAL RELATIONS AND THE KOREAN WAR

Although many European powers chose to recognize the new government of China in 1949–50, the United States refused to do so. Instead, it officially recognized Jiang's Taiwan government as the legitimate government of China, a decision that would not be reversed until 1979.

Treaty of Alliance and Friendship: This treaty between China and the USSR was signed in 1950; it provided for Soviet loans to China and the assignment of Soviet technicians to assist in China's modernization. The treaty was abrogated in 1958.

With little possibility of economic assistance from Western states, Mao turned to the USSR. In the winter of 1949–50, China's new leader made his first trip beyond China's borders. He visited Moscow to confer with Joseph Stalin and secure Soviet financial assistance for China's reconstruction. Stalin drove a hard bargain. Although the two men signed the **Treaty of Alliance and Friendship** the terms required China to repay the US$300 million in aid which was extended as a loan, not a gift. In addition, Stalin secured the rights to explore and develop natural resources in the Xinjiang region, directly across the USSR's far eastern border. The Soviets also retained the use of

Dairen (Dalian) and Port Arthur (today's Lushun City) on China's Liaodong peninsula. The agreement also resulted in some 80,000 Chinese going to Russia to study science and technology for various periods of time. An estimated 20,000 Russian and East European experts arrived to assist China in rebuilding heavy industry and other key ventures.

The alliance with the USSR also contributed to China's involvement in the **Korean War**, which began with the invasion of South Korea by Soviet-backed North Korea in June 1950. Rather than investing Soviet troops in the conflict, Stalin encouraged Mao to protect his eastern flank by assisting the North. As UN troops, about half of whom were American, landed in South Korea, China requested that the United States not intervene. Successive military victories brought the UN troops up the 38th parallel and then across it. China again issued a warning and began to mobilize troops. In November 1950, North Koreans, aided by thousands of Chinese troops, surprised the UN force and drove it all the way back to Seoul. General MacArthur, in charge of the operation, was recalled in April 1951 and a ceasefire was signed that summer. However, fighting continued until July 1953 when a truce was signed dividing the two Koreas at the same border as before.

Korean War: Conflict that began with the invasion of South Korea by North Korean Communist forces in June 1950 and ended with a UN-brokered truce in 1953.

The outcome of the Korean War was presented to the Chinese people as a victory, but it came at tremendous cost: 700,000–900,000 Chinese were wounded or killed; scarce resources needed for China's reconstruction were diverted to the war effort; and there were distractions from other programmes urgently needing government attention. It also included a personal loss for Mao, whose eldest son, Mao Anying, was killed in the conflict. Casualties for all sides were high: over 160,000 Americans; 520,000 North Koreans; and 400,000 South Koreans.

DOMESTIC POLICY: FIRST STEPS

The first priority was to consolidate control over all of China's territory. While the provinces of China proper were quickly occupied by CCP representatives and PLA units, the extension of CCP rule into the border regions took longer and required the suppression of anti-Communist forces, particularly in the Muslim northwest. Chinese troops also entered Tibetan territory and, as a result, secured an agreement with Tibet's representatives in 1951 [**Docs 2 and 3, pp. 131–3**]. Mopping-up exercises continued in some areas through 1953, with the strongest resistance coming from the minority peoples of the west and northwest.

Having established itself as the legitimate government of a unified China, the leadership began the implementation of policies in keeping with its

Agrarian Reform Law of 1950: Law authorizing the redistribution of land in China; half of the farmland was redistributed, mainly by confiscating the landholdings of wealthy families and allotting it to poorer families.

Landlord: A man who held larger than average amounts of land and hired farm labourers to work it, or rented his land to others. In the 1950s, landlords and their families became the target of various campaigns and landlord status disadvantaged any individuals so labelled for over three decades.

'Speak Bitterness' meetings: As part of the land redistribution process overseen by the CCP in 1950–3, villagers were encouraged to tell of their past abuse at the hands of local landlords, and these gatherings were thus an opportunity to speak of the 'bitter' past.

Three Obediences: In traditional patriarchal China, a woman was taught to be obedient to her father during her childhood, to her husband when married and to her son when she was widowed. These 'Three Obediences' meant that a woman would always be subservient to a male relative.

mandate for change. Foremost among these was land reform. In 1950, the new government adopted the **Agrarian Reform Law**; the law itself was of less immediate importance than the fact that the CCP used this initial reform to draw millions of peasant-farmers into the revolutionary process. Rather than simply distribute land to the landless, CCP workers, or cadres, were assigned to villages across China. After identifying the biggest landholders, or **landlords**, in the village, their task was to organize meetings of the villagers to discuss the 'bitterness' of the past and denounce the landlords as a symbol of the villagers' past oppression. Only after such **'Speak Bitterness' meetings** ended in a verdict on the landlords was the actual land reform carried out. In some instances, landlords judged by the villagers to be exploiters or bullies faced execution; those not considered enemies of the people were denounced and then released with only enough land to support themselves and their families. It is estimated that during the period of the land reform, some 2–3 million landlords were executed by peasant tribunals led by Party representatives. The landlords represented the rural elite, which effectively disappeared in village China, although their children, labelled 'son or daughter of a landlord', continued to bear the stigma of their new class designation. This exercise in class struggle initiated the ordinary peasant into the revolution, closing the door firmly on China's rural, feudal past [**Doc. 4, pp. 133–4**].

In the land-reform movement, approximately half of China's agricultural land was redistributed. The process did not result in equal landholding across China. In the north, where the population was less dense, the average family holdings in the early 1950s was as high as 2.3 acres; in the south, where the population density was very high, a family might have as little as 0.5 of an acre. Nonetheless, this was the first time any modern Chinese government had put the peasant first, and the popularity of the CCP was accordingly high among the rural population in the early years of CCP rule.

Another promise of the CCP was to address the long-standing inequality between men and women. China's old patriarchal order tolerated male dominance of women's lives, encapsulated in the old belief in the **'Three Obediences'** of women: obedience to her father when young; to her husband when married; and to her son in old age. Child marriage, concubinage and strongly held views against remarriage of widows all bespoke the low status of women before 1949. The CCP moved quickly in an attempt to rectify these long-standing abuses. The **Marriage Law of 1950** [**Doc. 1, pp. 130–1**] made men and women equal before the law, and proclaimed the right of a woman to seek a divorce from her husband. The legal marriage age for men was set at 20 years and for women at 18 years; no money or financial advantage was allowed either family under the new law and both parties were to marry only by choice, not by coercion or family mandate.

This law proved very controversial. As one observer noted, there were three main obstacles to its implementation: husbands, mothers-in-law and cadres. Some husbands felt they had the most to lose, as many men had paid money to their bride's family at the time of the marriage and their wives were thus a financial investment as well as mothers of their children and partners in fieldwork. A poor man could have seen the new law as a loss from which he might never recover. Mothers-in-law enjoyed power over their daughters-in-law and the new law threatened to upset this long-standing relationship. Finally, cadres found the law troublesome; village leaders feared alienating their neighbours if they pursued implementation of the new regulations too vigorously.

As women learned about their rights under the new law, the divorce rates in some areas rocketed. In response, local cadres often counselled couples to work out their problems. In some instances, the local officials would not grant divorces, especially if family hardship could be proven.

Complaints about the lack of implementation led the Party to renewed efforts to popularize the law in 1953. As the hold of the new government strengthened, the law was more or less enforced with regard to age and other provisions. Still, divorce remained a serious matter and often could be obtained by a woman only after repeated efforts. Women now 'held up half the sky' as Mao once said, but their social standing remained well behind that of men.

Although full equality for women was put on hold, the CCP made advances in other areas. Basic health care was a long-standing need in rural China and the CCP sought to establish clinics in each county and to train health workers to ameliorate the impact of some of the most common diseases. Young people were trained to recognize and report contagious disease and to give talks at the village level on the importance of hygiene and sanitation. The cost was modest; it had to be as China could ill afford to provide health care at anything more than a rudimentary level. The efforts made an impact, for by 1957 life expectancy had risen to 57 years, up from 36 years of age prior to 1949.

Education and literacy constituted another huge challenge to the new government. Literacy programmes for adults were begun in many villages, but this task was left to cadres who themselves often lacked much more than basic elementary education. Teachers in their teens were utilized in an effort to increase the people's educational level quickly, and plans were instituted to provide free universal elementary education throughout the country, although by the 1970s this goal had still not been met. The traditional form of Chinese characters was modified by scholars to make the language easier to learn, and gradually the simplified characters became the standard written form. CCP reports of the literacy rates for the 1950s now seem exaggerated,

Marriage Law of 1950: One of the first laws passed by the new CCP-led government, this made men and women legally equal, set minimum ages for marriage, and outlawed concubinage, among other practices. Its most controversial clause granted women the right to sue for divorce.

but it is likely that inroads were made, particularly as mass campaigns increasingly used simple slogans, characters for which were plastered on walls in public places all over China.

China's ethnic minorities were also an early subject of CCP concern. Although in terms of percentages, all the minority groups together constituted only 6–7% of China's total population, they were the principal inhabitants of over 60% of China's land. Teams of scholars were assigned the task of studying and identifying groups in order to determine which would receive the official designation of '**national minority**'. Over 400 groups petitioned the government for recognition, but the government initially only designated 40 groups as official minorities. The number eventually reached 55 where it has remained. The CCP's goal was to grant the most populous of the groups a certain amount of autonomy in their traditional homelands. These included the Tibetans, Mongols and Hmong (known as Miao in China) as well as peoples less well known in the West, such as the 6 million **Uighurs**, a Turkic Muslim group in the far northwest. Much less numerous minorities such as the Ewenki, the Hani and the Lisu (see table for a partial list of minorities) also received autonomy, although the administrative unit was the county rather than the province or region level [**Doc. 5, pp. 134–6**].

The **regional autonomy system** which was established in the 1950s was intended to offset the fact that, unlike the USSR, the new state did not allow any part of China to secede. As part of the new system, the central government announced plans to assist minority regions to advance. Although relatively little could be done toward this goal in the 1950s, the system held out the promise of financial support and a measure of local control over affairs to peoples who had been neglected or ignored by previous governments.

Hundreds of miles away from the minority areas, in urban China, the goal was to nationalize all privately held businesses and industries. In the initial phase, the new government bought a number of enterprises from their owners, some of whom remained as managers or supervisors. Managerial staff were retained at major industries and manufacturing plants. Slowly, China's urban business centres resumed production. Cities were cleaned of crime and vice, with brothels, gaming houses and drug traffickers put out of business. The new austerity of city life made it clear that the old order was, indeed, now gone.

The above policies were presented to the people through mass campaigns, led by local cadres whose job was to explain things at a level the peasants, many of whom were poorly educated or illiterate, could understand. The visionary goal of the Party leadership was to create a new socialist person who would see his or her loyalties as being first to the Party and the state and

National minority (shaoshu minzu): Refers to ethnic groups with official recognition and legal status as minorities.

Uighurs: Also spelled Uygur, Uyghur. A Turkic Muslim people, the majority of whom live in the Xinjiang-Uighur Autonomous Region in northwestern China.

Regional autonomy system: Established to give minority groups a voice, 'autonomous' governments were formed at the lower levels first, culminating in the formation of five autonomous regions; each level included representatives of all nationalities living in the area. In practice CCP domination ensured conformity with national government policy and allowed little deviation from Beijing-mandated policies.

Minority populations in the People's Republic of China

Name	Population	Location
Minority nationalities with populations over 1 million in 1990		
Bai	1,594,827	Yunnan
Buyi	2,545,059	Guizhou
Dai [Thai]	1,025,128	Yunnan
Dong	2,514,014	Guizhou
Hani	1,253,952	Yunnan
Hui	8,602,978	Nationwide
Kazakh	1,111,718	Xinjiang
Korean	1,920,597	Northeastern provinces
Li	1,110,900	Yunnan
Manchu	9,821,180	Northeastern provinces
Miao [Hmong]	7,398,035	Southeastern provinces
Mongolian	4,806,849	Inner Mongolia
Tibetan	4,593,330	Tibet, Qinghai, Sichuan
Tujia	5,704,223	Hunan
Uyghur	7,214,431	Xinjiang
Yao	2,134,013	Southern provinces, Hainan
Yi	6,572,173	South and southwestern provinces
Zhuang	15,489,630	Guangxi
Minority populations under 1 million in 1990		
Daur	121,357	Northeast, Xinjiang
Dongxiang	373,872	Gansu
Ewen [Ewenki]	26,315	Northeastern provinces
Gelao	437,997	Guizhou
Jingbo	119,209	Yunnan
Kyrgyz (Kirghiz)	141,549	Xinjiang
Lahu	411,476	Yunnan
Lisu	574,856	Yunnan
Maoan	71,968	Guangxi
Mulao	159,328	Guangxi
Naxi	78,009	Yunnan
Nu	27,123	Yunnan
Pumi	29,657	Yunnan
Qiang	198,252	Sichuan
Salar	87,697	Gansu
She	630,378	Fujian
Shui	345,993	Guizhou
Tadjik	33,538	Western Xinjiang
Tu	191,624	Qinghai
Wa	351,974	Yunnan
Xibo	172,847	Xinjiang
16 additional groups with populations of less than 25,000		
Total minority population	*91,200,314*	
Han Chinese population	*1,042,482,187*	
Total population	*1,224,882,815*	

Source: Adapted from *Renmin Ribao* [*People's Daily*], 14 November 1991, p. 3, and Gladney (1998).

then to the family. A selfless altruism was required to buoy the country and carry socialism to its final goal – the creation of a true paradise where all would be equal and all needs would be met.

Mass campaigns not only fostered patriotism and loyalty; they were also used to teach people the new, revolutionary vocabulary of the PRC. Individuals who did not embrace the new ideas of relations between men and women, for instance, were called **'Old Feudals'**. Oppression and its cause – the capitalist economic system – were taught to everyone through the political campaigns as well as in the schools. With the new vocabulary came popularization of the simplified Chinese characters that conveyed the new ideas, providing political lessons along with basic literacy.

Some campaigns aimed at fostering political ideas, but others were more pragmatic. The **Four Pests Campaign**, for example, called upon people to kill the four most common pests – flies, mosquitoes, sparrows and rats. The populace embraced this campaign with enthusiasm but, like some other early policies, it was not well thought-out. With the sparrow population diminished as a result of vigorous pursuit, many insects lost a natural predator and multiplied enormously, threatening crops. Still, the elimination of the other three pests may have contributed to somewhat better health statistics for the 1950s.

With these and other fundamental changes underway, the CCP turned to the larger issue of moving China toward a socialist economy. By the mid-1950s, the government had assumed total control of all enterprises. Growth in agricultural output had initially been strong as farmers relished their new landholding status. The organization of cooperative groups among villagers, called **mutual aid teams**, encouraged families to pool their tools and equipment. This step had been relatively successful, as many families who lacked basic equipment could now share the labour of a neighbour's water buffalo or plough to enhance their productivity. However, as the local cadres pushed farmers to pool their newly acquired land as well, forming larger, more efficiently farmed plots, resentments emerged. In 1955, only 14% of the peasants had joined the new units, called lower-level **Agricultural Producers Cooperatives (APCs)**. That summer the CCP was faced with a decision about the future of agricultural policy: should it move ahead more quickly toward a fully collectivized rural economy or give farmers time to adjust to the changes which had so recently occurred? Mao's decision was to move ahead more quickly. His impatience with gradual change and a more cautious approach pushed the Party leadership toward rapid change. By the end of 1955, almost all peasant-farmers were enrolled in some form of APC; the following year, rural China was dominated by the higher form of APC. The new APC system required that peasants not only share tools and equipment, but also pool all their land. Each individual therefore began to

'Old Feudal': A term used to describe anyone still adhering to old ideas after the Communist revolution of 1949.

Four Pests Campaign: A 1950s campaign of the CCP to eliminate common pests throughout China, including rats, mosquitoes, flies and sparrows.

Mutual aid teams: These small groups of villagers were organized in the early 1950s to formalize the practice of sharing tools and draught animals to facilitate agricultural production. Based on the success of the teams, the CCP quickly moved to a higher stage of shared ownership and production which was much less popular.

Agricultural Producers Cooperatives: Begun in 1955, these organizations called upon the peasant-farmers of China to pool all their resources and their land in order to increase production. These in turn led to the formation of the communes in 1958.

work for the state rather than for him or herself, receiving wages based on the amount of labour, tools, land and equipment given to the APC. Faced with little alternative, however, peasants joined the new APCs reluctantly; as a result, rather than increasing output, agricultural production reached lower than anticipated levels in 1956 and 1957. Thus, the CCP once more grappled with the issue of the pace of reforms.

Mao himself wanted faster change. Nonetheless, in 1956 he called upon CCP cadres to offer their comments and criticism. Initially, none stepped forward. Mao's stature as the head of the Party and the state was so great that any criticism of his policies was, for many loyal Party members, deemed disrespectful if not outright counter to the revolution's goals. Only after repeated urgings from Mao himself did criticism emerge in the spring of 1957. Called the '100 Flowers' Campaign, the movement derived its name from a classical Chinese phrase: 'Let one hundred flowers bloom, let one hundred schools of thought contend.' The goal was to have widespread discussion as a precursor to the major push toward a socialist economy, ostensibly as a way to identify and then rectify shortcomings in policy implementation.

At first, comments were relatively mild, but the number and the critical nature of the solicited remarks quickly grew as Party cadres urged members to speak up. People in and outside the Party reported abuses of cadre power, including bullying and forced compliance with directives. Minority cadres faced accusations of mistreating their own people in the border regions; intellectuals complained about the state of education and the plight of students. Looked at dispassionately, the critique of the Party offered in spring 1957 was hardly surprising given the enormous tasks at hand and the still evolving Party apparatus which relied on poorly trained local leaders and incomplete and/or inaccurate statistics for its economic planning. Nor should it have been surprising to the leadership that policy to date still faced numerous major and minor problems at all levels. In May and early June 1957, criticism continued to flow toward the centre at Beijing.

A week into June, Mao and the Central Committee called a halt to the campaign. To the consternation of many loyal CCP members, the Party announced that counter-revolutionaries within the country had used the opportunity of the '100 Flowers' Campaign to vilify the Party and its policies. The sharpest critics were detained and many individuals found themselves accused of being 'rightist' and against the Party [Doc. 6, pp. 136–7]. A new Anti-Rightist Campaign unfolded, and thousands of hapless CCP members found themselves sent into the rural areas for re-education at the hands of the peasant population. Their compliance with Party directions to offer a critique of the Party's methods and policies only brought what many must have seen as unwarranted retribution. Many cadres began years of labour at tasks such as raising pigs or planting crops. Some used the opportunity for

'100 Flowers' Campaign: Initiated in 1957 by Chairman Mao, this campaign called upon the people to offer criticism of policies and cadre behaviour; the programme was ended abruptly in early June 1957.

Anti-Rightist Campaign: A political campaign launched in the summer of 1957 to identify and remove from positions of power members of the CCP who were not adequately 'left' or pro-Communist in their thinking.

reflection on the revolution and its goals, but others simply suffered the penalty assigned by the Party, hoping that in time the 'rightist' label would be lifted.

Having effectively silenced all real and potential critics, Mao moved forward with plans for the rapid shift of all China to the commune system. An opportunity for open discussion and realistic appraisal of the Party's achievements was lost. Instead, Mao announced that China would now begin a 'Great Leap Forward' in order to catch up with European powers like Britain in just 15 years. What was to become the first great cataclysm to hit the PRC was thus launched by Mao and his supporters in 1958.

4

The radical Maoist phase, 1958–76

By 1958, eight years had passed since Mao declared the People's Republic. Mao himself was now 63. He had reason to be pleased with China's progress since the victory in 1949. China's agricultural production had returned to pre-Second World War levels, and the average life expectancy in China had reached 57 years of age. Modest improvements in health care and education augured well for the future. Technical assistance from the USSR had boosted China's industrial production as the 'Lean to One Side' policy bore fruit, although the Chinese relationship with the new Soviet leader, Khrushchev, was already severely strained. The international community saw China confront the United States and UN troops in Korea, and its stature among other developing states had increased as a result.

As the leadership assessed its overall position and weighed the impact of the 'rightist' element it believed had infiltrated the Party at various levels, Mao declared that the time had come to forge ahead rather than allow the Party to rest on its accomplishments. In the summer of 1958, China embarked on the **Great Leap Forward**, an ambitious economic plan to modernize all aspects of China's production capacity.

Great Leap Forward: An economic movement launched by Mao in 1958 to make China the equal of Britain in 15 years. It led to widespread famine and the deaths of millions.

To this end, all peasants were organized into rural communes in a matter of months. Huge in size, the 24,000 communes superseded the county-level governments as political structures. The new centralized economy called for the assignment of quotas to each commune. The state would collect a percentage from each commune while the remainder would sustain the commune members. Each individual became part of a smaller work unit, called a brigade, which in actual practice was often a reconstituted form of the village. Brigades were given work assignments and each member was paid in work points. These were tallied at year's end based on the amount of work done. Individuals then used work points in the commune stores for cloth, manufactured items and other goods; some families also received part payment in cash.

The single most important and enduring change brought about by the Great Leap Forward was the entry of women into the workforce. The new system required more full-time workers, and in rural China women were the answer. Women had always worked in the fields in some parts of China, but their work was often sporadic and seasonal because of their primary role in caring for children and running the household. In 1958, women began to work full-time in the fields. The average number of work points paid to a woman was lower than the rates paid to men, but with women's wages regularized, their financial contribution to the family was recognized as important. To free them from household chores, commune canteens fed the workers, sometimes offering as many as five meals a day and freeing women from this time-consuming task. Commune nurseries took over the care of infants and toddlers, and schools assumed daily care of children of school age. Chinese women became an integral part of the country's workforce, although it would still be some years before the principle of equal pay for equal work was embraced in rural and urban settings.

Mao's vision included the eventual self-reliance of each individual commune. Thus, ideally, each commune would have its own education and medical system, its own diverse agricultural production, as well as its own industries. Despite the illogic of requiring each commune to produce goods for which it had no locally available resources, the new campaign called upon commune members to embrace self-sufficiency by producing their own basic necessities, including iron.

The production of iron and steel consumed the energies of millions of Chinese peasants. They collected anything made of iron, from nails to cooking pots, and melted them down. To fuel the greedy, home-made furnaces, some communes denuded the landscape of trees and brush, at a huge environmental cost. The home-made furnaces also absorbed countless hours of labour as men and women tended the inefficient furnaces night and day. As an exercise in heightening revolutionary ardour, the push to make iron may have been a temporary success; however, the end product was tons of quite unusable metal.

Ignorance also led many communes into agricultural disaster. Cadres ignorant about the rudiments of agriculture advised on planting techniques and, in many instances, proposed impossibly high quotas that were intended to please their superiors and demonstrate enthusiasm for the new system. Intent on surpassing their quotas, some commune officials resorted to stratagems such as ordering the farmers to plant crops close together or to spread seed, or fertilizer, in thick layers, believing this would lead to enormous crops. The predictable result was that young plants had no space to grow and died before reaching maturity. The combination of peasant reluctance to criticize or challenge authority combined with over-zealous cadres' misguided advice contributed to a growing crisis in the countryside [**Doc. 7, pp. 137–8**].

The government-controlled media reported great increases in grain production. Based on inflated figures reported to the government by commune officials, the state took its mandated percentage of crops in tax. But because the actual amount of grain harvested was in reality lower, the amount collected by the state was a far larger percentage in real terms. As food supplies on the communes dwindled, grain and foodstuffs collected by the government rotted in warehouses.

By the spring of 1959, China faced food shortages. In sharp contrast to the reports of bumper harvests, urban residents found little food in the market. Rural China experienced acute shortfalls, but with travel in China restricted, the real dimensions of the crisis were not widely known except among higher Party officials. In July 1959, the Central Committee gathered at **Lushan**, in Shandong province, to assess the situation. The only outspoken critic was **Peng Dehuai**, a Long March survivor and admired military leader. His letter to Mao on the situation in the rural areas, which he personally had visited, indicated grave problems in policy implementation and outcomes, as well as growing food shortages [**Doc. 8, pp. 138–9**]. Although the tone of his letter was quite mild, it criticized the Great Leap and its chief architect, Mao himself. Mao's anger at Peng became public: the offending letter was copied and circulated to 150 top members of the CCP, and Mao demanded that Peng and his letter be repudiated. With no one in the leadership daring to counter Mao, Peng was effectively silenced, as were any other would-be critics.

A year before the meeting at Lushan, Mao had already decided he would step down from the position of head of state (President), a largely ceremonial position. At the Lushan Conference, the CCP accepted Mao's formal resignation from that position, although an attempt was made to divorce this move from the difficulties arising from the Great Leap – the worst of which was yet to come. Nonetheless, his resignation and subsequent shift away from the day-to-day workings of the government suggested Mao's tacit acceptance of responsibility for the deficiencies of the Great Leap. Liu Shaoqi, long regarded as Mao's successor, assumed the Presidency in 1959.

That summer, the inflated reports of bumper harvests continued, as did the foolhardy new planting methods, some of which were personally espoused by Mao. The result was deepening crisis. Crops that year failed, as they did in 1960 and 1961. Chinese came to refer to these as the '**Three Bitter Years**', for the impact on rural China was devastating. The very young and very old died first, but even the able-bodied weakened as a result of the severe shortages. An estimated 30 million Chinese died before the country began to recover (Becker, 1996). Peasants were forbidden to leave their communes and, as a result, millions of Chinese remained unaware of the widespread impact of the Chairman's Great Leap.

Lushan: A mountain retreat for CCP leaders and the site of the 1959 Lushan Conference at which Mao denounced his long-time colleague, Peng Dehuai, for criticizing the Great Leap Forward.

Peng Dehuai (1898–1974): PLA general. Peng gained prominence for his leadership during the Korean War, but his reputation was not adequate to protect him from Mao's denunciation of him in 1959, when Peng's negative appraisal of the Great Leap Forward was circulated to the Party elite. He lost his positions of power in 1959.

Three Bitter Years: The years of 1959–61 are referred to as bitter years because of prolonged famine and food shortages throughout China, as a result of both man-made and natural disasters. During this time, an estimated 30 million Chinese people died.

During this terrible time, Mao withdrew from politics and became increasingly isolated. He devoted himself to writing and to reading China's great classic literature. Liu and other top leaders were left to deal with the disastrous aftermath of his policy.

Liu was in an awkward position, given the fact that Mao's stature and position as Chairman of the CCP still gave him precedence over all other Party figures. After 1959, it was up to Liu and others in the government to salvage Chinese agriculture and mitigate the disaster. One step was to allow private plots so that farmers could augment their families' diet from their own individual gardens after completing their work for the commune. Bonuses and other incentives rewarded the most diligent. Administratively, Liu divided the huge, unwieldy communes into smaller, more manageable units. The number of communes thus grew to over 70,000. Food and cloth were rationed in an effort to stretch resources. Factory and industrial workers also saw their bonuses and incentives restored in an effort to boost production. Slowly, China began to recover. Production levels rose once more as the resilient peasants and workers rescued the country from poor central planning.

TIBET

Dalai Lama: The highest-ranking religious leader in Tibetan Buddhism. Having fled China in 1959, the 14th Dalai Lama established a Tibetan government in exile at his refuge in Dharmsala, India.

Following the victory of the PLA in 1949 and the establishment of the new government, Chinese military units moved to occupy Tibet and, from a position of military strength, signed an agreement with representatives of the young **Dalai Lama**, the temporal and spiritual ruler of Tibet. Part of that agreement assured the Tibetans that no socialist land reform would be carried out in Tibetan territory [**Doc. 2, p. 131**]. The CCP kept their promise, but their reorganization of provincial boundaries resulted in many Tibetans living outside the new Tibetan borders. Tibetans who now found themselves residents of the Chinese province of Sichuan were required to participate in land reform like their Han neighbours. When local authorities moved to enforce the land reforms, Tibetan resistance became violent and open fighting erupted in late 1955. As a result of the fighting in Sichuan, Tibetans fled to Lhasa, demanding both protection and action from the Tibetan government which they expected to uphold what they saw as their right to retain their personal landholdings. But with little military strength available to assert his people's claims, the Dalai Lama sought to calm the situation and solicit support from outside as a counter to Chinese strength.

The situation remained tense, continuing into 1957. Mao himself assured the Dalai Lama that he would delay land reform in China for another six years and possibly longer. Unimpressed with Chinese assurances, however, factions within Tibet began arming themselves, some with assistance from the United States (Goldstein, 1997). The situation was brought to a head in March 1959 when Tibetan leaders decided that the Dalai Lama would only be safe outside Tibet. He and his top advisers fled to India under cover of darkness. A bloody uprising against Chinese rule erupted but was quickly suppressed. From exile in India, the Dalai Lama declared the **17-Point Agreement** invalid, as did the Chinese government.

> **17-Point Agreement:** The agreement signed in 1951 between representatives of the Tibetan leader, the Dalai Lama, and the new Chinese government. Both sides eventually repudiated the agreement which was in effect from 1951 until the spring of 1959.

Once fully in control of the region, the CCP and the PLA subjected the region to intense campaigns aimed at breaking the power of the religious elite. Monasteries that engaged in any form of resistance were destroyed and the monks forced to return to secular lives. A massive propaganda campaign denounced the old feudal society of traditional Tibet. From the CCP perspective, the Tibetans were now liberated and free to travel the socialist road. From the viewpoint of many Tibetans, however, the year 1959 marked the beginning of Chinese efforts to obliterate their culture and religion [**Doc. 3, pp. 132–3**].

THE SINO-SOVIET SPLIT

The situation in Tibet and the growing problems stemming from the Great Leap were only two of several serious issues confronting China in 1959. Mao's growing disagreement with the new Soviet leader, Khrushchev, who was pursuing a policy of peaceful coexistence with the United States, now deepened. In addition to the policy toward capitalist states, Khrushchev also asked for concessions from China, such as the right to build a radio station in China and to refuel ships in China, all of which were rejected by Mao in 1959. Mao also believed that Peng Dehuai's criticisms of the Great Leap had been influenced by the USSR.

By 1960, the growing divide was an open **Sino-Soviet split**, and that summer the USSR ordered Russian advisers in China home. From that time onwards, the two Communist powers' interaction was marked by varying degrees of hostility. Not until 1989 was a Soviet leader welcomed in China.

> **Sino-Soviet split:** This famous rift in Chinese–Soviet relations occurred in 1958 when Mao, angered at the Soviet leadership's attitude toward China, broke off relations.

THE SEEDS OF THE CULTURAL REVOLUTION

Having stepped down as head of state in 1959, Mao played a decreasing part in the work of the government. He was no longer as visible as he had been, and was less available to old friends or even formerly close advisers. He became a remote and distant figure, although he continued to live near other top leaders in **Zhongnanhai**, a guarded compound next to the old imperial palace in the centre of Beijing. His third wife, Jiang Qing, lived in the compound in separate quarters, as did Mao's daughter by his second wife, He Zizhen, and his daughter by Jiang Qing. Later, his family circle expanded to include a nephew, Mao Yuanmin.

Zhongnanhai: The private, guarded compound in Beijing which houses China's top leaders. It is located on Changan Boulevard, just to the west of the former imperial palace of the Qing dynasty.

During this hiatus, Mao became increasingly disturbed by the efforts of the Party leadership to resurrect the battered Chinese economy. Rather than carrying the goals of the revolution forward, he came to believe that the Party was straying off the socialist path. Behind the compound walls, Mao conceived a new campaign to prevent the derailing of the revolution and to ensure a new generation of revolutionary successors from among those coming of age in 'New China'. Called the **Socialist Education Campaign**, the goal of this new mass movement was to rekindle revolutionary fervour.

Socialist Education Campaign: This political campaign to instill proper socialist values in the Chinese population was ordered by Chairman Mao in 1962, but the outcome fell short of his expectations, leading him to launch the Cultural Revolution in 1966.

With China finally recovering from the Great Leap, Mao's new campaign was launched in 1962. Workers and farmers studied Mao's works and attended rallies and meetings. All were exhorted to apply Mao's words and many dutifully attempted to do so. Whether the masses reciting slogans could be entrusted with the future of the revolution, however, remained an open question. Mao himself was clearly not satisfied with the way in which the campaign was carried out and increasingly questioned the commitment of the Liu government to the revolution as he envisioned it. The lacklustre campaign, the emergence of what Mao saw as capitalist tendencies in a system that offered bonuses and other incentives for workers, and his own increasing distance from the daily routines of government business all contributed to Mao's dissatisfaction with the political climate of the early 1960s.

The situation created opportunities for some within the Party who sought to bolster their own position through zealous support of Mao as the country's 'Great Helmsman'. Minister of Defence **Lin Biao** catered to the image of Mao as supreme leader by publishing a book, *The Quotations of Chairman Mao*, later popularly referred to as the **'Little Red Book'** because of the bright red plastic that covered the pocket-sized volumes. Everyone in the military was required to read and memorize the quotes. Under Lin's direction, the PLA became a stronghold of Maoist teachings [**Doc. 9, pp. 139–40**].

Lin Biao (1907–71): General in the People's Liberation Army (PLA) and Minister of Defence under Mao. A leader of the Cultural Revolution, he prepared the 'Little Red Book' of Mao's quotes used by thousands of PLA soldiers and Red Guards. Lin was accused of plotting against Mao and died in 1971 when his aeroplane was shot down over Mongolia as he fled China after a failed coup attempt.

Others, particularly intellectuals within the Party, saw in the changed atmosphere an opportunity to critique Mao. Although none would openly accuse Mao of making mistakes, more subtle means could be found. One such means was the publication of a play, *Hai Rui Dismissed from Office*. The author was a well-known intellectual, Wu Han, who enjoyed strong ties to influential members of the CCP, including the President, Liu Shaoqi, and the CCP Secretary-General, Deng Xiaoping. Wu also served as deputy mayor of

'Little Red Book': Officially entitled *The Quotations of Chairman Mao*, this pocket-sized book.

Beijing, under Mayor **Peng Zhen**. Ostensibly, his play was about a loyal official of the Ming period who was wrongfully dismissed for telling the emperor the truth. The parallel with Mao's dismissal of Peng Dehuai, the most outspoken critic of Mao's Great Leap, was hard to miss. In 1965, Mao decided to act. In what some scholars view as the opening volley of Mao's last great political campaign, the Cultural Revolution, Mao ordered a critique of Wu Han's play, but compliance was repeatedly delayed, much to Mao's annoyance. Finally, spurred on by repeated urgings from his wife, Jiang Qing, Mao had a critical review published in Shanghai. Mayor Peng Zhen, who had managed to protect Wu Han for a time by asserting that the play was 'only' literature, could no longer do so.

By the spring of 1966, Mao and his closest supporters had won. Mao, aided by his wife and her leftist supporters, prepared to launch the last great campaign of his life.

Peng Zhen (1902–97): Former mayor of Beijing and member of the CCP Central Committee and Politburo. Purged in the Cultural Revolution, Peng returned to a position of influence under Deng Xiaoping in the 1980s.

THE GREAT PROLETARIAN CULTURAL REVOLUTION

At the age of 72, Mao initiated what became a violent and destructive campaign that set Party member against Party member and generation against generation. All across China, violent confrontation marked this effort to destroy, once and for all, the old society, and replace it with a new, socialist order led by the generation born and raised under the Communist system. This new generation of 'revolutionary successors' became the vanguard of the new radical campaign, the **Great Proletarian Cultural Revolution**, led by Mao and his wife.

In August 1966, the CCP's Central Committee, under the direct leadership of a newly energized and publicly visible Mao, issued a directive calling for a great 'cultural revolution' to begin [**Doc. 10, pp. 140–1**]. The directive called for an open attack on all remnants of the old society so that a new, truly revolutionary society could emerge. The call to destroy the '**Four Olds**' resonated among young people in ways that even Mao must have found unexpectedly powerful.

To jump-start the new movement, young people were directed to form revolutionary groups called Red Guards. All over China, young people answered this call. To impress upon them the importance of their task as the leaders of the new movement, Red Guards were invited to come to Beijing where they could catch a glimpse of the Chairman as he greeted massed audiences in Tiananmen Square. The frenzied gatherings stirred young people who vowed their undying loyalty to the Chairman. The cult of Mao,

Great Proletarian Cultural Revolution: A political movement launched by Chairman Mao Zedong in 1966 which became a violent assault on those considered disloyal to Mao and the Communist movement. Although the most extreme phase ended in 1969, the aftermath continued to affect the lives of millions until Mao's death in 1976.

'Four Olds': Denounced during the Cultural Revolution, the four 'old' practices were old habits, customs, culture and thought. As part of this onslaught on the past, young Red Guards destroyed temples, religious sites, books and Western goods such as pianos and clothing.

fostered by Lin Biao and other radical leftists, swept across China as thousands of young people converged on Beijing to see their hero. Far from being spontaneous occasions, however, the marshalling of large numbers of Red Guards in the square and their movement in and out of Beijing was orchestrated by the military and radical factions in the Party. The young revolutionaries would spend the night in quarters arranged for their temporary use and would then be quickly sent on their way out of the city so that new arrivals could be accommodated.

Many of the young people who flocked to Beijing in 1966 saw themselves as saving China from the burdens of the oppressive past and upholding the truth of **Mao Zedong Thought**. They carried their 'Little Red Books' as a sign of their devotion and sported 'Mao badges' of all shapes and sizes which they pinned to their shirts and jackets.

Mao Zedong Thought: Also, Maoism. The political thought of Mao Zedong, including his interpretation of Marxism and Leninism, and derived from his various writings on socialism, capitalism and communism.

Honoured by Mao's call to action, the youngsters began their onslaught on traditional Chinese culture. Teenage leaders spouting Party slogans and rhetoric attacked their designated targets of 'old culture, old ideas, old customs and old habits' with great enthusiasm. Elderly Chinese who had kept clothing or objects from the past were subjected to lectures and harangues by youngsters who burst into houses and apartments at will to search for any goods from the 'old' categories. Some items were taken away, others were smashed, destroyed or burned with great fanfare out in the street.

Not only mementoes and heirlooms suffered Red Guard attentions. Party leaders, teachers and professors found themselves under attack for any casual remark that suggested disrespect to Chairman Mao or the CCP. Students whose parents wore the 'rightist cap' as a result of previous campaigns, or those with relatives in Taiwan or Hong Kong, were singled out for abuse by their classmates. Terror descended for both Party loyalists and anyone formerly given a 'black' label as the hunt for supposed counter-revolutionaries spread across China [Doc. 11, pp. 142–3].

The Red Guards did not constitute a single entity. Initially, children of Party cadres took the lead in organizing Red Guard groups; children of the 'black' categories, such as those from landlord families, were not allowed to join. In the autumn of 1966, however, the Party lifted restrictions on who could join the Red Guard movement and the number of groups proliferated. Youngsters whose background had excluded them could now also demonstrate their loyalty to Mao. Like others from politically acceptable categories, they, too, danced the loyalty dance and confessed all their innermost thoughts to China's Great Helmsman, Chairman Mao. All chose names for their local groups that reflected their loyalty to Mao, such as 'Protectors of Mao Zedong Thought Red Guards' or 'August First Red Guards'.

In 1966, as fervour grew, the Party continued to facilitate the movement of young people around the country. Any young person with an armband declaring him or her to be a Red Guard (*Hongweibing*) could board a train for Beijing or Shanghai, or other 'revolutionary' destinations. Remembering those days years later, many participants noted that they had never known such freedom. Thousands took advantage of the sudden opportunity to see places they had never dreamed of visiting. Troops of young people formed their own 'Long March' contingents to 'gain revolutionary experience' as the Party exhorted them to do, and marched on foot along routes where Mao and the PLA had fought for the revolution.

Throughout the course of the Cultural Revolution period, some young students simply followed their own local leaders and many did little more than chant slogans and turn up for rallies (Jiang and Ashley, 2000). A minority proved zealous participants, attacking any adult, regardless of social status, who was deemed by them to be anti-Maoist. Beatings and humiliating parades through the streets awaited some victims; less fortunate targets died at the hands of China's young in the name of Mao's revolution.

Girls and women became equal participants in the movement, leading their own Red Guard bands, travelling on the trains 'to make revolution', and in some instances leading or participating in attacks on hapless victims of the movement. As daughters of the revolution, they wore the same pseudo-military clothes as the male participants, and chanted the same aggressive slogans. It appeared that this new generation of young Chinese women were fully enfranchised members of the new order.

Mao used the opportunity of widening chaos to attack his own chosen targets. Liu Shaoqi and his wife, **Wang Guangmei**, both became victims. Liu disappeared by the end of 1966; he died in 1969 as a result of his persecution. His wife was vilified before a huge crowd in Beijing and then sentenced to years of solitary confinement in Beijing's prison system. Another major target proved to be Deng Xiaoping, who was attacked as the country's 'number one **capitalist roader**', an unlikely epithet for a man who had, since his teens, been dedicated to the socialist cause. Nonetheless, he, too, disappeared. Although he and his family suffered during the most virulent phase of the Cultural Revolution, he re-emerged in 1973 (see discussion in the next chapter) and was later restored to his position on the Politburo.

In 1968, competing groups of Red Guards began to fight among themselves, with each group declaring itself the true protector of the Chinese revolution and Mao Zedong Thought. Former and active members of the PLA joined forces with student groups, increasing the level of violence. Stones and bricks gave way to guns. In pitched battles both sides suffered casualties; thousands died in fighting between army units ordered to restore calm and armed student groups intent on victory for their own Red Guard faction. Some of the worst fighting occurred in the western province of Sichuan and in the central China city of Wuhan. By 1969, competing Red Guard groups closed businesses and disrupted transport and distribution of food and goods in towns and cities all over China.

Wang Guangmei (1922–2006): American-born wife of Liu Shaoqi, Wang was detained in solitary confinement between 1967 and 1979, accused, like her husband, of opposing the Maoist revolution.

Capitalist roader: Epithet used during the Cultural Revolution against those in positions of authority deviating from the Maoist line. Among those so accused in 1966 were Liu Shaoqi and Deng Xiaoping.

That same year, in the northwestern Muslim region of Xinjiang, a brief shooting war broke out between units of the USSR and the PLA on the Sino-Soviet border. This threat to the nation's security led the CCP to announce an end to the Cultural Revolution in Xinjiang. That summer, Mao decided that the movement had reached its objectives and declared victory over counter-revolutionary forces. Officially, the movement was over. But while the military quickly ended Red Guard activities in Xinjiang, stopping the chaos elsewhere took more time.

To curtail Red Guard activities, the CCP ordered young people to return home. When students on some urban university campuses continued to hold rallies and fight, the PLA was sent in to stop them. Arrests eliminated the most outspoken supporters of the movement and a harsh crackdown brought quiet to the campuses at last. To limit young activists further, hundreds of young people were sent down to the rural areas to work on communes and on huge state construction projects. The harsh conditions and poor diet quickly drained youthful energies as manual labour replaced political rallies (Jiang and Ashley, 2000). By the summer's end calm was returning to China. Mao declared the movement a success, but how he measured that success was not immediately apparent, even to Party stalwarts.

In 1969, Mao was again the most powerful man in China. His views on the need for maintaining revolutionary zeal and guarding against all enemies who would dare impede the progress of the country toward socialism seemed unchallengeable. To prevent a return of the bureaucratic style of those now condemned as 'taking the capitalist road', Mao called for a new kind of government organization. Former titles and positions disappeared; in their place were revolutionary committees which now ran governments, communes and industries. Typically, these included a worker, a cadre and a member of the PLA. Leaders of many provinces and regions had disappeared in the Cultural Revolution, replaced by men and women loyal to the goals of Mao's new radical agenda. With China's culture now supposedly revolutionized and remnants of the feudal past destroyed, or at least badly damaged, the Party hierarchy turned inward to continue the struggle for power behind closed doors once more.

The violent phase of the Cultural Revolution, from 1966 to 1969, deeply marked Chinese society. In addition to the estimated half a million people who died from torture, beatings and forced suicide, thousands more were brutalized as a result of the frenzied activities of Red Guard factions who inflicted untold physical and psychological damage. Young people raised without the supervision of parents who had been sent away for re-education lived hand to mouth on the fringes of society. Those whose elders returned from years of hard labour witnessed the enormous physical and psychological toll, from which some never recovered. Many young people who inflicted the humiliating verbal abuse and public beatings on neighbours and former teachers in the name of the revolution would later hear the CCP's apology to some of their victims, leaving the former Red Guards to reflect on why they had been urged to commit such outrages on people who were now deemed to be innocent of all charges against them. For a whole generation, the realization that their loyalties earned them only manual labour jobs in rural China and that their supposed 'counter-revolutionary' targets were exonerated contributed to changing attitudes toward the Party and its ageing leadership.

Economically, the country also suffered. Because the major struggles were in urban areas, production fell as workers spent their time in political struggle. Agricultural production in many areas also dropped, and income stagnated. One of the few positive developments was that the urban turmoil brought opportunities for small town and village enterprises, which produced necessities such as chemical fertilizer and small consumer goods that city factories, absorbed with political activity, failed to supply. Overall, however, Mao's plans for a strong economic and military state in his own lifetime suffered yet another major setback as the Cultural Revolution finally drew to a close.

All of this generated a new cynicism about the CCP and Mao's revolution. Because the times required it, ordinary Chinese became adept at attending meetings and saying little; at hiding all real feelings and guessing what the local leadership wanted them to say and do. 'Politically correct' slogans and jargon were the order of the day. Even formerly stalwart members re-examined their long-held views. Although the majority of the people who suffered during the movement were ultimately rehabilitated and readmitted to the Party ranks, the cynicism remained [**Doc. 12, pp. 143–5**].

Even the return to some semblance of normal life after 1969 was shattered in 1971 for many Chinese with the amazing announcement that Mao's designated successor, Minister of Defence Lin Biao, had attempted to assassinate Mao. In what came to be called the '**571 Affair**' China's official press reported that Lin and his family had plotted to blow up Mao's house, killing him and his entourage. When the plan failed, largely as a result of Lin's own daughter informing the Party of her father's plans, the Chinese news media reported that Lin had been shot down in an aeroplane flown by his son, an officer in the Air Force. A photograph of the crash site somewhere in Mongolia purported to show the remains of the plane, but the 'official' picture revealed little more than burned wreckage in an unidentifiable locale.

'**571 Affair**': Shorthand for a plot against Mao by his Minister of Defence, Lin Biao, in September 1971. A full account of the incident has yet to be written.

Party members and former Red Guards heard this news with a sense of shock. The infallible Mao had personally chosen Lin. How could he have made such an enormous mistake – trusting a man who could plot his death? People who had been taught that every word Mao uttered was true, now had to confront the fact that Mao was, after all, only human. Despite the jolt to the Party faithful delivered by the revelation of Lin's plot, Mao remained at the pinnacle of CCP power – he was too commanding a figure and, furthermore, his radical supporters appeared to hold firmly to power at every level in the country. Those who no longer respected their ailing leader's decisions now bided their time as Mao's health began to deteriorate.

Then, in 1972, came another surprising piece of news: China would host the American President, Richard Nixon. Mao and Nixon represented polar opposites. Mao presented himself and China as the only true Communist movement and continued to denounce the USSR, just as it denounced American imperialist intentions and its capitalist system. Equally committed at the other end of the spectrum, Nixon held strongly anti-Communist views. Nonetheless, both men considered other internal and international factors in making an about-face and agreeing to meet. Nixon's decision was not the result of any great foresight or political acuity, as is suggested by many American sources, but instead was a result of shifting power relations within the international community. For over two decades, the United States endorsed the fiction of Taiwan's Nationalist Party, still under the leadership of the defeated Jiang Jieshi, as the sole legitimate government of China. This fiction was wearing thin as China continued to gain support among the world's nations for its admittance to the United Nations. Year by year the vote to admit China and oust Taiwan from the UN and from its US-backed seat on the Security Council shifted toward China. By 1971, it was clear that the United States would soon lose the vote over Taiwan. Nixon simply read the extremely large writing on the wall. Of necessity, the United States had to begin talks with China. Rather than allow this to look like a defeat for his administration, Nixon turned the tables and presented his visit to China as a breakthrough in international relations. Clearly, it would only be a matter of time before the United States recognized the PRC as China's legitimate government.

For Mao, the menace of the USSR was paramount. The 1969 fighting on the western border led to military build-up on both sides, but other borders also had to be guarded. The USSR remained an ally of North Korea on China's northeastern border and, in the south, was allied to North Vietnam. Further, relations with India were also strained during the Cultural Revolution, constituting yet another sensitive strip of border. China, therefore, could benefit from improved relations with the United States, however slight that improvement might be.

Go-betweens arranged the talks. In February 1972, the two sides met in Beijing, where Nixon received a muted public reception. Most of the Chinese residents of the capital city were not aware of the American President's visit, although it was extensively and ecstatically reported in the American and world press. The results of the exchange between Mao and Nixon were encapsulated in the **Shanghai Communiqué** which called for continued talks and movement toward normalization of Sino-American relations. Although such normalization would not come until 1979, the Nixon visit signalled a new era in Sino-American relations.

After the Nixon visit, Mao's various illnesses continued their assault on his health: Parkinson's disease, heart disease and other maladies weakened the leader. Other elderly comrades-in-arms also battled illness. The first to succumb was Zhou Enlai, who died of cancer in January 1976. A great outpouring of national grief met the news of his death. A few months later, Mao's long-time military commander, Zhu De, also died. The dragon year of 1976 was also Mao's last: he died on 9 September 1976, leaving as his most important legacy a unified state – achieved at a great cost to millions of his countrymen.

The nation now waited to learn who would succeed Mao. In October, the startling news came that Mao's widow, Jiang Qing, and her three closest supporters in the Cultural Revolution had been arrested. In the Chinese press, the group was called the '**Gang of Four**' and together stood accused of crimes against the state. A further surprise was the announcement that a relatively unknown Party member, **Hua Guofeng**, would now lead China into the post-Mao era.

ASSESSING MAO'S IMPACT ON CHINA

Decades after his death, the image of Mao is once again an important symbol of the Chinese people's struggle for national unity and pride. Despite his legacy of the disastrous Great Leap Forward and the chaotic Cultural Revolution, Mao remains an icon for many Chinese, who honour him as China's greatest twentieth-century leader. Beyond China's borders, however, references to Mao and his accomplishments are less laudatory. Some popular accounts have portrayed him as a tyrant and a dictator, comparable to Stalin or Hitler. However, the most highly regarded biographies place Mao in historical context and credit him for his achievements as a revolutionary leader who unified and strengthened China after years of devastating warfare. None ignores his role in events that led to enormous loss of life, but all seek a broader understanding of the man and the system which led to such tragic outcomes (Terrill, 1993; Short, 1999; Spence, 1999).

Any assessment of Mao must take into account his whole career, both before and after 1949. Clearly, his career as a revolutionary is inseparable from the period of dramatic changes that marked his adult life prior to 1949. Better than any other leader of his day, Mao understood how great the need

Shanghai Communiqué: An agreement signed between the United States and China in 1972, declaring their mutual intention to open talks and explore the possibility of resuming official diplomatic relations.

Gang of Four: Consisting of Chairman Mao's wife, Jiang Qing, and her three key supporters in the Cultural Revolution, this 'gang' was blamed for the excesses of the Cultural Revolution. In a show-trial, Jiang Qing was sentenced to death for her actions; the sentence was commuted to life in prison.

Hua Guofeng (1921–2007): Hua rose from relative obscurity to become Premier of China following the death of Mao in 1976. He was soon eased out of his top positions by Deng Xiaoping and replaced by Deng's own hand-picked men.

was for fundamental change in the countryside. But he also believed he had discovered the means to bring about that change – through leadership of the majority of the Chinese population, the peasant-farmers in China's vast countryside. To coalesce the power of the peasantry, Mao tapped into traditional views of authority and government that included loyalty and self-sacrifice as central values. To sway students and intellectuals, Communism was presented as a set of modern scientific principles that could resolve China's seemingly insurmountable problems. China's heightened sense of nationalism and unified efforts to fight Japan during the Second World War were also explicitly harnessed by Mao and the CCP to expand their appeal. By the end of the war, Mao and the CCP emerged with a strong following in northern China that laid the foundation for their 1949 victory over Jiang and his forces. The great feat of wresting control from the GMD and the creation of a strong, centralized state earned Mao and the Party great respect and admiration. Regardless of later misjudgements and errors, Mao enabled China to 'stand up', and that accomplishment alone places him in the category of national hero to many Chinese.

Mao's impact on China must also be assessed in terms of economic and social changes in China after 1949. Despite the setbacks of the Great Leap and the Cultural Revolution, overall China's economy made decided advances during the Maoist period. China's industrial sector grew rapidly and agricultural output was once again showing increases by the time of Mao's death. China's infrastructure expanded with the addition of new railways and improved roads. Electricity became available in all but the most remote villages. Life expectancy reached 65 years by the time of Mao's death, a remarkable increase over the 1949 figure. Under the new laws of the PRC, women held equal status with men and, as a result of the commune movement, worked outside the home. Although efforts to expand education stumbled repeatedly because of political campaigns, the number of literate men and women climbed as schools and colleges grew in number throughout the period. These accomplishments are part of the legacy of the first generation of revolutionary leadership.

At the same time, Maoist policies exacted an enormous human cost. Misguided policy decisions of the Great Leap Forward claimed millions of lives. Whether this cost was levied unintentionally or not, Mao himself chose the policies that led to human disaster and he cannot be absolved of responsibility for the outcomes. When the records of the CCP are someday made available for objective examination, both the Chinese people and the world community will be able to assess more clearly the circumstances that led to the greatest tragedies of the Maoist period and how that experience influenced China's current economic reforms and its political direction.

Despite the disasters that marked the last decade of Mao's life, and the deeply flawed policy decisions made by him and his closest associates, China soon recovered. The resilience of the Chinese people can be clearly seen in the revival of the economy and Chinese society as a whole during the reform era initiated by Deng Xiaoping, as discussed in the next chapter.

5

Building reform-era China, 1977–89

DENG REVERSES THE MAOIST DIRECTION

From the death of Mao in September 1976 until 1978, manoeuvring for power occupied the top government and Party leaders. By 1978, it was clear that Deng Xiaoping and his supporters were the victors in a struggle played out largely behind closed doors. Until his death in 1997, Deng orchestrated a series of reforms that give this era its name.

Yuan: A general Chinese term for money. Officially, the currency today is called *renminbi*, or the people's money.

Major problems faced the new Deng administration: the government now had a 6.5 billion **yuan** deficit; 20 million Chinese were unemployed; and an estimated 100 million were undernourished. The military was woefully out of date, as was China's own technology and scientific research. Thousands of CCP members and wide segments of the population questioned the decisions of the Party leadership. The radical approach of the Maoists, who called for a successor generation of Party faithful more 'Red' than expert, managed to leave China far behind other countries in Asia where the standard of living greatly exceeded that of the average Chinese. If the legacy of the revolutionaries was to mean anything, new approaches to China's many problems were imperative.

Zhao Ziyang (1919–2005): Former Premier of China. Zhao was hand-picked by Deng Xiaoping to serve as Premier in 1980 and to reform the commune system. Zhao's introduction of the contract responsibility system brought rapid agricultural expansion, and helped to launch China's economic revival.

Deng and his supporters realized that without economic advances, the future position of the CCP would be untenable. The goal therefore became the succinctly stated 'Four Modernizations' originally put forward by Premier Zhou in the 1970s: modernization of agriculture, industry, national defence, and science and technology. The most important of the four was the modernization of agriculture because 80% of the population derived their living primarily from agricultural production. Unlike the earlier Maoist policies, which were hastily designed and quickly implemented, the new approach called for experimentation with changes in just a few areas before beginning wider reforms. To oversee reform in this vital area of the economy, Deng appointed a close personal supporter, **Zhao Ziyang**.

Zhao was of a somewhat younger generation of the CCP leadership. Born in 1919, he was only 18 when Japan invaded China in 1937. While still in his teens, he joined the Party and fought in the Second World War. After the 1949 victory, he rose through the Party ranks in Guangdong province and, after a stint in Inner Mongolia during the Cultural Revolution, was reassigned to Sichuan, which had suffered tremendously from the violence and chaos of the Cultural Revolution years. In order to speed economic recovery there, in 1975 he began modest reforms which proved very successful. A popular slogan in the province was 'Yao chi liang, zhao Ziyang', meaning, 'If you want food to eat, find Ziyang', the latter phrase being a pun on Zhao's surname which, in the ditty, can be understood as either a surname or the verb 'to find'.

The system used in Sichuan called for renting commune land to individual farming families. The farmers' crops had to be sold to the state at state-mandated prices. Initially, land could be leased for only 1 year, but the early result was so successful that the periods of the lease were extended to 3, then 5 and then 15 years. Also, only a percentage of produce had to be sold to the state. The remainder could be sold by the family at newly established 'free markets' which sprang up in towns and villages throughout Sichuan. Called the **contract responsibility system** or responsibility system, the incentives contained within the new system quickly and dramatically increased crop production. Rural incomes doubled. By 1983, 98% of the country's peasant-farmers had shifted to the new system. The communes became a part of the past, an economic and social experiment that failed to deliver the pre-1949 promised paradise of the CCP.

Even before the new system was instituted nationwide, Zhao was given a more important role in Deng's new government. In 1980 he was appointed to the state council and, as the success of the reforms in Sichuan became apparent, he was named Premier, replacing Hua Guofeng who disappeared into obscurity.

In the 1980s, agricultural production increased an average of 9% a year under the new policies. Equally important to many farm families was the rise of town and township enterprises. By 1989, these small enterprises produced textiles, small electronics or component parts, and plastics; together they accounted for 58% of the total value of rural output. An estimated 25% were run by rural women whose financial contribution to family income increased considerably. For the first time in many years, farm families had money to build new houses or new additions to existing homes. The arrival of electricity to even the most remote rural areas allowed the introduction of such luxuries as cassette players, washing machines and televisions. While not every area enjoyed an equal measure of prosperity, the changes in the early

Contract responsibility system: Adopted in the early 1980s, this system allowed peasant-farmers to lease land and plant crops of their choice. Because of its success in increasing agricultural output, it replaced the commune system.

1980s were so dramatic that it was almost like a second revolution. The new slogan was 'To get rich is glorious', and the Chinese embraced the movement with great enthusiasm.

Modernization of industry was more difficult to accomplish. Unlike the farmers, the urban workers had been the primary beneficiaries of the Maoist period. They enjoyed many benefits that derived from their jobs as workers. An individual was employed by a *danwei* or work unit. In addition to wages, workers had job security, subsidized housing, medical care, pensions and other benefits from their employer, the state. It was virtually impossible to be fired, and lateness, shoddy work or frequent absence were common abuses. Of all urban workers, 96.8% enjoyed such privileges, which could also be passed on to children who were given preference in hiring at their parent's *danwei*.

A majority of government-run enterprises made little or no profit. To change this, in 1984 the government granted autonomy to many state enterprises. Over 400,000 such organizations could now set wages as well as prices; profits could be reinvested to upgrade equipment or to offer workers bonuses. Pressure on unprofitable ventures grew to improve their products and cut losses. Despite the new directives, some ventures continued with business as usual except that complaints and foot-dragging strategies were offered rather than profits. Workers resisted the loss of their **'iron rice bowl'** jobs which provided a lifestyle many rural Chinese envied.

But the Deng government was adamant: in the mid-1980s it warned that enterprises that did not make a profit would be closed. To encourage profits, the government lowered the tax on total revenues of an enterprise to only 33%, down from 55% in 1983–4. Still, the progress toward shifting industry to the new system was not smooth. By 1990, 54% of industry remained state-owned and concerns over rising urban unemployment placed further changes on hold.

FOREIGN INVESTMENT AND THE SEZs

As a further stimulus to the economy, in 1980 China secured its first loans from the International Monetary Fund (IMF) and the **World Bank**. Money became available to upgrade machinery and establish new manufacturing and industrial development. At the same time, another Deng initiative opened China further to Western investment: the **Special Economic Zones (SEZs)**. In 1979, the Deng government opened four southern coastal towns and villages as SEZs: Zhuhai, near Macao; **Xiamen**, across from Taiwan;

Danwei: Chinese term for work unit. In the Maoist era, every worker belonged to a *danwei* which not only paid his or her salary, but also provided health care, housing, child care and other services.

Iron rice bowl: A term used to designate a permanent position, literally an unbreakable 'bowl' that guaranteed basic livelihood or 'rice'.

World Bank: Formed at the end of the Second World War to finance the rebuilding of war-torn states and the development of former colonies, the Work Bank loans money to its member-states for projects all over the globe. China became a major borrower in the 1990s.

SEZ (Special Economic Zones): Instituted by Deng Xiaoping to jump-start the Chinese economy in the reform era, these zones offered foreign investors generous terms in the form of tax relief and low costs.

Xiamen: Chinese coastal city in Fujian province designated an SEZ as part of the reform era efforts to attract foreign investors to China.

Shantou; and **Shenzhen**, just across the border from Hong Kong. A fifth, Hainan Island, off the southern coast, was added in the 1980s. The advantages of these areas for investors were considerable: the 15% tax was waived for the first and second years of profitability and a 50% tax exemption provided further incentive in the third and fourth years. No import duties were attached to production materials or equipment.

By far the most successful has been Shenzhen, which clearly benefited from its proximity to Hong Kong. The primary foreign investors were Hong Kong and Taiwan Chinese whose investments created a boom town out of a small rural village in a matter of a few years. Attracted by good training and high rates of pay, workers flocked to the town, which boasted the highest annual economic growth rates in all of China by the end of the 1980s. The other SEZs developed more slowly but each boosted local industry to some degree as well as attracting foreign investments. In addition, the government authorized 14 coastal cities to offer special privileges to foreign investors as a further sign of China's new desire to stimulate growth of technology and international trade.

Shenzhen: Former village just across the border from Hong Kong, Shenzhen was made an SEZ in 1980; in the next two decades, its population grew to 4 million, including a large, well-trained workforce employed by international corporations manufacturing a wide range of goods.

DENG AND THE REORGANIZATION OF THE CCP

Deng himself had been a victim of the extreme Maoist line during the Cultural Revolution. He was aware of the shortcomings of a CCP leadership that had become isolated from the people, just as he was aware of the problems caused throughout China because of poorly educated and inept cadres. Within the Party itself, cadres who had limited education but were considered politically reliable still remained in place at the upper levels of government. At the very highest levels, a small number of elderly men still clung to their positions of power in the Politburo of the CCP's Central Committee. Deng himself was in his 80s, as were several other Party stalwarts.

In 1982, Deng initiated a plan to encourage senior members of the Party to retire. By 1986, a total of 1.8 million had done so. Furthermore, he sought to cleanse the ranks: between 1983 and 1987 the CCP expelled over 150,000 cadres for various forms of wrongdoing (MacFarquhar, 1997: 362). Deng also moved to raise the overall level of education of cadres; as a result of his efforts, 60% of the Party membership below the level of the Politburo soon consisted of younger men and women with college educations. However, some elderly members remained at the top of the power structure; Deng appointee Premier Zhao Ziyang, for example, was in his 60s, as was Secretary-General of the CCP Hu Yaobang, another Deng protégé (MacFarquhar, 1997: 336–7).

While the CCP moved to reform itself, Deng remained a committed Communist. He reaffirmed this in proclaiming the Four Cardinal Principles: first, China remained committed to following the socialist road; second, China remained a 'dictatorship of the proletariat' as it continued toward Communism; third, the CCP's leadership was inviolate; and, lastly, Deng proclaimed the supremacy of Marxist–Leninist–Maoist Thought. Any observers who thought they were witnessing the dismantling of China's socialist system needed only to be reminded of the Four Cardinal Principles which, officially at least, maintained the fiction of a government still following the old revolutionary road. Certainly, the CCP maintained its hold over China's society despite the relaxation of economic controls. This power is illustrated in the discussion (below) of social policies in the 1980s.

FAMILY PLANNING AND THE 'ONE-CHILD' POLICY

The government's concern with a burgeoning population in the 1950s initially led to limited campaigns to persuade couples to have fewer children. But it was not until after the Cultural Revolution that greater efforts were made to publicize the need for lowering the country's fertility rate. In the 1970s, the campaign to curtail population growth adopted the slogan '**Wan xi shao**'. '*Wan*', meaning late, asked couples to delay marriage and child bearing; '*xi shao*', meaning fewer, referred to waiting longer between children and bearing fewer children overall. As part of this campaign, peasant families were asked to limit families to three children; by 1977 the number dropped to two. This phase of the campaign was successful, lowering fertility rates from six to three children per woman (Greenhalgh, 1994).

Wan xi shao: Chinese slogan translated as 'later, fewer, further between', which was used with the new family planning regulations in 1980s.

A new version of the 1950 **Marriage Law** was announced in 1980, requiring all married couples to use a form of birth control. The law did not specifically call for a 'one-child' limit, but local regulations and national publicity campaigns made it clear that one child per family was the goal of the new campaign. The actual implementation of the law varied from province to province, and each area could establish rewards for compliance as well as penalties for ignoring the new regulations. The five autonomous regions' minority populations were initially exempted from the new one-child limit, but by 1986 these areas, too, were urged to institute one-child limits in urban areas and two-children limits in rural districts.

Marriage Law of 1980: This revision of the original 1950 law raised the minimum age for marriage to 22 for males and 20 for females. It also required all married couples to practise birth control, among other provisions.

The pressure on urban populations all over China was great. Penalties could be harsh, including fines of up to 15% of a family's annual income and no free schooling or health care for an unauthorized second child. There were abuses of power as local family planning officials struggled to adhere to quotas imposed by higher authorities: forced late-term abortions and abandoned baby girls were part of the price of the new policy in some instances. Most family planning authorities preferred women to use an **IUD** (intrauterine device) which, from their viewpoint, was cheaper and more reliable than other forms of contraception as well as having the advantage of giving control of a woman's fertility to the doctor who inserted and removed the IUD. Only with permission could a doctor remove an IUD and allow a second pregnancy.

IUD: Intrauterine device. A contraceptive device inserted by a physician to prevent pregnancy. This is the most commonly used method of birth control in China.

Undermining the national efforts to control population, however, was the new economic system. As China reverted to family farms, the family once again became the basic economic unit in the countryside. The more sons in a family, the more hands to work the land and the more income the family would share. In the 1980s, girls still 'married out', following the traditional exogamy of village China; a family with only a single daughter would lose that pair of hands upon the girl's marriage, while a son would not only remain at home, but would also bring in another worker, his wife, to increase the family's fortune. By reinforcing the patriarchal values of China, the family-planning policy undermined earlier efforts to improve the status of women and to break away from old patterns of male dominance (Jacka, 1997).

Some groups found ways around the rules. The 'floating population' was not monitored by family-planning officials because it was transient; children born to women who joined this migratory group were thus outside the plan. Even peasant families found ways around the regulations, and the policy clearly did not have 100% compliance. Nonetheless, China's official rate of population growth fell to 1.1, one of the lowest in the world. In 1988, many rural areas modified their policies so that rural families whose first child was female usually received permission to have a second child.

THE 'OPENING' OF CHINESE SOCIETY IN THE 1980S

During the 1980s, China's new openness allowed many Chinese their first glimpses of the wider world beyond China's border. Access to translations of Western literature and the arrival of Hollywood films in towns across China boosted the demand for publications and entertainments of all kinds. Chinese authors and film producers found new audiences for their work as government regulation at last relaxed. One popular new genre was the 'scar' literature that detailed the misery that had afflicted so many during the period of the Cultural Revolution. One shared theme in much of this writing was the devastating impact of the movement on individual lives. These accounts made clear the authors' views that they had been manipulated into joining a movement that cost some of them their families, their chance for a good education and their self-respect. A growing number of these works found their way into English as the '10 lost years' of 1966–76 became a part of history (Liang and Shapiro, 1983; Yue, 1985; Gao, 1987; Ma, 1996) **[Docs 11 and 12, pp. 142–5]**.

As workers and peasants at last prospered, new styles of clothing in brighter colours emerged on China's streets. Privately owned restaurants offered appetizing food and snacks, and roadside vendors sold fruits and vegetables grown in local gardens. Music tapes of Hong Kong and Taiwan singers circulated through the country, along with China's own rising generation of rock musicians. Discos opened in many cities, although the official hours usually required such establishments to close relatively early. Dancers and practitioners of traditional exercises, like the slow movements of *taijiquan* (t'ai ch'i) and *qigong*, gathered in public parks in the early morning hours to enjoy decidedly apolitical activities. Although these new pleasures were small, everyday matters, the chance to enjoy daily life was, in itself, a sign of renewal.

Taijiquan (t'ai ch'i): An ancient form of flowing physical exercise practised by many Chinese for general health and well-being.

Qigong: Ancient form of breathing exercises mixed with physical movements to enhance health and prolong life.

The more open atmosphere also meant less oversight of officials at all levels in the vast Chinese bureaucracy. Some officials found opportunities to enrich themselves and their friends in the changed atmosphere. Among the crimes officially reported and denounced in the press during the 1980s were embezzling state property, smuggling Western-made products and taking bribes. Periodically, police crackdowns resulted in large numbers of arrests; those convicted often received stiff penalties, from years in prison to death. Nonetheless, large- and small-scale corruption continued as China's economy expanded at an ever-faster pace.

Long-suppressed crimes such as prostitution and drug trafficking also re-emerged, along with the economic reforms. The punishments for both of these crimes could be as extreme as the death penalty, but as profits from these activities grew, the number of people willing to take the risks involved also increased. Sales of pornography and increasing incidences of sexually transmitted diseases reinforced conservatives' claims that China had gone too far in opening its doors to the decadent West.

CHANGES IN MINORITY REGIONS

China also witnessed a new restlessness among its minority populations in the 1980s. Although the policy of regional autonomy was considered China's solution to 'the nationalities question', the policies of the Maoist period had confirmed for some minorities their belief that the Han Chinese did not respect or value minorities or minority culture. Minorities welcomed the reforms of the 1980s, as did other Chinese citizens, but their welcome quickly changed to dismay as the central government announced new plans to develop the rich natural resources of some of the autonomous regions. Beijing also appeared to encourage Han Chinese to move to the border regions, and as word spread of readily available land and other incentives, the numbers of Chinese heading west increased. In response, students in minorities areas organized demonstrations in major towns and cities. Just as Han Chinese students in China proper demonstrated for change, so did minority students who also hoped for true autonomy in addition to greater democracy and economic freedom.

Of particular concern to the government were activities in oil-rich **Xinjiang**, home to the Uighurs, a Muslim group numbering some 8 million people in the 1980s. Xinjiang was the site of secessionist governments in 1933 and 1944, both of which sought to overthrow Chinese dominated provincial governments and establish an independent East Turkestan Republic. The last of these still controlled three of the region's districts in 1949 when the PLA marched into the area and struck an agreement with the Nationalist officials still holding on to power there. In an effort to gain support of the Uighurs and other Muslim groups in Xinjiang, the PRC promised cultural autonomy and assistance with economic development. Instead, it sent hundreds of poor Chinese who were relocated to the region by the government in the late 1950s. Many of these new settlers scratched out a living on land reclaimed from the deserts, while others worked in the region's oil fields or coal mines. The Cultural Revolution brought more Han to the region, along with fighting, desecration of Muslim mosques, burning of the **Qur'an** and prison sentences for outspoken Uighurs and other minorities. Although the military restored order in Xinjiang in 1969, the aftermath of the violent phase of the Cultural Revolution continued with the suppression of religious activities through to 1976. It was not surprising therefore that even after Uighurs and other Muslims were finally allowed to worship publicly once more, relations between the Chinese population and the Muslims remained strained.

When the reform era began, Xinjiang's Muslims sought to make their voices heard. Demonstrations became a part of urban life in the major cities; even the regional capital, Urumqi, which was a Han Chinese stronghold, saw student demonstrations in the 1980s. Some of the students' complaints mirrored those elsewhere in China: corruption, inflation and abuses of power. Other complaints were more specifically related to the region's minority status: Uighurs opposed the population-control policy; they wanted an

Xinjiang-Uighur Autonomous Region: China's largest minority region, Xinjiang is home to Muslim peoples such as the Uighur, Kazak, Tajik and Kyrgyz. Han migration into the region since 1949 has drastically changed the ethnic composition: from 5% of the population in 1949, Han accounted for an estimated 40% in 2010.

Qur'an (or Koran): The sacred book of Islam, containing the teachings of the Prophet Muhammed, dating from the seventh century CE.

Lop Nor: A lake, now a dry lake-bed, in eastern Xinjiang; the area is the site of China's nuclear-testing programme.

Takla Makan Desert: Located in the southern area of Xinjiang, the Takla Makan is one of the world's most arid places; it contains enormous natural gas and oil deposits, and is therefore marked for exploitation in the early twenty-first century.

Hui: Chinese who follow Islam. Some Hui people trace their roots to the arrival of traders from the Arab world during the Tang dynasty (618–906 CE). This 'foreign' origin is cited as a reason for the Hui being classified as a minority group.

end to Han migration which had increased Han presence from 5% to 40% of the population; and they demanded that nuclear testing in the **Lop Nor** area of the **Takla Makan Desert** stop. The government condemned the demonstrations and increased vigilance and arrests, rather than acknowledging the legitimacy of these requests.

Other minorities fared better in the reform era. For example, Muslim Chinese, or **Hui** as they are officially called in China, reacted vigorously when books deemed insulting to Islam appeared on bookstore shelves in their autonomous area, Ningxia. In that instance, the offending book was pulled from bookstore shelves and the Muslim leaders were mollified with apologies. Privileging one minority group over another, however, was viewed in some quarters as a 'divide-and-rule' tactic which meant that each group struggled alone for privileges or concessions from the government. With the CCP ultimately determining policy in minority areas, the prospects for true autonomy over local cultural affairs still seemed as remote as ever.

THE DEMOCRACY MOVEMENT AND TIANANMEN SQUARE

As the reform era continued to breathe new life into China's economy, many observers of these dramatic changes could be forgiven for thinking that the economic liberalization of the government would inevitably have to extend to greater personal freedom and a more democratic and open political system. Certainly, students and intellectuals across China equated economic reform with political reform. The younger generation especially welcomed the changes initiated by Deng.

Dazibao: Chinese term for 'Big Character Poster'. A poster containing opinions and/or political slogans pasted on to walls in public places.

Democracy Wall: Located in central Beijing on Changan Boulevard in 1978, this wall was covered with Big Character Posters in the early years of the democracy movement in China. After 1980, the wall was off limits.

Their increased expectations quickly turned to public calls for greater changes, in particular democratization. Even as the first reforms were being announced in 1978, students began posting *dazibao* or Big Character Posters on university campuses calling for rapid advances toward political liberalization. In the fall of 1978, the southern walls of the Forbidden City on Changan Boulevard in the centre of Beijing carried student and worker posters calling for more freedoms and faster change. Dubbed '**Democracy Wall**', the area became a meeting place for students and urban residents of all walks of life who gathered at the wall to listen to speeches and voice their own complaints about the existing system. In December of 1978, posters criticizing Deng himself began to appear, but despite this new provocation, no action was taken to curtail the movement. With the inauguration of what became known as the democracy movement in 1978, it appeared that a new era had indeed begun.

One of the more outspoken leaders was **Wei Jingsheng**, a young worker who called on the Deng government to institute a **'Fifth Modernization'**, democracy. Wei's call was taken up by students who continued to flock to the wall in early 1979. Abruptly, on 29 March 1979, the government arrested Wei and accused him of crimes against the state. A one-day show-trial in October 1979 ended with Wei receiving a 15-year sentence, most of it to be spent in solitary confinement. In December, 'Democracy Wall' was moved to a more remote and inaccessible part of Beijing. The next year, the **'Four Big Rights'**, dating from the Cultural Revolution period and included in the 1978 constitution, were revoked: citizens no longer had the rights of *daming*, *defang*, *dabianlun* and *dazibao*, the rights to speak out freely, air views fully, hold great debates and write Big Character posters. At the same time, the government began quiet investigation and detention of the most active supporters of the democracy movement. An estimated 100,000 people were arrested and sent for re-education in rural areas. Those from outside the major cities had their residence permits revoked, a measure intended to limit further the concentration of pro-democracy advocates in urban areas.

These efforts to quiet, or at least tone down, critics inside China did not work. Increasingly disenchanted with the pace of the reforms and the refusal of the government to allow greater personal and political freedom, outspoken individuals continued to challenge the government. Among them was the highly regarded physicist **Fang Lizhi**, a popular professor at the **China University of Science and Technology (CUST)**, in Hefei, Anhui province. The Russian-educated Fang had once worked on a top-secret government project, a heavy-water nuclear reactor. In 1957 he was expelled from the Party for criticizing the politicization of the physics curriculum: his physics text quoted Lenin who, for political reasons, rejected the theories of renowned physicist Niels Bohr. Nonetheless, China's great need for educated individuals meant that Fang was eventually allowed to work at CUST. During the Cultural Revolution, however, he was labelled a 'stinking intellectual' and was relegated to the countryside where he laboured in rice fields and helped dig a railway tunnel. After the death of Mao, he was reinstated and even allowed to go abroad to attend scientific conferences. His stature as a scientist led to his appointment as Vice-President of CUST where he enjoyed the support of many of his colleagues and students in the 1980s. In 1985, a student demonstration at his university drew over 17,000 people who called for greater reform. The following year, Fang gave a speech in which he said that the socialist movement was a failure and that China needed not only modernization but also Westernization if the country was to advance (Fang, 1991). This time, he was relieved of his duties at CUST and, in 1987, was appointed to a research institute in Beijing where he could be watched more

Wei Jingsheng (b. 1950): Accused of opposing the Chinese government, Wei was sentenced to prison in 1979. After his release, he once more spoke out against government polices and was rearrested. In 1998 he was released on medical grounds and currently lives in the United States.

Fifth Modernization: Democracy. Students called for the addition of this fifth item to the official 'Four Modernizations' of the early Deng era, demanding that the government not only modernize industry and agriculture, but also the government itself.

Four Big Rights: In the 1978 Chinese constitution, the Chinese people were given the rights of *daming*, *dafang*, *dabianlun* and *dazibao*, which meant, respectively, the right to speak out freely, air views fully, hold great debates and write Big Character Posters. These were all revoked in 1980 as part of government efforts to curtail the emergent democracy movement.

Fang Lizhi (b. 1936): Astrophysicist at China University of Science and Technology (CUST). His outspoken criticism led to his being blamed for the student demonstrations of 1989, after which he was forced to leave China.

CUST: Acronym for China University of Science and Technology, a major technological university in the central Chinese province of Anhui.

Liu Binyan (1925–2005): Dissident journalist and author. Liu worked as a journalist for the CCP newspaper, the *People's Daily*. Appalled by increasing corruption in the Party, he wrote a series of exposé articles for which he was finally expelled from the CCP. He chose to leave China and worked as a human rights activist and writer in the United States.

Hu Yaobang (1915–89): Secretary-General of the CCP in the 1980s. Hu was among the men chosen by Deng Xiaoping to inaugurate reforms. However, in 1987 his support for student activists led to his dismissal from his post. His death, from natural causes, in April 1989 touched off the student demonstrations that marked the beginning of Beijing Spring.

closely. Despite the government monitoring, he continued to speak out, calling for more reforms [**Doc. 13, pp. 145–7**].

Fang was not alone in his outspoken comments. Others also criticized the system and suffered accordingly. For example, **Liu Binyan**, a journalist, investigated stories of official corruption and, for his efforts, was expelled from the CCP. He left for the United States where he became an active member of human rights organizations.

Despite the dangers involved and the possibility of severe repercussions from the authorities, intellectuals continued to speak their minds. In an effort to dampen student interest in hearing such views, in 1986 the government announced new regulations for all college graduates which required two years of assigned labour before they began their chosen careers. Worse, from a student perspective, was that 30% of each graduating class had to accept jobs assigned by the government. Students saw this for what it was: a means by which to curtail criticism from China's best-educated people. Angered by the new rules and disgruntled over low stipends (virtually all university students at that time were supported by monthly government payments) and poor living conditions, student dissatisfaction simmered.

Disagreements emerged within the higher echelons of the Party. **Hu Yaobang**, Deng's hand-picked leader of the CCP, made no secret of his opposition to the new rules. As a result, Hu was dismissed from his post in 1987. China's students immediately embraced him as a hero for championing their cause.

In 1988, student organizers decided to circulate a petition calling for greater reforms. Stirred by the daring speeches and writings of men such as Fang Lizhi and their own student leaders, their list of demands began with a call for modernizaton and democracy. The summer of 1988 saw demonstrations in cities across China; during the academic year of 1988–9 campus unrest continued.

The catalyst for the massive demonstrations that led to the dramatic and tragic events in Beijing on 4 June 1989 was the unexpected death of Hu Yaobang on 15 April 1989, from a heart attack. His loss galvanized students, who organized a mass memorial service in Tiananmen Square, at the very centre of the nation's capital. What began as a memorial for Hu quickly grew into mass demonstrations. Day after day that April, students, workers and ordinary Beijing residents paraded to the square, calling on the government to institute greater democracy and end the growing corruption among officials. Some marchers carried signs to air grievances or to criticize specific government policies.

Although the government repeatedly ordered the marchers to disperse and to leave the square, students and their supporters continued to gather there. On 26 April 1989, the government denounced the students in an editorial in China's official newspaper, the *People's Daily*. The still-peaceful demonstrators were called 'conspirators' and their actions were labelled illegal. By officially denouncing the students and their allies, the government raised the stakes. Students now feared reprisals. To protect themselves by legitimizing their demonstrations, students not only continued to rally in Tiananmen Square, but also demanded a dialogue with top government leaders to present their views. On 27 April, over 50,000 students and their supporters crowded the streets of the capital, cheered by residents. The movement was dubbed **'Beijing Spring'** and appeared to augur a new age of democracy for China.

Many among this generation of students saw themselves as heirs to the **May Fourth Movement** of 1919. In honour of that earlier generation, which had also sacrificed so much in order to save its country 70 years earlier, the students held yet another major demonstration on 4 May 1989. Police efforts to control the massive demonstration were ineffectual, and students flooded into the centre of the national capital once more.

The CCP clearly faced a difficult predicament. To complicate matters further, in the middle of May, Mikhail Gorbachev, the architect of Soviet reforms and *perestroika*, was scheduled to arrive in Beijing, the first visit to China by a Russian leader since 1959. This historic visit would be covered by the international news media, representatives of which had begun to arrive in Beijing. The occupation of the city centre by thousands of students was becoming more than a national embarrassment for the CCP: it would now be televised for an international audience. Unrelenting, the students decided to call a hunger strike and in doing so galvanized even greater popular support and sympathy. Ultimately, the Gorbachev visit took place as scheduled but the usual welcome ceremonies in Tiananmen Square had to be abandoned. To the great embarrassment of the leadership, students held up signs calling for *perestroika* and Russian-style *glasnost* as foreign media filmed the student-jammed square.

It is important to note that Beijing was not the only city to experience what came to be called the 'Beijing Spring'. Students in other major cities followed the example of their friends in Beijing and launched their own demonstrations. Some students made the long and expensive journey to Beijing to record the impassioned speeches, interspersed with rock music by some of China's biggest rock stars, and then returned home to play the recordings over loudspeaker systems at their home universities. Thousands of students all across China were joined by workers in mass demonstrations calling for greater government reform, and cities such as Shanghai, Wuhan, Guangzhou and Xian witnessed an outpouring of criticism mixed with the exuberance of popular music.

Beijing Spring: The period of April, May and early June of 1989 when student-led demonstrations in the capital city of Beijing appeared to be pushing the CCP toward greater democratization.

May Fourth Movement: This political and intellectual movement takes its name from the 4 May 1919 protests against the Treaty of Versailles. The student-led protests throughout China led to a new intellectual awakening and the rise of Chinese nationalism.

On 18 May, the stand-off in Beijing took a new turn. The Prime Minister, **Li Peng**, agreed to a televised interview with student leaders, including some still on a hunger strike. Wang Dan and Wu'erkaixi were among the student representatives chosen to meet the top leaders of the CCP. The exchange between the youthful leadership and the top men of the CCP included repeated student demands for the government to listen to the people and to enter into a dialogue with them about China's future. The stony face of Prime Minister Li, filmed at the end of the interview, suggested that the patience of the Party leadership had come to an end.

What must have been an angry and frustrated Central Committee finally voted on 20 May to impose martial law. Only Zhao Ziyang, Deng's appointed heir-apparent, opposed this move. As a result, he lost his standing in the CCP and was dismissed from his post as Secretary-General on 24 May. He was subsequently placed under house arrest. As for the students, they simply ignored the announcement and continued their occupation of Tiananmen Square.

To boost morale and keep the number of demonstrators high, celebrity rock stars visited the square. They also provided a welcome diversion for the hundreds of students with impromptu rock concerts which served to draw even more onlookers and participants to the centre of the city. Art students from Beijing contributed a statue they called the Goddess of Liberty, which they erected just opposite the painting of Chairman Mao over the central gate at the north end of the square. The atmosphere combined the tension of a political movement with the spirit of a rock concert.

At the end of May, students still occupied the square, but word spread that troops were arriving in the capital. The situation became extremely tense. Student leaders called for a vote on whether or not they should remain in Tiananmen Square, where hunger-striking students had drawn new supporters to their cause. Although at one point the majority voted to end the demonstration, a minority of student leaders were joined by newly arrived students who wanted the movement to continue. So, despite the efforts of professors sympathetic to the students to persuade them to end their occupation, hundreds of students chose to remain.

On 3 June, troops brought to the Beijing area from outlying regions began to converge on the centre of the city. On 4 June 1989, in the early hours of the morning, armed units advanced on the square itself, shooting at random to disperse onlookers who threw stones or shouted epithets. Gunfire thus preceded the military push to clear demonstrators from Tiananmen Square once and for all. Shocked Beijingers rushed bloodied victims to local hospitals and, as the troops advanced, the toll of dead and wounded rose. Last-minute negotiations between the students and the military allowed the final band of demonstrators gathered at the south end of the square to leave. As they marched away, leaving behind the debris of weeks of occupation, they sang the international anthem of Communism, the 'Internationale'.

In the chaos of 3 and 4 June, the number of dead was impossible to ascertain. Later estimates varied from hundreds to thousands, and even a decade later the final number of fatalities was still disputed. But the grisly photographs of that night and the day after show bodies still caught in wreckage around the city of Beijing as well as bodies piled in some Beijing hospital corridors. The military secured the square and cleaned up the mess in the days that followed. The official press in China denounced the entire movement as 'counter-revolutionary' and castigated its leadership [**Doc. 14, pp. 147–8**]. The government-controlled media publicized the arrest warrants issued for student leaders and outspoken critics such as Fang Lizhi, who sought refuge in the US embassy with his family. He remained there for a year before being allowed to leave China. Student leaders fled underground, and a number of them eventually made their way abroad. The latter included Wang Dan and Wu'erkaixi, a young Uighur whose name is more accurately romanized as Erkesh Devlet. Both had been among the student representatives to interview Li Peng on television just weeks earlier. The most prominent woman leader, Chai Ling, also escaped, eventually making her way to the United States. Less fortunate students were caught in the crackdown that followed in the summer of 1989. Some of China's most promising young students soon began prison sentences; while the most outspoken sat in solitary confinement, others were sent for *laogai* or 'reform through labour' in the often harsh conditions of labour camps.

The international aftermath included broken cultural exchanges and a temporary halt to foreign investment. The most pessimistic observers felt that in one horrific night the CCP had lost all that it had gained in the preceding decade. Certainly the hoped-for democratization of China was seen as an evermore distant dream, as the optimistic 1980s ended in Beijing's Tiananmen Square.

6

Deepening reform: China in the 1990s

Following the Beijing Spring of 1989, the CCP teetered on the edge of another dramatic policy shift, away from the economic reforms that had improved the lives of so many. Conservatives in the Party reasserted their position, warning once more of the dangers of change and using the example of urban disorder in support of their claims.

However, instead of a reversal, other events in the Communist world shifted the balance toward a continuation of the reforms and the 'opening up' of China to the outside. In 1991, the USSR collapsed under the weight of growing internal political issues and a shattered economy. The constituent republics of the former Communist giant found themselves independent for the first time in 70 years, and Russia itself began a new life as a republic. China's former mentor and economic model was gone, and its failings were exposed for all to see.

In response to these dramatic international events, Deng moved quickly to reinvigorate the reforms of the 1980s. His highly publicized visit to the dynamic southern province of Guangdong in 1992 signalled that China would press on with its new direction, away from a centrally planned economy and toward an increasingly market-driven system. Although Deng was 88 years old that year and no longer active in the day-to-day affairs of the Party, his decision to move forward with China's reforms ensured the continuing expansion of the Chinese economy.

At the head of the government was the newly appointed **Jiang Zemin**. Born in 1926, Jiang represented what is referred to in China as the 'third generation' of CCP leadership. Jiang joined the CCP during the Second World War and served in the military. After 1949, he was among the young Chinese sent for education in the USSR where he learned Russian and received a degree in engineering. After a stint working in an auto plant, he held a series of central government posts, and by 1985 his experience earned him the position of mayor of Shanghai, where he also held the top Party post. His technical training helped to launch Shanghai's renewal: the city had

Jiang Zemin (b. 1926): President of China 1993–2003; Secretary General of the CCP, 1990–2002; head of the Chinese military 1989–2004. An engineer by training, Jiang's political career began in the 1950s, leading to his 1986 appointment as mayor of Shanghai. In 1989, Deng Xiaoping brought him to Beijing and supported his elevation to the top positions in the country.

languished for years with little government support to the former stronghold of colonialism and imperialism. Under Jiang, Shanghai began its renaissance, paving the way for its key role in international trade and foreign investment in the 1990s. In 1987, he was appointed to the CCP's Politburo. During the student-led demonstrations of 1989, Jiang managed to defuse the situation in Shanghai, which could have been the site of a Tiananmen-style crackdown without Jiang's cautious reponse. This success doubtless contributed to Deng's decision to bring Jiang to Beijing to replace the disgraced Zhao Ziyang in June 1989. As a transitional figure between the old guard and the new, Jiang was well prepared to continue Deng's efforts to accelerate modernization and economic reform.

Also at the top of the Party hierarchy in the 1990s was Prime Minister Li Peng. Born in 1928, Li's father was executed by the Nationalists for his leftist sympathies in 1930. Li became the adopted child of Zhou Enlai and his wife, **Deng Yingzhao**, who raised a number of children whose parents died in the political and military struggle prior to 1949. Like Jiang, Li was also educated in the USSR, returning to China in 1955 with a degree in engineering. With Zhou's support, he rose through the Party ranks and by the 1980s was serving as one of five Vice-Premiers under Zhao Ziyang. When Zhao was moved to the post of Secretary-General of the CCP in 1987, Li was promoted to Acting Premier and then Premier of China. After 1989, Li was widely blamed for the shootings at Tiananmen Square and rumours that he was to be removed continued throughout the 1990s.

Deng Yingzhao (1904–92): Government official and activist, known for championing women's rights, particularly through the Chinese Women's Federation. The wife of Zhou Enlai, Deng held positions in the Party in her own right after 1976.

Behind both men, however, was Deng himself, who continued to counter the complaints and protests of the ageing coterie of conservatives whose numbers continued to dwindle as the decade progressed. In 1997, weakened by illnesses associated with advanced old age, Deng passed away at the age of 93. Although some observers in and outside China had surmised that President Jiang would falter without his powerful backer, such was not the case. Jiang consolidated his position in the Party and with the military to remain firmly at the top of the power structure. His guidance continued to move China along the path of economic reform and away from the destructive policies of the Maoist years.

ECONOMIC GROWTH IN THE 1990S

By 1995, headway had been made in dismantling the inefficient and unprofitable government-run enterprises. Approximately 34% of businesses and industries were run by the state; another 37% were classified as collective ownership, which referred to an array of ownership forms ranging from small village or township businesses to workshops run by the workers or local governments; 29% were classified as privately owned and operated. In 1996, China's State Statistical Bureau reported that more than 1 in 12 workers were employed by private (*siying*) enterprises, and that over 25 million individual businesses and 650,000 privately run enterprises produced 14.6% of China's **GDP** (Parris, 1999: 267) [**Doc. 15, p. 149**]. China's state-run enterprises, which continued to employ two-thirds of China's urban workforce, contributed less than half of China's economic output. The private sector was clearly the most dynamic part of the economy and it was the source of wealth for China's first multimillionaires: 2–5% of all the private enterprise owners had incomes over 10 million *yuan* by the middle of the 1990s (Parris, 1999: 267).

Siying: Chinese term for private enterprises.

GDP: Acronym for gross domestic product. A figure produced by deducting the value of income earned on investments made by a country's citizens abroad from a country's total GNP; usually based on annual figures.

This new system of public and private ownership was referred to as 'socialism with Chinese characteristics' in China, but outside the country another term was coined to describe the hybrid system – 'authoritarian capitalism'. Both terms have come to describe a system that is partly under close government control, particularly in banking and internal trade of commodities, but also partly free to expand and develop new products and new markets. China became a land of joint ventures, enterprises with foreign funding and/or investors but with Chinese public agencies as partners. In addition, the SEZs (introduced in Chapter 5) continued to draw new foreign investment to China and to provide training for hundreds of Chinese workers.

During the 1990s, the number of agricultural workers steadily declined as more and more opportunities were created by the burgeoning economy. From a high of some 70% employed in agriculture or related work at the beginning of the reform era, the numbers steadily declined to less than 50% by the middle of the 1990s (Goldman and MacFarquhar, 1999: 41). With better-paid options in the towns and cities available, and more mobility for the working population tolerated by the government, the urban population also grew during the 1990s. As a result, parts of rural China experienced a marked '**feminization of agriculture**' as young men sought seasonal or even permanent work in the cities, leaving their wives and children to manage the family's leased farmland.

Feminization of agriculture: The predominance of female labour in agricultural work which was low-paid and low-status labour. Young men sought better pay and status in town or city enterprises, leaving women to work the family's leased land during the reform era.

Young women seeking an escape from what could be harsh conditions in rural areas also sought work in the city. Usually, they ended up in low-paying factory jobs but, from their viewpoint, these were still desirable as their salaries allowed them to enjoy some of the pleasures of city life as well as to send money to their parents back home. Factories in Shenzhen, for example, took advantage of this labour pool by hiring young women on short-term contracts that did not require the company to provide the benefits that went with hiring long-term employees. Any worker who proved difficult could be easily fired and replaced from the readily available pool of rural women hoping for a period of adventure before marrying and settling down (Lee, 1998).

INCREASING DISPARITY BETWEEN URBAN AND RURAL CHINA

The greatest economic prosperity of the 1990s occurred in the urban areas and, in particular, along China's coast. As these cities courted foreign investment and encouraged new housing, roads and transport systems, the look of China's urban environment changed dramatically. In the 1990s, some cities called themselves 'city of cranes' because of the great number of building cranes that crowded China's urban skies. The pounding of pile-drivers reverberated through downtown Shanghai and Beijing as new high-rise buildings rose from what had been neighbourhoods of old-style tile-roofed houses. Privately owned apartments offered all modern amenities to their new owners, who also frequented the new nightclubs and restaurants in places such as Nanjing and Guangzhou. Cell phones and pagers became de rigueur for the up-and-coming young businessman. Those who had succeeded in the new economy also bought personal computers and by the end of the decade over 17 million Chinese subscribed to an internet service. For a new generation of young educated Chinese, the 1990s clearly offered the kind of life inconceivable to those of their parents' generation.

While urban incomes rose, however, rural incomes changed more slowly. On average, city dwellers enjoyed double the income of their rural counterparts in the 1990s. Unlike urban and coastal China, the hinterland still had areas without an adequate electricity supply, elementary schools or health care. Conditions in the poorest areas remained difficult, and the possibility of a comfortable lifestyle still seemed an unobtainable goal.

Adding to the woes of some poorer areas, farm families without good connections found themselves the target of increasing exactions from local officials. Although the terms of a farm lease called for set amounts in taxes and rent, local officials increasingly added levies of various kinds. Some of these funds were ostensibly to be used for local roads or irrigation projects, but other taxes or fees, simply labelled miscellaneous or occasional taxes, made people both angry and suspicious. They believed that the money they worked so hard for was disappearing into the pockets of lazy and corrupt officials. Peasant-farmers resented these additional payments, but many found themselves unable to avoid the added financial demands. As in previous periods of change in China, those at the bottom once more found themselves at the mercy of local officials. Complaints against these exactions led some angry farmers to demonstrate in town centres and to denounce local officials publicly. The usual response from the government was to arrest the farmers who were considered to be the ringleaders of the demonstration and to allow local officials to remain in their posts. Without local accountability of officials, the levies appeared likely to continue.

It was therefore of great interest to observers both in and outside China when the CCP moved to allow a more open elective process to develop at the local level. Moves in this direction began with the **Organic Law of Villagers' Committees**, which came into effect in 1988. The law was intended to allow villagers a greater say in the management of their village and greater autonomy for elected village officers. According to the law, all adult residents of the villages had a right to vote and stand for election to a three-year term on their village committees, which varied in size from three to seven members. Although the 1989 demonstrations in Beijing threatened to derail this reform, in the 1990s many villages did, indeed, hold elections in which they chose their local officials from among competing candidates. In 1997, the CCP leadership reaffirmed its commitment to the Organic Law which, for the first time since 1949, gave rural residents the power to rid themselves of the most incompetent or corrupt village officials. Although corruption (discussed below) continued to influence village elections at the end of the 1990s, the new rules offered the prospect of greater accountability among officials at the lowest level.

Organic Law of Villagers Committees: Passed in 1988, this law was intended to give local villages more autonomy. Through village-level elections, competition for local offices increased and gave villagers the opportunity to vote corrupt or incompetent officials out of office.

CHINA AFTER DENG XIAOPING

After Deng's death in 1997, President Jiang moved out from under his predecessor's shadow. Although domestic matters took precedence, President Jiang took on an increasingly visible role in international relations. His understanding of international affairs was arguably stronger than that of all earlier leaders, including Deng Xiaoping, and Jiang seemed relatively more comfortable on foreign visits. His ability to speak English even enabled him to give the occasional interview to visiting English-speaking journalists. In the 1990s, both his sons went to the United States to study and returned with American graduate degrees. Jiang himself visited the United States in 1997. Despite clear differences with the American leadership over issues such as human rights, the visit heightened his status at home.

After 1997, Jiang's position was further strengthened when Li Peng followed constitutional law and stepped down as Prime Minister. Li was still widely blamed for the shootings at Tiananmen Square in 1989, and some observers saw this as a positive development for Jiang's presidency. Li did not disappear; he became Chairman of the National People's Congress during 1999–2000, and remained popular among Party conservatives. However, his position was weakened in 2000 when his protégé, Cheng Kejie, Vice-Chairman of the NPC, was executed for corruption.

Jiang replaced Li with a valued colleague from his Shanghai days, the dynamic and reform-minded **Zhu Rongji**. Zhu was promoted to Executive Deputy Prime Minister in 1993 and to Prime Minister in 1998. Additional Jiang supporters in key government positions included a woman, Chen Zhili, who became Minister of Education, and Zeng Peiyan, Minister of State Development and Planning Commission, and close adviser Zeng Qinghong, who became head of the CCP's Organization Department in 1999 (Gilley, 1999: 249–50).

Like all Chinese leaders, Jiang's position at the head of the Party and the civilian government also made him the commanding officer of all branches of the military. To ensure continuing military support for his presidency, he provided additional funding for much-needed modernization of all branches of the military establishment.

Jiang's administration also remained dedicated to Deng-style reforms. To continue forward momentum, Jiang reaffirmed the need for China to upgrade its production methods and management techniques. China's economy continued to grow, although the Asian economic crisis of 1997–8 slightly slowed the percentage of growth. Nonetheless, China made remarkable strides in expanding its economy, and by the end of the decade, China enjoyed the world's third largest GDP, measured in purchasing power parity (Meisner, 1999: 245).

Zhu Rongji (b. 1929): Prime Minister, 1998–2003. He held a number of national-level posts before becoming Shanghai's mayor in 1989. In 1990, he moved to Beijing and was named Prime Minister in 1998. His major task was to deepen China's economic reforms while maintaining political stability.

POPULAR CULTURE IN THE 1990s

As China continued its opening process and the reforms of the 1990s deepened, new forms of entertainment and pastimes emerged. From the young, post-Mao generation to the retired workers who had seen such dramatic changes in their lifetimes, people participated in voluntary spare-time activities that brought pleasure rather than political indoctrination.

One strong indicator of the degree of change was the emergence of new forms of literature. The 'scar' accounts of the 1980s gave way to the 1990s 'beautiful writers', young women who wrote of their careers and, in a bold departure from earlier writings, of their love life. The new atmosphere in China fostered a more outspoken and adventurous urban woman, who attracted young reading audiences despite the fact that the books themselves were often quickly banned by the authorities. The resulting cachet seemed to add to, rather than detract from, their followings.

Young people were increasingly drawn to discos and clubs in towns and cities all over the country. Western-style rock music, by both Western and Chinese groups, made buildings vibrate late at night. More sedate but no less popular were the dancing clubs organized by older citizens: in the early evenings, groups of retired folks performed traditional dances to the accompaniment of drums, enjoying themselves on warm summer nights. Other new sounds in China included karaoke clubs, which, as elsewhere in Asia, subjected audiences to fractured versions of classical and modern music from the East and the West.

Some newly available forms of entertainment were of a more educational nature. Urban families enrolled their single offspring in innumerable after-school activities such as piano, dance or martial arts lessons as parents sought to give their child the opportunities and pleasures they themselves never had. Although rural children continued to work on the family farm after school, the aspirations of parents with smaller numbers of children also rose in village China, where the modest pleasures of a generally better diet and wider access to radio and television brought colour to the lives of millions.

Sports, always popular in China, drew new recruits. The possibility of joining a professional or semi-professional sports team encouraged young men to hone their skills. Sports leagues formed to compete with neighbouring towns or provinces, and posters of sports stars were included in many of the new magazines available on streetcorners all over the country. Thousands of people simply enjoyed the opportunity for a game of table tennis, billiards or various forms of chess.

In many ways, the decade of the 1990s was a pivotal one for Chinese society. Although it had begun with many people still in shock over the 1989 shootings in Tiananmen Square, it ended with greater prosperity, for larger numbers of people, than in any other decade of the twentieth century. Ironically, that dramatic change was possible only because of the rejection of Mao's vision of creating a socialist society in just one generation.

7

Challenges in the 1990s

Many of the changes in China after the death of Mao in 1976 received broad popular support from the majority of the Chinese people and, in general, the last two decades of the century were decades of hope. Prosperity reached into the countryside as farmers set their own prices for their products and built new homes or added new rooms to the old ones. More opportunities for education, and even for travel within China, opened new doors for many, who saw the new government policies as the answer to China's – and their own – future prosperity.

Yet the changes gave rise to unanticipated problems and new challenges for the CCP. Surveyed below are challenges that emerged in the 1980s and 1990s for Chinese society as a whole and for the CCP in particular. These include China's growing levels of environmental pollution and their consequences; a continuing increase in crime and corruption; discontent among minorities over limits on religious practice; and the need for greater equity in access to education and employment.

POLLUTION AND THE ENVIRONMENT

China's environmental problems were not atypical of nation-states undergoing rapid modernization. In the 1950s, the Great Leap Forward contributed to the process of environmental degradation through over-hasty policy decisions which did not take into account their impact on the environment. Cutting of trees and brush to fuel the backyard steel furnaces sped deforestation all over China and compounded the annual flooding as denuded ground shed water. In the north and northwest, there was an increase in desertification as China's major deserts threatened to cover precious arable land. The use of coal to fuel and heat homes meant that pollution continued to harm air quality; as the urban population grew in the reform period, the increased emissions intensified the pollution levels, as did an increase in the number of vehicles, none of which were required to have pollution-reducing catalytic converters.

The increase in small and middle-sized enterprises in the late 1970s and throughout the reform period placed further stress on waterways which were already polluted by industrial waste from state-run enterprises. Farmland run-off included 'night soil' (untreated human faeces) which was still used as the most common fertilizer in rural China. Added to this was a mix of fertilizer and insecticide chemicals that entered rivers and streams as farmers attempted to force crops from marginal land.

State Environment Protection Administration: Created in 1998 to address increasing environmental pollution problems, the SEPA is to enforce laws and policies dealing with environmental protection.

The growing problem obviously needed attention, and in 1998 the government created the **State Environment Protection Administration** to address poor air and water quality. The new agency was empowered to enforce existing laws, and in a number of cases it imposed fines on polluters. Unfortunately, the payment of the fine did not always end the polluting practice.

China also attempted to provide protection to some of the country's endangered animal species. A national and international campaign raised money to preserve the panda's natural habitat, but as of 2000 the endangered black-and-white herbivore was still safer in a zoo than in the wild. The same was true for northeastern China's Siberian tiger. In central China, the Yangzi river dolphin remained in difficulty despite efforts to protect it from fishermen. As ecotourism gains in popularity in China and elsewhere, China may find greater incentives to preserve the rarest aspects of its natural heritage.

China's efforts to raise the standard of living also meant that some ambitious projects threatened further damage to the environment. One of the most controversial issues of the 1990s, both in and outside China, was

Three Gorges Dam: The world's single largest dam. Located in Sichuan province on the Yangzi River, the resultant reservoir flooded acres of farmland, submerged historic sites, and entire villages, requiring the relocation of millions of people. It supplies electricity to western China where demand is enormous.

the **Three Gorges Dam**, which, when completed, would become the world's largest hydroelectric project. At a cost of US$24.5 billion, the new dam would also be the world's most expensive. Among the varied impacts of the project were the relocation of 1.2 million people, whose homes and farmland would be inundated, and the loss of important archaeological sites. Conservationists and critics warned that the dam's location over a seismically active area was also a time bomb. Further, the Yangzi River, the world's third longest, carries a great deal of sediment which could threaten the actual workings of the dam. Further, because much of the upstream water contains untreated human waste, the build-up of pollutants could contribute to yet another disastrous consequence. However, if the project were to work as planned, it would supply one-tenth of all China's electrical power. It was also hoped that it would help control flooding all along the river and increase the amount of shipping tonnage throughout the Yangzi River valley, a distance of over 1,000 miles.

CRIME, CORRUPTION AND VICE

Overall, the crime rate in China compared with that of developed countries remained low during the 1990s. As noted in one study, China has also had a smaller number of people in prison relative to the size of its population than in the West: the United States, for example, imprisons people at double the Chinese rate (Seymour, 1999). However, Chinese law allows much harsher penalties: its criminal law code called for execution as punishment for over 200 crimes. The judicial system was also accused of tolerating the use of brute force in dealing with prisoners and of a lack of due process. For example, in the **'Strike Hard' Campaign**, which began in the middle of the 1990s, police increased the rate of arrests across China, detaining thousands of men and women whose crimes ranged from petty theft to arson and murder. The campaign was clearly a warning to criminals that it would be a mistake to interpret the new economic freedoms as an invitation to engage in illegal activities. Although the campaign had its internal critics, in general many Chinese supported it, as well as the harsh treatment meted out to criminals. The persuasive rationale was that strong punishment is necessary if China is to enjoy relative stability.

Despite the efforts of the 'Strike Hard' Campaign and continuing vigilance, there was nevertheless an increase in the number of people willing to test the law. The new profession of long-distance truck driver, for example, facilitated the transportation of drugs from drug-producing areas of Southeast Asia through southern China to Hong Kong, from where they could reach a wide international market. Drugs also flowed from Afghanistan and Pakistan into western China. A quantity of hard drugs such as heroin remained in China to feed local demand, but most of the drug shipments made their way to coastal cities for transport overseas.

Drugs were not the only commodity trafficked. As China's economy raised expectations for a better life, it became more difficult for men in poorer villages to find a wife. To fill this need, kidnappers lured young country girls recently arrived in the cities with promises of good jobs. Instead of jobs, however, the girls would be threatened and intimidated into accepting as a husband a man who might pay as much as 8,000 *yuan* (US$1,000) for a kidnapped 'bride'. Laws forbidding this practice included stiff penalties, but despite the punishments the practice continued. With opportunities for good jobs in rural areas scarce, girls continued their trek to the city and risked capture by such predators.

Related to cases of female exploitation was an increase in prostitution. Virtually eliminated in the Maoist period, this profession quickly re-emerged with the increase in freedom of movement and increasing urban affluence. Penalties were severe, but the temptation to make what some young women

'Strike Hard' Campaign: A police campaign which began in the mid-1990s intended to crack down on crime throughout China. The increased presence of policemen on the streets and in highly populated areas such as markets and parks was noticeable, but complaints of less public crimes, such as bribery and the embezzling of public funds, continued.

saw as 'easy money' drew them to take the risks involved. Those included the risk of contracting a life-threatening illness as the rate of HIV-AIDS cases soared toward the end of the 1990s to an estimated 600,000 people. Infected blood collected by private companies was also identified as the source of numerous infections, even in some predominantly rural areas of provinces such as Henan and Shaanxi. Adequate medical care and counselling for those infected was almost non-existent.

While drugs and trafficking in women clearly represented a threat to some segments of Chinese society, of greatest concern to all groups was the increase in corruption among Chinese officials. Under the old Maoist system, not only were the amounts of money an individual official controlled much smaller than during the reform era, but also the kind of lifestyle money could buy at that time was hardly opulent. With the advent of the economic reforms, however, opportunities quickly expanded, and many officials, on fixed wages that soon left them economically behind, succumbed to temptation. In some instances, an official simply looked the other way. Far more serious were economic crimes including the embezzling of millions of *yuan* from state enterprises. The greatest public opprobrium was reserved for officials at the very top of the Party structure who used their positions to enrich themselves and their relatives. The highly publicized arrests and trials of such individuals were clearly intended to send a message to those lower down the ladder that such behaviour would not be tolerated. As of 2000, however, such crimes continued to be reported in the Chinese press, suggesting that the lure of wealth remained seductive.

The authorities found crime a challenge. They also paid close attention to the emergence of popular religion in the reform era. The presence of a growing foreign business community and an increasing number of foreign journalists resident in the county meant that China's policy on religion was opened to international examination and, as discussed below, the issue of religious freedom continued to draw worldwide attention.

Buddhism: A universal, world religion based on the teachings of the historical Buddha of the sixth century BCE. The basic tenets focus on escape from the pain and suffering which marks all human life and ending the cycle of repeated birth and death by following moral precepts and, ultimately, attaining a state of enlightenment.

Daoism (or Taoism): An ancient school of thought in China derived from the observation of nature and the belief in dual forces of *yin* and *yang*, respectively, represented by the moon and the sun, the negative and the positive, and the dark and the light. Daoism is one of the *san jiao*, or Three Teachings, of China; the other two are Buddhism and Confucianism.

RELIGIOUS POLICY

Because the Communist movement is atheist, Chinese constitutions have made a point of stressing that while there is freedom of religion in China, citizens have the right to believe or not to believe in any religion. Religion is invariably referred to as 'backward' and a form of 'superstition' which belongs to the past and not to present-day, modern China. Officially, five major religions are legally allowed to practise: **Buddhism**, **Daoism** (Taoism), Islam, Catholicism and Protestantism, each of which has official spokespersons recognized by the government. These individuals are responsible for any activities among their adherents. As a result of this 'watchdog' status, the leaders of the officially recognized religions are seen by many as mere ciphers. Certainly, the need to be accountable to the government makes the position of religious leaders very difficult.

Since 1949, policy toward religion has reflected the political climate. Thus, the relative tolerance of the 1950s gave way to the extreme suppression of all religious belief in the period of the Cultural Revolution. Young Red Guards, born after the 1949 liberation, participated in a widespread onslaught against religious sites, defacing what they could not totally destroy. It seemed that all religion would be obliterated in the process.

However, with the advent of the reform era, policy shifted once more. Accusations against religious leaders were withdrawn and a measure of freedom was accorded to religious institutions. In some cases where damage to religious structures had been extreme, money was provided for rebuilding churches, mosques and temples. In particular, historically important Buddhist sites were cleaned and repaired at public expense. Muslim sites were also restored, some with government funds and others with support only from the members of the affected congregation.

Christianity, in particular, suffered under the constraints noted above, but difficulties that attended its practice were more profound and stemmed from different roots. As a Western import, Christianity was closely associated with the old unequal treaty system of the nineteenth century. Missionaries of the twentieth century sought to overcome residual antipathy toward their religion through activities related to the **social gospel** movement which emphasized educational and medical services as an aspect of their ministry in China. But Communist attitudes toward missionaries and their Chinese converts led to their attacking Christian groups in the 1920s and 1930s and, not surprisingly, this enmity continued and intensified with the CCP victory. Only those members of the Christian church willing to place themselves under Party supervision could practise their religion publicly.

Social gospel: The Christian Protestant movement to include education and medical services as part of its evangelical efforts in China prior to 1949.

The advent of the reform era allowed Chinese Christians to resume religious activities more openly. Churches in major coastal cities reopened first, largely because of the increasing numbers of foreigners residing in Shanghai, Beijing and Guangzhou. Some church buildings that had been confiscated and used for other purposes once again became houses of worship, although the elderly predominated in most congregations.

Protestant churches in general fared better than Roman Catholic ones. The latter remained in a difficult position because of the requirement of the government that priests' first loyalty be to China, not the Pope. Those refusing to accept this were not allowed to represent Catholicism; as of 2000, a number of priests remained in prison for refusal to accept this 'patriotic' official policy [**Doc. 16, pp. 150–1**]. In contrast, Protestant groups operated with comparative freedom. Western Protestant missionaries developed new methods of proselytizing: dedicated Protestant Christians simply went to China to work, often as teachers, and used the opportunity of friendship with local people to introduce Christianity, holding religious services in private homes. The government periodically cracked down on those foreigners believed to be active missionaries, but the often young and determined Western Christians were willing to teach for low pay and were therefore tolerated within certain limits.

Even religious movements that claimed traditional Chinese rather than foreign roots had legal problems. In the 1980s, revivals of quasi-religious practices such as *qigong* were at first widely tolerated. This ancient practice emphasized the cultivation of good health through breathing and physical exercises as well as meditation. However, a modern variant of this old form, called **Falungong** (variously translated as the Law of the Wheel or Buddhist Law), made itself unwelcome, despite its seemingly innocuous system of belief. Its leaders promised not only good health and the ability to defeat diseases such as cancer, but also spiritual salvation and even world peace through its practices. Because of its large membership, estimated by some observers to be as high as 10 million, and its public practice of meditation techniques, the CCP viewed its members as troublemakers. In April 1999, some 10,000 members gathered for a silent demonstration in front of the gates of Zhongnanhai, the Beijing enclave housing the top CCP leadership, to protest against the detention of some of their fellow believers. When this and other demonstrations in the capital were suppressed, *Falungong* members in other cities staged their own silent but nonetheless, for the government, embarrassingly public demonstrations. On 22 July 1999, the organization was declared illegal and all public and private observance of its rituals banned. The leading figure associated with the movement, Li Hongzhi, who had left for the United States sometime earlier, was denounced as a criminal. Neither that accusation nor the official ban stopped members from practising their religion, and thus demonstrations and arrests continued.

Falungong: Also known as *Falun Dafa*, variously translated as the Law of the Wheel or Buddhist Law. A late twentieth-century spiritual movement based on the ancient teaching of *qigong*, a system of breathing exercises and physical movements, and on a mixture of Buddhist and Daoist beliefs.

While the general population could follow their religious beliefs within the limits described above, CCP members were expected to end any religious affiliation. In minority areas in particular, the government was adamant in requiring formerly Muslim or Buddhist cadres to repudiate their beliefs. In some cases, instruction in atheism was offered to minority cadres [**Doc. 17, pp. 151–2**]. But because religion was seen by many minority groups as an important component of their national identity, leading cadres who no longer followed their people's religious practices risked isolating themselves from the people they were supposed to represent.

EQUITY IN EDUCATION

One goal of the PRC was to provide education for all its citizens. Efforts began in the 1950s, but were interrupted by economic and political campaigns. Nonetheless, progress was made in reducing the rate of adult illiteracy and in providing a primary school education to both boys and girls. By 1980, millions of young Chinese had been given the chance to improve their lives through greater educational opportunities.

Officially, China established compulsory education for those aged from 7 to 17. Unofficially, however, many students who began elementary school never finished, in part because during the reform period schools of all levels began assessing fees. Although the amounts charged were very modest by Western standards, the fact that their child's education would cost the family money has meant that poorer families tended to remove their children – usually daughters – from school after only a few years of education. The government's pride in its public statistics, such as the often-cited fact that 90% or more of China's children attended primary school, did not report the number withdrawn from school and never finishing. It was in urban areas that a child was most likely to receive 12 years of schooling, but the cost of going to a good middle and high school could be astronomical. For example, in northeastern Chinese cities, a family could pay several thousand American dollars for a year of high school education in a highly regarded 'key' school. Even more modest middle and high schools charged fees that some families found beyond their means. Nonetheless, in the 1990s more Chinese were receiving a basic education than at any other time in the twentieth century, and this was a major step forward for the country and its people.

The number of Chinese students studying abroad also gradually increased as families earning money in the new economy found ways to fund a son or daughter with the right qualifications. Most went for graduate-level training and, of these, a small number returned to China where family ties and business opportunities provided incentive. The majority, however, chose not to return, often because of a lack of work in the area of their graduate training but also because of a continuing wariness about their prospects in China.

THE CHALLENGE OF EMPLOYMENT AND THE 'FLOATING POPULATION'

During Mao's lifetime, employment was determined by the government. The commune system, intended to provide security to all rural residents, absorbed millions of farmers and relocated urban workers. Cities were not accessible to rural residents as the government maintained a strict system of registration which did not allow individuals to change their place of residence except in very specific circumstances. Even marriage to someone with urban residency rights did not automatically allow a rural resident to move. The CCP's goal was to prevent the emergence of huge **conurbations** – and the many problems associated with highly concentrated urban populations.

Conurbation: Densely populated urban area that includes a major city, its outlying suburbs and small towns.

The reform era changed this system. As farm families began to lease land for their own crops and explore sideline production, families sought opportunities for maximizing their income. One means by which to do this was to allow the men in the family to seek occasional work in town to augment the family income. By the 1990s, young men from many of China's rural areas travelled in search of seasonal work, joining what has come to be called the 'floating population'. Initially, men travelled for seasonal agricultural or construction work but, as demand rose for these workers, the ranks of men leaving the countryside grew. Because they were 'temporary' workers, the usual permit system did not apply. Many of these workers were housed in temporary shelters on the worksites of new hotels and apartment buildings in towns and cities across China. When a project finished, the men moved on to the next construction site.

The 'floating population' was blamed for many things. Police sought suspects of petty crimes in the workers' shelters; local residents blamed them for fighting and generally misbehaving. When women joined the ranks, they, too, were viewed as being troublemakers. As these women were also beyond the control of their village family-planning committee, officials saw them as potential violators of the one-child policy, although there are no statistics to indicate that this was so. Overall, these seasonal labourers became a key component of the workforce that made possible the rapid construction of new buildings and roadways all across China. Despite the sometimes harsh conditions they endured, the number of workers in this 'free' labour population continued to grow.

During the 1990s China also witnessed another new phenomenon. As pressure increased on state-run enterprises to make profits not losses, workers were laid off in an effort to gain control of company finances. To make room for younger workers and reduce unemployment rates, government and businesses encouraged women to retire at the age of 50; retirement for women was mandatory at the age of 55. While workers understood the rationale behind this, losing one full-time worker's income caused considerable financial difficulties for families that relied on two incomes to maintain a relatively stable lifestyle. For men who were abruptly laid off, there was little or no unemployment insurance to support their families; those on government pensions could not survive on the small amounts allotted each month. People who had been taught to expect that the government would provide a life-long job now saw their own and their family's future jeopardized by the new economic system.

The numbers of disaffected and unemployed workers grew throughout the 1990s. Northeastern China was hit particularly hard, as this region had a large number of industrial and manufacturing cities reliant on government-owned enterprises. The younger and more enterprising among those laid off joined the 'floating population' but others were unable to do so, because of age or family responsibilities. With no means of livelihood available, many unemployed workers staged demonstrations and demanded that the government provide assistance. Efforts were made to help some individuals, but the problem was not alleviated. The issue of employment for millions of Chinese remained a major threat to the continuing stability of the country through the decade. The government's reliance on China's fast-paced economic reforms to absorb excess labour in the long term offered little comfort to those still seeking a means to support themselves and their families.

All the issues raised above constituted new challenges to the government. One response by the CCP was to push forward toward a stronger economy and also to cultivate a new sense of national pride in China. This also meant there was a shift away from the teachings of the old ideology and its stress on Marxism, Leninism and Maoism, and a move toward encouraging nationalism and patriotic feelings among China's people, as discussed below.

CHINA'S NEW NATIONALISM

Despite the problems outlined above, which constituted pressing issues for China's government and the CCP, the PRC's new prosperity engendered a growing pride in the country's rapid advance and its many achievements. The lack of religious freedom and the persistence of what are seen in the West as human rights abuses worried some Chinese but, on the other hand, many saw these as a relatively small price to pay for the opportunities at last available as a result of the economic reforms. The chance to build a good life for one's family and pride in what the Chinese people have accomplished contributed to the spread of a new kind of Chinese nationalism.

Criticism of China by Western nations not only contributed to this new nationalism, but it also brought out a defensive posture that the government used to good effect. In 1995–6, several influential publications appeared on the theme of a strong and powerful China which deserved respect from foreign states rather than heavy-handed criticism. Although the readership of these Chinese works was largely male and urban, the ideas they expressed showed how much some young intellectuals had changed in the short period since the events at Tiananmen Square. One of these books, *Megatrends China* (*Zhongguo daqushi*), included articles originally published by the State Statistics Bureau. The unifying theme of the articles concerned American efforts to contain China and thereby limit its growth, both domestic and international. America's constant attacks on China's human rights record were presented as just one example of how the United States interfered in China's domestic affairs.

While government agencies could be expected to author such views, another nationalistic salvo came from five young men of the Tiananmen Square generation. Their book, famous under its English title as *A China That Can Say No*, became a Chinese bestseller in the summer of 1996. The authors asserted that Western countries, particularly the United States and Great Britain, opposed China's economic and political clout and therefore sought to dictate China's domestic policy. They portrayed opposition to Beijing's bid to host the Olympic Games and America's hard bargaining over trade issues as part of a conspiracy to dominate and humiliate China. While Chinese intellectuals may have been unimpressed with the extreme nationalist rhetoric, many Chinese supported its anti-Western sentiments and its nationalistic agenda.

Another example of this new trend came a decade after Tiananmen Square when a new generation of students and young Beijingers participated in a different kind of demonstration, this time in support of their country. Following America's bombing of the Chinese embassy in Belgrade during the days of warfare in the Balkans, protestors threw stones and chanted anti-American slogans as they marched through Beijing's diplomatic quarter in May 1999. Pride in the achievements of their country over a remarkably short time-span of two decades gave this new generation a sense of national awareness that not only measured China in comparison to the recent past, but also in terms of its international standing.

By the end of the century, there was a generation that had only known the reform era and its relative prosperity and openness. Despite the unequal distribution of incomes, the opportunity to earn money and control one's economic life were eagerly embraced as individuals and families chose to *xiahai*, or 'jump into the sea' of the new economy and make it on their own. Urban residents under the age of 30 could choose from a growing number of options for education and employment, and many took pride in the changes that had brought China back to relative economic prosperity [**Doc. 18, pp. 152–4**].

By the end of the 1990s, even the youthful student leaders of the 1989 Beijing Spring had moved on. Some had suffered greatly for their roles in the student movement, but others now embraced some of the same economically driven agendas as did other Chinese of their generation. Among those who

Xiahai: Chinese term which literally translates as 'into the sea', but which came to mean leaving government positions to 'jump' into the new economy of the 1990s.

suffered the most was Wang Dan, the soft-spoken leader of the early phase of the student occupation of Tiananmen Square, who initially left China but then chose to return, as a result of which he was forced to endure time in prison for his role in what the government viewed as a 'counter-revolutionary' movement. In 1998 he was released on medical grounds after serving a total of seven years. He arrived in the United States and, a decade later, was pursuing his PhD at Yale University. Wu'erkaixi, the most outspoken and irreverent of the young men who had demanded dialogue with top government officials in May of 1989, also fled China in the aftermath of the Tiananmen Square shootings. However, after some years in the United States, he returned to Asia, married a young Chinese woman from Taiwan and went into business there. During an interview given in 1999, he spoke of the *naïveté* of the students and of how they had collectively miscalculated the depth of discontent in 1989 China. Chai Ling, the most visible of the young women leaders of the student movement, made the most dramatic change. In China, she was a graduate student, married to a fellow activist, Feng Congde. Both were the children of doctors and had therefore suffered during the period of the Cultural Revolution as offspring of the 'stinking intellectual' class. At the time of Beijing Spring, Chai Ling had already applied to go to the United States for graduate study. After 4 June 1989, she was smuggled out of China and arrived in the United States in 1990. By 1996, she was living in Cambridge, Massachusetts and working on her MBA at the Harvard Business School. Divorced and leading a distinctly American lifestyle, in 1999 she became chief executive officer of an internet company, backed by major American corporate interests. Her success in the United States, and her frequent trips to Taiwan to criticize the CCP, led some to label her an opportunist. Certainly, like other prominent young leaders of Beijing Spring, she had moved on, far from the days in which a stunning act of violence ended a movement whose time had not yet come.

Whatever her personal motivations, Chai Ling's economic success was what many of China's younger generation aspired to at the end of the twentieth century. Economic success was the new focus of youthful ambitions, not a high post in the government or Party. Civic-minded individuals turned to their careers rather than politics, and as they prospered, they gained a share in supporting the system that made their prosperity possible. For its part, the CCP continued to emphasize the importance of economic growth and pride in China, as well as a national commitment to making China a strong economic and political power. Mao's words of 1 October 1949 still carried great power: the Chinese people, he said, had stood up. The rhetoric of the 1990s affirmed that this, indeed, was the case.

8

Contemporary Chinese society

The PRC celebrated its sixtieth anniversary in 2009. In the preceding decade, China experienced further social changes and, in response, government policy sought to address problems arising from the rapid economic growth that continued to transform the country and the lives of its people. Among the new developments was the formation of a burgeoning middle class, while at the top a small, wealthy, elite class emerged in the great coastal cities. Life in some rural areas also improved but the lure of the city drew ever-increasing numbers of young people, leaving the fields to the middle-aged and elderly. At the bottom, an estimated 200 million people still struggled with meagre incomes and limited resources.

The most important social changes and new or revised policies to address emerging social needs are surveyed in this chapter. Topics include the formation of new social classes, education and health care, women and the family, minorities and environmental issues. Of growing importance to the generation born since 1980–90 was access to the internet and new forms of entertainment and culture, a topic addressed at the end of the chapter.

POPULATION AND SOCIAL CHANGE

The massive social changes underway in China affected people of all classes and ethnic groups, but the process was deeply influenced by the massive size of China's population which reached 1.35 billion in 2009. While the sheer number of people posed its own challenge, it was also this hard-working population that spurred the country's phenomenal economic growth by offering a seemingly endless supply of low-cost labour. The Chinese people also supplied the drive and ambition to improve their own lives and, in the process, propel China to the forefront of the world's economies. Despite a remarkable work ethic and a climbing GDP, huge economic inequities continued and, in some aspects, intensified.

A major issue was the expanding income gap between rural and urban populations. In the 1990s, urban residents earned two to three times the average income of rural residents who then constituted some 70% of the population. After 2000, urban workers earned closer to four times more than rural residents whose numbers declined to under 50%. Given the income disparity, it was no surprise that young people increasingly chose the factory over the farm, leaving rural areas to the older generation.

The continuing rural–urban income disparity helped to fuel what became the single greatest population migration in modern history. China's rate of rural-to-urban movement is roughly three times as great as that of migrants moving from Europe to the United States at the end of the nineteenth and early twentieth centuries. Some 200 million people left farms and small towns for the city; China expects rural migration to the cities to continue well into the middle of the twenty-first century.

Although China's population continued to grow, in 2002 the country had one of the world's lowest birth rates in the world at 0.6%. (Taiwan, still separated from China in 2010, had nearly the same population growth rate, 0.65% in 2000.) The family-planning policy remained in force, but most rural families could have two children, particularly if the first child was a girl. Gradually, enforcement of family-planning regulations relaxed as the government considered eliminating the policy altogether. If the 2009 fertility rate of 1.7 (that is, an average of 1.7 children per woman) continues as expected, China's population will stabilize in 2030 and then begin to drop. (In comparison, India's fertility rate of 2.8, if continued, means India will replace China as the world's most populous country by 2040.)

SOCIAL CLASSES

The Maoist goal of creating one vast classless society after 1949 dramatically transformed Chinese society. Wealthy families suddenly found themselves at the bottom rung of the social ladder. Hard-working peasant-farmers and urban factory workers occupied the highest rungs. Ironically, the Party that had the avowed aim of ending the class system altogether, virtually set class status in stone, with personal dossiers that detailed class background determining people's access to education and jobs.

The reform era dramatically reversed this social order, turning the Maoist-imposed ranking system on its head. Entrepreneurs and investors became the most highly regarded segment of the population as China's class structure increasingly mirrored that of states with market-driven economies.

In the first two decades of the reforms, China's uppermost elite still came from the *gaoganzidi* or children of high-ranking cadres. By the 1990s, many of these privileged children chose new careers in business, benefiting directly from their family connections. Some *taizi* or princes, children of the highest leaders in the PRC, chose to pursue high Party, government or military positions, or kept one foot in the government and another in private business.

After 2000, newly generated wealth in the coastal cities created the new elite of business leaders and entrepreneurs. In the 1990s, many businessmen aligned closely with local Party officials whose permission was vital to business expansion (Pearson, 1997: 115). The admission of entrepreneurs to the Party after 2002 was recognition that many Party members were already in private enterprise. Younger people also began to join the Party, although their motivations in doing so increasingly reflected the need for good relations with Party officials to succeed in some areas of business rather than a desire to follow Communist ideology.

The growth of China's new middle class accelerated sharply after 2000, although definitions of middle- and upper-class status varied. Defined in China as those having household assets over US$18,000, their number grew from 15% in 1999 to 19% in 2003, or over 250 million people. The China State Information Centre defined those earning 50,000 *yuan* per year (US$6,227) as middle class, and estimated that 25% of the population would attain this level in 2010. Outside observers estimated the middle class as being somewhat smaller, between 100 and 250 million. Regardless of which number had the greater validity, the growing middle class constituted a new element in China's social structure. Holding salaried positions in Chinese or international corporations, the aspirations of middle-class men and women became those of other well-off young professionals in other countries. The latest cell phones and computers, international travel, designer clothing, privately owned housing, private schools for their children and a family automobile or two became the norm for this expanding segment of China's newest class [**Doc. 19, pp. 154–5**].

Despite the growing number of middle-class Chinese, over 800 million people still did not meet the middle-class threshold in terms of income. Of these, an estimated 200 million people subsisted on low annual incomes of under US$1,000 a year, many in the most remote rural regions of the country. In urban areas unemployment and inadequate pensions meant severe financial struggles for some families. The poor constituted a large underclass that government policies had yet to reach. Nonetheless, millions of the poorest citizens improved their lives relative to earlier decades: the

World Bank credits China with bringing an estimated 200 million out of abject poverty since 2000.

China's new wealth was also unevenly distributed in geographical terms. The country's riches were concentrated along the 'Gold Coast' which stretches from Guangdong in the south to Liaoning province in the north. The rest of China's provinces and regions lagged behind in terms of per capita incomes as well as in economic development. Although the number of Chinese living in rural inland areas shrank every year, with less than 50% of the population earning their livelihood from agriculture in 2008, rural farmers remained firmly at the bottom of the class structure in terms of their meagre share of China's growing riches.

Policies to assist some of the poorest rural areas became the focus of much attention in 1999 when China announced its 'Opening Up the West' (*Xibei dakaifa*) campaign to encourage development in the western provinces. Attending to China's education system, health care and its abused environment (all discussed below) also gained new urgency as the rural–urban divide continued to grow and potentially threaten both Party authority and on-going economic growth.

WOMEN AND THE FAMILY

Changes for women had already taken hold in the 1990s. Overall, their education level had increased, with half of women between 18 and 64 having a middle school or higher level of education by 2000. Among urban women under 30, the number of years in school reached 10.4 in 2000, about the same average as men. Rural women, however, lagged behind, with an average of seven years, roughly one–two years less than rural men.

The new economy brought more opportunities for women at all levels of society. A fortunate few led major international corporations, aided by ties to the CCP elite. Li Xiaolin, daughter of retired CCP leader Li Peng, became Vice-President of China Power Investment Corporation, for example. Other wealthy women chose to work for charitable organizations: one example was the American-educated granddaughter of Deng Xiaoping, Deng Zuoye, who raised money for causes such as the Sichuan earthquake and for disabled children.

At the other end of the spectrum, female factory workers still faced poor working conditions. Many girls in their teens came from rural areas to work in the cities. Initially, they were a small percentage of the rural migrant workers lured by good-paying jobs in the cities. After 2000, the number of female migrant workers rose to roughly one-third of all such migrants. Referred to as *dagongmei* or 'working sisters', many of these young women worked to support parents at home or brothers heading off to school.

After the turn of the twenty-first century, a new pattern emerged. Instead of returning home to marry, as had been common practice, ambitious girls took night classes in the rapidly proliferating private commercial schools, acquiring skills that allowed them to seek employment beyond the factory floor. These girls reflected a growing trend among rural teens whose motivations to leave home were no longer limited to helping their families. As author and journalist Leslie Chang pointed out, the new waves of migrant women and factory girls were often the best-educated young people in their home villages. Few had any direct experience of farming, having begun factory work directly after leaving school, and a growing number did not wish to return to what they saw as the drudgery of rural life (Chang, 2008).

Among middle-class women, expectations for an increasingly comfortable lifestyle rose. Family consumption increased as career women and wives bought the latest in household appliances and electronics. While households in China on average still saved around 25% of their post-tax income, spending on a wide range of domestic and internationally manufactured goods increased.

In terms of earning power, Chinese women did well in comparison to women elsewhere in Asia. In 2000, women in South Korea earned 58% of the average man's salary and in Japan it was 70%. According to the Chinese government, in 2005, Chinese women with a junior high school diploma earned 68% of that earned by similarly educated men; this rose to 78% for those with a senior high school diploma, 80% for those with junior college and 83% for those with a college education. These positive numbers boded well for greater equity in earning power, although discrimination against women in the workplace remained an acknowledged problem.

Changes in the law also affected women's status. Revisions to the 1980 **Marriage Law** were announced in 2001. New provisions recognized extra-marital affairs as a cause of divorce and implemented penalties against the offending party, a provision that provoked criticism before and after it was passed into law. Other grounds for divorce included bigamy, abuse, gambling and drugs, all of which suggest a range of behaviours pinpointed as weakening the marriage bond. In recognition of the new wealth in some families, the law also included clauses on prenuptial agreements [**Doc. 20, pp. 156–7**]. Women also received new protection in the division of common property and custody of children. As the divorce rate climbed in China, some blamed the new law for making it too easy to get a divorce, but others suggested a range of factors including rising incomes, for women as well as men, and a degree of selfishness that appeared to characterize children born under the

Marriage Law revisions of 2001: While retaining clauses from the earlier versions, the 2001 law had new clauses on division of marital property, prenuptial agreements and penalties for a spouse who caused a marriage to fail.

one-child policy. Overall, divorce became more common, increasing from 341,000 in 1980 to 1.4 million in 2007, but still relatively low by international standards.

Since 2003, marrying couples have not needed permission from their work unit to marry, as previously required. In addition, some major cities no longer required couples to register for family planning. Increased privacy, greater access to information, and individual choice of employment brought women and men a greater sense of personal freedom. Officials had less and less influence over residents who could now change jobs, buy a condo or choose a private school for their children without having to first apply for permission.

Women's lives overall benefited through new laws and work opportunities, but society as a whole remained patriarchal. Employment law still allowed an employer to limit some jobs to men or women only and could also stipulate the age range for potential employees. While women had already been given certain protections in the workplace such as guaranteed maternity leaves for instance, these laws also worked against women in that some employers refused to consider women workers because child rearing could entail loss of time at work. Because men still had a very limited role in child care or household duties, it was understood that a woman would carry a 'double burden' of her job and her family responsibilities.

Further evidence of patriarchal preferences could be seen in a lop-sided sex ratio that resulted from family-planning policy. The ratio remained at around 119 males to 100 females throughout the decade. A natural birth rate would be 106 males to 100 females. Pressure on rural women to produce a male heir continued and may be at least partly to blame for the rate of suicide among rural women – three times the rate for women in the urban areas.

A related matter was the prevalence of spoiled single children, or 'little emperors', indulged since birth by parents and two sets of doting grandparents. The '4–2–1' syndrome became shorthand for 'one child, two parents and four grandparents'. Because retirees often relied on their children for support in old age, having an only child meant that a single child would not only care for his or her parents in old age, but also the ageing in-laws of his or her spouse. Such care was not optional because providing care for parents was stipulated in the Marriage Law. This looming financial burden may also have a role in government reconsideration of the one-child policy.

A worrying trend after 2000 was the number of women involved in prostitution. The fast-expanding entertainment sector included private clubs and karaoke bars often linked to prostitution (Zheng, 2009). This lifestyle offered an extremely high income to young women who ignored the risks to health and safety associated with it.

Other crimes involving women also grew, particularly trafficking in women for prostitution or for sale as unwilling brides. Gangs kidnapped women and sold them to men in poor, remote areas who would force them to agree to a marriage. Because of shame, some women simply submitted. Although the total number of women forced into marriage in this way is not known, revisions to the Marriage Law in 2001 specifically mentioned the phenomenon, suggesting that it was common enough to warrant inclusion in the law code.

MINORITIES

The advances and reverses for women could also be seen among China's minorities. In terms of numbers, most minority populations thrived for, unlike the majority Han Chinese, most did not have to follow the one-child policy (see a partial listing of groups and their estimated 1990 populations on p. 31). Numerically small groups such as the Ewenki and Tajiks, for instance, continued to have large families. The Kazakhs of the northwest had the highest birth rate with an average of five children per family. Altogether, the combined numbers of minority groups reached 130 million, or roughly 10% of China's population in 2010.

Some minority groups and individuals took full advantage of China's form of affirmative action with little apparent worry over a possible threat to their cultures or their identity by doing so. Among the advantages given to minorities is admission to universities with lower exam scores than those of Han Chinese students. A growing number of minority men and women completed undergraduate degrees, PhD degrees or became doctors or lawyers.

In 2005, the government issued an official White Paper on regional autonomy, reviewing existing laws and noting advances for minorities. Part 3 on the rights of self-government of ethnic autonomous areas noted that training new minority cadres had been a fundamental goal and that, as a result, at the end of 2003 there were 2.9 million such cadres and specialized personnel. The report also declared that the percentage of minorities in the **National People's Congress** had reached over 13%, exceeding the actual percentage of all minorities in China. Each ethnic group also had one or more deputies in the congress. The report also noted that autonomous areas had enacted their own laws and regulations, particularly in the areas of Marriage Law, Land Law and Grassland Law, the latter being especially important in nomadic areas of the north and west.

Efforts were also made to portray minorities as a historical component of China's diverse population [**Doc. 21, pp. 157–9**]. In some textbooks published after 2000, minorities received special attention and, having been

National People's Congress: This body is the highest legislative authoritative body in the People's Republic of China, but in practice the congress convenes for only one–two weeks, making it impossible for its nearly 3,000 members to provide oversight of government policy or its implementation. The 11th Congress convened in March of 2009.

largely absent from such accounts before, were praised for their contributions to modern China. They were also enjoined to support the CCP principle of 'national unity', a slogan that, nonetheless, fell short of full support among some minority groups.

China also made efforts to unite the country through better transportation. Projects that began after 2000 directly affected minority regions in Qinghai province and Tibet. In 2006, completion of a new railway line from Xining (in Qinghai province) to Lhasa meant that rail travel was now possible all the way from Beijing to Lhasa, the Tibetan regional capital. Speculation that this would bring new Han migrants to the previously remote region proved only partly correct, but concerns remained that the new rail line would allow greater economic integration of Tibet with the rest of China as well as enhancing control by the central authorities.

Despite improvements in the living standards and education of minorities overall, tensions continued in Tibet and Xinjiang. In Tibet, the region's worst violence in three decades occurred in March 2008, prior to the Beijing Olympics. An unknown number of Tibetans were killed or injured, with an unknown number arrested and imprisoned for inciting anti-government activities.

The worst incident of ethnic-related violence occurred in the Xinjiang region in the summer of 2009. Sparked by the beating to death of two Uighur migrant workers in southern China, protests in Urumqi left nearly 200 dead and over 1,600 wounded, many of them Han Chinese. Despite a massive police and army presence, unrest continued into August and September of the same year. In these and other instances, the government cut communications, closing down internet access and also limiting travel to and from the region. In 2010, the Beijing authorities reassigned the region's Han Chinese Party secretary who had advocated harsh measures to maintain control. His replacement was expected to help boost economic development in the oil-rich region as well as maintain stability.

EDUCATION

One route to self-advancement in China has always been linked to education. As surveyed below, access to education became more difficult for those with limited family resources, while rich families took advantage of expanding educational options in the new economy.

A new concern in the reform era was the availability, affordability and quality of education for young people. During the Maoist era, education was provided by the state from the first grade through university. Exams taken at each level decided which child could continue to middle school and high school. Most Chinese had at least an elementary education prior to 1978; a small percentage continued on to high school and even fewer on to college. Entrance to colleges and universities was open to those few who had received high entrance exam scores or whose families had connections. As China moved away from state-supported schools, gradually responsibility for funding education devolved to local authorities and to parents.

Officially, the government instituted a minimum requirement of nine years of education in the 1986 Compulsory Education Law. As a general principle, education was free, but parents paid for books and other supplies. In poorer counties and villages, parents also contributed to the upkeep of the local schools and, in some instances, helped pay the teachers' salaries. In the 1990s many poor families enrolled their children in school as required by law but withdrew them within a few years to assist the family in the fields or other home enterprises. It was not uncommon for young girls from poorer inland provinces to be sent out to work rather than finish middle or high school, often to help finance a brother's education.

New avenues for further training and education emerged as part of the expanding number of commercial or business schools set up outside the official education system. Young people who did not do well enough in the entrance exams to get into good high schools or colleges found possibilities for self-improvement in private commercial schools that proliferated in urban areas, particularly in factory towns. These institutions trained students in specific skills valued in the marketplace: English; computer skills; machine operation or repair; and writing skills useful in supervisory or management positions. Mastery of these allowed young workers to move beyond the factory floor into white-collar jobs or higher-paying types of factory work. This private educational system, generally unregulated and uneven in the quality of education provided, was a direct response to the aspirations of young, ambitious, rural migrants who chose not to return to their home villages but opt for new lives in the city.

For those students who did well in the public school system and whose families could afford the tuition, a university education was the ultimate goal. In the Maoist era, a university education remained the prerogative of a small minority; in 1980, less than 1% of Chinese held a university degree. The government worked to increase these numbers as the need for highly educated individuals jumped in the new economy. In 2004, some 2.5 million students graduated from college, and in 2010, the government announced that a record 6.3 million students would receive degrees. The costs of such an education began to climb in the 1980s as funding for universities shifted from the government to educational institutions. In 1992, the government allowed universities to set their own fees, opening the way to rapidly rising costs. By 2000, only students from families with the financial ability to support a full-time student could expect to enter college. Many institutions added new graduate degrees, such as the MBA, to provide ambitious students with internationally recognized credentials.

A college degree not only paved the way to new careers, it also became a requirement for entry into China's political elite which, by the late 1990s, was predominantly college-educated (see further discussion in Chapter 9 on the government and the CCP). Chinese students educated abroad also began returning to China where the opportunities in the burgeoning economy promised rapid advancement and high salaries as well as living conditions as good, if not better than, those in major international cities.

Overall, Chinese government figures assert that the average amount of formal education for its citizens reached 11 years in 2006. Given the widely held view that education offers the best route toward advancing both the individual and the family, the number of high school graduates will undoubtedly climb in coming decades and a growing number will aspire to an education at college level.

HEALTH CARE

Health care, like education, was once the province of the commune or work unit. Hospitals and smaller health facilities received government funds to operate, and everyone was covered through a basic cooperative medical system. Between 1949 and 1978, the overall level of care was basic, with few trained physicians and nurses to staff hospitals and clinics. Nonetheless, there were improvements in the overall health of the Chinese, as measured in the statistics for infant mortality, which dropped from 200 to 34 per 1,000 live births, and in life expectancy, which rose from 35 to 68 years.

When the old socialist system was dismantled, health care was left first to local government units and then to the family and individual. By the 1990s, it was largely privatized. The most significant result was that most of the rural population was effectively uninsured. Health-care expenses became an enormous burden for all but the most well off. Although the government instituted regulations on the amount that medical practitioners could charge for certain services and pharmaceuticals, hospitals and clinics nonetheless became 'for profit' enterprises and led to a crisis in the availability of medical care.

The government response to this crisis came in 1998 when it mandated employer insurance schemes. These consisted of medical savings accounts to which the employee and employer contributed specific sums. However, some employers refused to follow the new rules on the grounds that they could not afford to contribute, while others found ways to avoid compliance altogether. The government persisted with the programme, however, and by 2007 asserted that basic medical insurance covered some 180 million urban employees.

Self-employed farmers still went without basic health insurance until, in 2003, the Ministry of Health launched the rural cooperative medical insurance system. At first, residents made a modest annual contribution while the state, province, city and county governments supplied additional funds. In 2009, the payment by an individual was 20 *yuan* (US$2.50) with the government contributing 80 *yuan* (US$10). The resulting pool of money provided partial payment to cover certain health-care services, although it did not provide for primary care or protection in instances of catastrophic illnesses. According to government reports, the plan covered 814 million rural people, or 91.5% of its target population by 2008. Plans are to increase the basic medical insurance to cover 90% of both the rural and urban populations by 2011.

In the same year, anti-discrimination laws to protect the rights of people with HIV-AIDS were enacted, although anecdotal stories of discrimination continued to surface. The latter group received an especially sympathetic hearing because of publicity which pointed out the accidental infection of rural residents who sold blood drawn with unsanitary needles, leading to their infection.

Research on the state of China's health revealed a negative side to the impact of China's changing diet. A 2007–8 study reported that the country was facing a major public health problem because of the rapidly increasing rate of diabetes. An estimated 92.4 million adults had developed the disease and another 148 million were diagnosed with prediabetes (Yang *et al.*, 2010). With 1 in 10 people diabetic, China's health-care system will need to prepare for this and other illnesses more typical of developed countries.

In sum, the health system in China mimicked that of other capitalist nations where the wealthiest sector of the population enjoyed access to the highest standard of care while the majority had basic health care providing limited medical coverage. Major illnesses or accidents still resulted in extreme financial hardship for the vast majority. This new inequity may figure prominently among the urgent issues for the government to tackle, as it does in much of the world.

THE ENVIRONMENT

Since 2000, vast tracts of western China, where ethnic minorities are a majority in many counties, have been targeted for greater development. Concerns expressed within China over the impact on the environment suggest internal opposition to these plans, but as discussed in the following section, China's national concern over the environment led to new governmental efforts; private individuals and non-governmental organizations (NGOs) also emerged as a new force to lead China toward a sustainable environment.

As noted earlier (p. 72), concern over the environment led to the founding of the State Environment Protection Administration in 1998. Since then, government policies have changed dramatically as the country tackled major environmental issues.

Water sources were an urgent concern. Many rivers carried untreated human waste as well as the pollutants from riverside factories. For example, the Huai River of north China had become so badly polluted that its foul waters turned black in the 1990s. Despite officially backed cleaning efforts, the Huai suffered another calamity in 2001 when some 38 billion gallons of badly polluted water entered the river, making it unfit for human use. Overall, in 2002, 75% of the water in China's rivers was judged unsuitable for drinking or fishing (Economy, 2005).

Both flooding and water shortages added to worries. In 1998, 3,000 people died when the Yangzi River flooded, covering 52 million acres. The culprit in this instance was over-logging in western Sichuan, a practice that the government ordered stopped. The new Three Gorges Dam, which was completed in stages between 2006 and 2009, did not end all flooding but it did lessen the severity. In sharp contrast to the Yangzi floods was the fate of China's other great river, the Huanghe (Yellow River). Once known as 'China's sorrow' because of frequent disastrous floods, so much water had been diverted away from the river for agriculture that it often ran dry in the 1990s: in 1999 the river ran dry for 42 days, depriving farmers of the north China plain of water for their crops.

Previous governments of China had considered the possibility of diverting southern rivers' water north where aridity had long limited farmers' productivity. After 2000, plans for such a diversion were again revived. The 'South-to-North Water Diversion Project' is the largest such water diversion system ever undertaken. It will link the Yangzi River with the Yellow, the Huai and Hai Rivers of the north for an estimated cost of US$62 billion, twice as much as the cost of the Three Gorges Dam on the Yangzi River. Approved in 2002, it is estimated that the massive canal system will be completed in the middle of the twenty-first century.

In terms of air quality, China became the world's leading producer of greenhouse gases, and China's reliance on coal remained a major factor in the country's badly polluted air. Over two-thirds of China's energy comes from coal, some of which contains high levels of contaminants. Not only does coal fuel the factories that create China's growing wealth, but it is the heating fuel for nearly half of all Chinese homes. The reform era dramatically increased reliance on coal so that use doubled from 600 million to 1.2 billion metric tonnes in 2000. In 2002, China had six out of the world's ten most polluted cities, as a result of the use of coal and factory discharge.

Automobiles are another, newer source of urban air pollution. Until the reform era, automobile use was restricted to members of China's elite, but numbers began to grow quickly in the 1990s. In 2000, there were still only 13 vehicles per 1,000 people but the vehicles were big polluters because China's domestically produced cars were not required to have catalytic converters. They emitted 10–20 times more pollutants than US or Japanese cars. In 2001, China took a major step toward cleaner air by finally banning lead from gasoline (Economy, 2005: 194).

Spurred by the Olympic Games of 2008, Beijing began its 'Blue Sky' project in order to raise public awareness of the need to curtail all sources of pollution. The goal was to increase, year by year, the days in which the city enjoyed blue sky, rather than the dust, dirt and chemical pollution that was the more usual atmosphere of the badly polluted city. There has been success, with the government reporting a steady if slow increase in the number of days with mostly blue sky.

Land degradation and encroaching deserts were another area of major concern as China's western deserts appeared to be shifting slowly to the east. One cause was over-grazing of grasslands which in turn was caused by a growing demand for meat as Chinese incomes increased. Another cause was cultivation of marginal lands. Pastoral areas in Qinghai and Inner Mongolia, for example, lost some 4.4 million hectares of pasture as new Han migrants moved in to build farms, despite a reduction in the availability of drinking water. Grasslands north of Beijing so deteriorated from overuse that desert sands had reached within 250 kilometres of the capital. A shelterbelt project, dubbed the 'Great Green Wall', resulted in the planting of hundreds of trees as a way to stop further desert encroachment and improve air quality. At a cost of US$6.3 billion, this kind of project was expensive, particularly when some forms of grass might have been more effective. In 2004, the Ministry of Agriculture used a combination of planting grasses and a grazing ban to restore some 70 million hectares. Victories such as this were being declared year by year as governmental and citizen groups spread the word about environmental sustainability.

Increasingly concerned about the environmental impact of rapid economic growth, the government also established a number of new agencies and commissions to address these concerns after 2000. At the top is the ministerial-level State Environment Protection Administration, linked to province-level and lower bureaus established to monitor and guard the environment. China also passed stringent environmental laws. Unfortunately, the administrative structures remained underfunded and do not have enough workers for the gargantuan task of monitoring and enforcing regulations. Efforts thus far are promising, but much hinges on the strengthening and enforcing of existing regulations.

In 2002, China ratified the Kyoto Protocol to help curb greenhouse emissions. China also became the largest recipient of environmental aid from international sources such as the World Bank and the Global Environment Facility, although such assistance has been reduced because China no longer qualifies for International Development Assistance (IDA). Its close neighbour, Japan, also provided aid for environmental projects, particularly with a view to limiting the flow of polluted air generated in China and affecting Japan's air quality.

Small but growing numbers of the Chinese public share a worldwide concern over environmental issues and global warming. The idea of citizen groups united for special causes was virtually unknown in China prior to the reform era, but the numbers of such groups are a new social phenomenon dating from the 1990s. China's first environmental NGO was founded in 1993 by Liang Congjie who proved an effective, dynamic leader. A grandson of influential Chinese intellectual Liang Qichao, his background and political connections contributed to the success of his group, Friends of Nature.

Television programmes on the need to protect and respect the environment began to appear regularly, and environmental groups sponsored events on Earth Day, for example, to publicize the need for citizen support. The government generally welcomed these and other activities because the most successful among them attracted international funding for environmental projects, assisting the government in its on-going efforts to curtail pollution and move toward green policies.

In 2004, environmental groups claimed a victory when the Chinese Premier, **Wen Jiabao**, announced that planned dam construction on the Salween (Nu) River, which flows through China to Burma and Thailand, would be suspended pending further study. As the dams were close to a World Heritage site, international agencies had also backed the activists in their request for reconsideration of projects that would both displace people and endanger protected plants and animals.

Wen Jiabao (b. 1942): Educated as a geologist in Beijing, Wen worked in Gansu province until reassigned to Beijing in 1982 where he worked with reformers Hu Yaobang and Zhao Ziyang. When Hu became President, Wen was elevated to the position of Premier.

The need for greater international cooperation over global warming received Chinese President Hu's support in 2009 when he addressed the UN General Assembly on the issue of climate change. He indicated that China would take determined and practical steps toward tackling the problem by conserving energy, cutting carbon emissions and developing renewable energy, among other practices [**Doc. 22, pp. 159–60**].

Overall, as Elizabeth Economy of the US Council on Foreign Relations has written, there has been a 'sea change' in Chinese environmental protection, in both attitudes and practices (Economy, 2005: 215). Continued efforts marked by stronger penalties and more stringent inspections could help improve the lives of the millions of Chinese reliant on environmental protection.

THE ARTS, ENTERTAINMENT AND POPULAR CULTURE

The reform era witnessed a renaissance in the arts and, despite censorship of some creative endeavours, the talents of outstanding individuals began to flower. After 2000, a new generation influenced both by the re-examination of classical China and a new openness to the West gained world prominence in music and film, while Chinese authors, inside China and abroad, claimed an increasing audience for their work.

The international art world welcomed Chinese artists in all media with unbridled enthusiasm [**Doc. 23, pp. 160–1**]. Prices for Chinese paintings rose into the millions of dollars, and installation art by avant-garde artists appeared in major art galleries around the globe. Films made in China garnered world attention as the fourth and fifth generations of film-makers found a world stage for their work. Zhang Yimou and Chen Kaige won international acclaim for their cinematic creations, as did Taiwan-born Ang Lee whose award-winning film *Crouching Tiger, Hidden Dragon* added cachet to Chinese film production and praise for actors Zhou Yunfai (Chow Yun-fat) and Zhang Yi. John Woo, Hong Kong's best-known director, showcased action films that drew millions of fans, in Asia and around the world.

Classical musicians proved themselves masters of Western as well as European and Chinese forms. For example, renowned pianist Lang Lang received standing ovations for his performances of European classical music, a genre forbidden in China during the Maoist era. Composers Ye Xiaogang and Tan Dun, whose music for the film *Crouching Tiger, Hidden Dragon* gathered domestic and international accolades, enjoyed new-found fame and acclaim for their music. An upcoming young generation excelling in musical expression promised to add even further lustre to the growing ranks of Chinese stars.

Popular music followed international trends and, after years of resistance from the authorities, Western rock groups began to add China to their international tours, albeit with occasional censoring of lyrics by the government. Hip-hop, rap and other forms of contemporary music found eager fans, with home-grown Chinese groups forming and dissolving as quickly as in the rest of the pop world. Television programmes modelled on European and American shows which feature hopeful musicians and dancers before live and cyber audiences of voters contributed their own share of new stars. Musicians and singers from Hong Kong and Taiwan remained popular, with music and musicians moving far more freely throughout Asia than ever before. Artists such as **Cui Jian**, whose songs were heard by young protesters during the Tiananmen Square demonstrations of 1989, appeared on stage in China and abroad.

In the realm of literature, Chinese regulations once banned many Chinese and foreign literary works; at one time, possessing such literature was a dangerous enterprise. Rules on publication gradually relaxed in the reform era. By 2010, the range and type of literature available to the reading public represented a massive transformation. China also published a huge number of books and magazines every year, including many in Chinese and in foreign languages. Popular books included computer manuals and scientific studies. Censorship did not totally disappear, but the relative freedom of access to a broad range of materials was taken for granted by young Chinese able to pursue their interests in a way not possible for their parents' generation.

Sports fans, sporting events and sports stars became a greater phenomenon, with Chinese soccer players becoming national heroes. The Beijing Olympics in 2008 showcased world-class, dedicated athletes and China's record number of 56 medals led the awards list. Chinese athletes also went international in professional sport, including world-renowned Yao Ming, whose popularity and fame in China extended around the globe when he became a major NBA player.

Cui Jian (b. 1961): Beijing-born musician, songwriter and vocalist. He was among the most popular young musicians to perform in Tiananmen Square during Beijing Spring of 1989.

TECHNOLOGY AND COMMUNICATIONS

The Chinese government had a major role in the rapid expansion of technology and communications by encouraging and facilitating their growth. Its role as a cyber censor drew critics both inside and outside China, but the fact that its leaders actively pressed for adoption of the newest technology and encouraged the fast-paced development of China's 'knowledge economy' has been a key factor in China's technological revolution.

After 2000, the number of Chinese with access to cell phones, e-mail, instant messaging and online social networks grew at breakneck speed. In 2001, China had over 140 million cell-phone users, more than America's 118 million in that same year. By 2006, the country had 400 million users, more than the entire population of the United States.

Cell-phone use differed in some respects from other parts of the globe. In China, cell phones became the primary means of accessing the internet, with

Baidu: Literally meaning '100 degrees', Baidu is China's premier Chinese-language internet search engine and is the world's largest in terms of the number of users. Its founder, Robin Yanhong Li, is one of China's new multibillionaires.

use for conversation a distant second. The major service providers were China Mobile and China Unicom. The Chinese company **Baidu** was the most popular search engine; in 2010, it had more users than any other system in the world. Yahoo! and Google held only small shares in the booming China business. Google's differences with China over censorship led to it temporarily moving its PRC operations to Hong Kong, but in July 2010 it re-entered the China market providing a limited number of internet services.

Personal computer ownership rose more slowly, primarily because of cost but also because of easy and inexpensive access to the web via China's ubiquitous internet cafes, even in some of the more remote regions of China. In 2007, 137 million Chinese used the internet via computer, with educated, urban males the single largest group of 'netizens'.

The rise of the cell phone and fast communication raised new issues for China's government, which sought to control the flow of information on any topic of national political sensitivity, particularly information on Tiananmen Square in 1989, Tibet and Xinjiang. Websites on these topics were routinely blocked by the government. China required all internet providers to monitor for any efforts to access forbidden information. Since 2000, government officials have been appointed as monitors of websites and e-mails in an effort to prevent access to, or the spread of, information it does not approve. The periodic arrest of journalists for what they have written or shared privately online continued to remind users of the government's still powerful role in regulating information.

Despite government efforts at controlling the web, it remained invaluable to many Chinese who accessed information online or used it to communicate with friends and family. Especially popular web hosts were Sina.com, sohu.com and netease.com, which offered international and domestic news as well as access to individual blogs. Chinese bloggers proliferated, although not to the extent they have in the West. Many valued the opportunity to write online about issues of personal or national concern such as environment and social policy. In 2010, however, the government indicated that it would no longer allow anonymous blogs or postings on the web, a practice that was previously tolerated, and the impact of this pronouncement remains to be seen.

Emphasizing that even the top leaders of the country understood the value of e-media, in February 2010, Premier Wen Jiabao held an unprecedented online chat with internet users via two major portals: the central government's website at www.gov.cn and their official news website, www.xinhuanet.com, the Xinhua News Agency.

Despite the government embracing the web to address people directly, the fact that anyone with a cell phone is able to send video and still images across China challenges the government's level of control over communications.

There are several documented instances of the internet and cell-phone cameras being used to record ethnic violence, for example, before sharing these images with the world. Images of violence in Tibet during March 2008 and in Urumqi in the summer of 2009 reached the world within minutes. Some were posted to YouTube where they remained available for a global public. Although the government cut electronic access with these regions, the advent of instantaneous communication undermined government efforts to control the news. Events that previously could be confined to the realm of rumour now required a fuller and more persuasive official response.

China's increasing technological sophistication relied on its best universities to produce a new generation of trained technology and communication personnel. At the top of the list is Qinghua (also spelled 'Tsinghua') University, in Beijing, from which many of the top Chinese political leaders graduated, and Shanghai Jiaotong University, which attracted many top students in computing. The government also benefited from Chinese students who went abroad to study at some of the world's finest universities. Some observers believe that the nature of the web and the increasingly well-educated men and women who use it will contribute to a more open society. It already appeared, in 2010, that the government may be fighting a losing battle as more people find ways to breach the governmental firewall in order to access unfiltered and uncensored information.

9

Government, politics and the economy since 2000

The impetus for China's dramatic rise to its position as an economic powerhouse derived from government policy and the Beijing leadership, which unleashed the Chinese entrepreneurial spirit and allowed millions of Chinese to pursue lifestyles unthinkable for an earlier generation.

Reforms also continued to move the country further away from the socialist ideals of the 1949 revolution and the Maoist era. But far from threatening the CCP's political domination, as some observers predicted, the reform era continued under China's one-party system, with the CCP holding tightly to its monopoly on political and military power. It continued the long-standing policy of limiting freedom of political expression, in the name of national stability and economic growth. Although demonstrations at the local level sky-rocketed after 2000, the central government maintained its hold over all political matters and reified the pre-eminence of the CCP.

GOVERNMENT, PARTY AND MILITARY

While the structure and practices of the government and CCP continued to follow established forms, major changes occurred. One of the most significant was the educational levels and backgrounds of Party members and government officials. Prior to the reform era, advancement through the political ranks had depended on factors such as personal connections and seniority in the CCP as well as a commitment to Marxism and an appropriately proletarian 'class background'. The high value placed on these qualities meant that the overall level of formal education among the leadership at every level was very low (Li, 2001: 33). As late as 1982, over 50% of CCP members had only an elementary education or were illiterate.

By 1986, major changes had begun. Some 1.3 million senior Party cadres retired and were replaced with a new cohort of nearly 500,000 college-educated men and women (Li, 2001: 33–5). In the 1990s, the move to a more professional and better-educated bureaucracy was well established. In 1998, more than half the top Party leaders held university degrees. Under President Hu, a growing number of the highest officials held advanced degrees, and recruitment of Party members from the growing middle and entrepreneurial classes increased the average level of education among both Party and government officials.

The most remarkable change within the CCP began in 2000 when President Jiang Zemin announced his policy of the 'Three Represents', the three referring to categories of people previously unwelcome by the CCP: entrepreneurs, intellectuals and scientists. Despite initial internal Party opposition, the CCP ultimately embraced the policy, making it possible for members of all three groups to join the Party. As one observer noted, 'It made little sense to exclude the people whose success was the result of following the Party's policies' (Dickson, 2004: 149).

Inclusion of capitalists in the CCP was followed by a much anticipated move to protect private property. This was affirmed in an amendment to the Chinese **constitution** which had been adopted in 1982. Approved in March 2004, the fourth amendment, article 11, stated that: 'The State protects the lawful rights and interest of the non-public sectors of the economy, such as the individual and private sectors of the economy.' Article 13 took individual rights a step further by stating that: 'Citizens' lawful private property is inviolable' [**Doc. 24, pp. 161–2**]. Although the right of the government to expropriate land in certain circumstances (and with appropriate compensation) also remained on the books, these new amendments unequivocally established the right to own private property.

CCP membership also changed as the door to entrepreneurs opened. Party membership had always been a small percentage of the total population. Membership was, and remains, only available to certain applicants and a careful vetting of background and employment was required. With more categories of people now eligible for membership, the number of Party members grew; between 2002 and 2007 membership rose by 10%. From some 10 million members in 1956, total membership rose to 64 million in 2000 and 75 million in 2009, making the CCP the single largest political party in the world.

The composition of the CCP's membership illustrated the increasing educational level of party members. In 2007, 32% had a college education or higher. The percentage of women members rose to 20% and nearly 24% were 35 or younger.

Constitution of 1982: China had three previous constitutions adopted in 1954, 1975 and 1978, respectively. The 1982 constitution reflected the early reforms that took hold after 1978 and its four amendments expanded and confirmed new rights, such as the right to have and to inherit private property.

The most common field of study for top Party and governmental leaders was engineering; many shared the common experience of studying at the prestigious Qinghua University in Beijing. Despite changes at the top, senior leaders with limited formal education nonetheless remained influential into the twenty-first century. The last of the Maoist era leaders was BoYibo who died in 2007 at the age of 98 (*New York Times*, 17 January 2007, C14).

The government itself was the focus of administrative reforms initially outlined by Premier Zhu Rongji in 1998. These sought to shrink the size of the central government and also strengthen the role of the state in the areas of finance and regulation (Cheek, 2006: 111). Reforms of the legal system also began in the 1990s when numerous laws were passed concerning the roles and powers of the police, the judiciary and lawyers. In 1996, changes to the Law of Criminal Procedure constituted a major step forward as new laws recognized the presumption of innocence and right to legal defence as well as access to legal aid for certain eligible individuals. As the civil law code underwent changes, Chinese ventured into the long-neglected legal profession in growing numbers. As one noted analyst of the changes that reshaped the legal system writes, it was no exaggeration to state that 'never in the twentieth century did Chinese citizens enjoy a degree of legal protection and security similar to what they enjoy today' (Muhlhahn, 2009: 294). Implementation of the reforms remained uneven, but they indicated another important shift that affected all social strata in changing China.

Changes in the law and in government were accompanied by new opportunities to join NGOs. Internationally recognized groups such as chambers of commerce, professional associations and social groups of many kinds all attracted strong memberships. Politically acceptable causes, such as environmental activism and disaster-relief efforts, drew increasing numbers of volunteers, some organized through online social networks [**Doc. 25, pp. 162–3**]. These new social groupings suggested the emergence of a new civil society after 2000.

Hu Jintao (b. 1943): President of China, 2003–present; Secretary-General of the CCP and head of China's military. Hu rose through the Chinese Communist Youth League and held top Party positions in Guizhou and, in 1988, in Tibet. In the 1990s, he was moved to Beijing where he served as President of the Central Party School and as a member of the Politburo before his election as president.

In 2003, China witnessed the peaceful transfer of power from President Jiang Zemin to his successor, **Hu Jintao**. A member of the powerful Political Bureau of the CCP, Hu had assumed the top Party post of Secretary-General in late 2002. He officially began his term as President in March 2003. As stipulated in the Chinese constitution, Hu was elected by the National People's Congress, rather than by popular vote. Cementing his status as China's most powerful man, in 2004 he also became head of the Central Military Commission which controls China's military establishment (see further discussion, below). Hu Jintao thus held all three of China's most powerful positions. Following established practice, other top Party leaders held the top posts in the government, making the Party and the government in full accord on policy matters.

Born in 1943 and educated at the prestigious Qinghua University, Hu represented the 'fourth generation' of leaders since the 1949 revolution. The first generation was that of Chairman Mao and Zhou Enlai; the second, Deng Xiaoping; and the third, Jiang Zemin.

President Hu came to power at a very tense time in international relations. The war in Iraq began within days of his taking office. The **SARS** outbreak was spreading in China, although initial government reports denied its severity. There was yet another crisis over North Korea's development of nuclear power.

SARS: Severe Acute Respiratory Syndrome. Illness caused by a virus affecting the respiratory system; also referred to as swine flu. An outbreak of SARS led to hundreds of deaths in Hong Kong and China in 2003.

Hu's response was uneven. China initially expressed its opposition to the war in Iraq, but following a visit to China by American President George W. Bush, China agreed to join the 'war on terror'. The handling of the SARS epidemic received poor marks from members of the medical establishment in China and elsewhere, but subsequent efforts to deal with threatened outbreaks of infectious diseases improved. China sought to persuade its North Korean neighbour to abandon efforts at expanding its nuclear power, with halting success (see further discussion in Chapter 10 on foreign relations).

In handling these and other challenges, Hu relied on key individuals, particularly Premier Wen Jiabao. Wen previously worked with the reformers Hu Yaobang and Zhao Ziyang in the 1980s, and subsequently with Jiang Zemin (see entry for Wen Jiabao in 'Who's who'). The close alliance between Hu and Wen was marked by their very public commitment to on-going reforms in the government and Party as well as maintaining the stability necessary to China's continuing economic expansion. They became known for what some refer to as their populist approach, repeatedly reminding the public of the needs of the less fortunate and appealing directly to the people for support in building China into a great power. They also declared that reducing the urban–rural income gap was a central tenet of their administration, although success in this area proved elusive. Premier Wen personified the government's concern for the unfortunate, and his visits to poor regions and disaster sites, such as that of the 2008 Sichuan earthquake, became part of the government's new efforts to persuade the population of the leaders' personal concern for people's welfare.

After 2000, the expanding role of the internet provided a new avenue for the government to present itself and its new policies to the people. The Chinese Communist Party inaugurated a website in 1997, and websites for governments at all levels began appearing online, some to lure Chinese and foreign tourists and some to highlight their area's welcome to business investors. Even top government leaders found the web a useful vehicle for their own messages of concern for the people's welfare. As previously noted, Premier Wen appeared on Chinese television for an online chat, responding to questions from the public.

The Chinese central government's official website indicated the possible direction of future governmental reforms. Under 'Presidency', a section on the election of the President states that 'as the political democratization process continues, the single candidate practice will gradually be replaced by a multi-candidate election' (www.gov.ch).

While this statement suggests a government goal of future democratization, no significant opposition parties exist. The eight long-standing political parties referred to on government websites are regarded as affiliates of the CCP and thus offer no challenge to its authority. Efforts by Chinese citizens to organize new and independent political parties saw no more success than in earlier decades. For example, the China Democracy Party (CDP) was founded in 1997, but in 1999 key leaders were arrested and imprisoned while others fled abroad (Wright, 2004: 129). In 2007, the New Democracy Party of China was founded in Nanjing, but its leader was quickly arrested for subversion and sentenced to 10 years in prison.

Liu Xiaobo (b. 1955): Professor and dissident author. Liu participated in the Tiananmen Square movement after which he became an out-spoken advocate for fundamental human rights in China. Imprisoned in 2008, he was awarded the Nobel Peace Prize in 2010.

The 2009 case of **Liu Xiaobo**, a university professor and one of the leaders of the 1989 democracy movement, was a reminder of the dangers of publicly criticizing government policy. Liu was detained immediately after 1989 for several months and then released, but in the years that followed he was repeatedly in trouble for publishing articles advocating human rights and greater political reform. He was arrested in 2009 and sentenced to 11 years [**Doc 26, pp. 164–5**].

That same year the government announced China's first human rights action plan, in keeping with a call from the UN in 1993. Issued by the State Council Information Office in April 2009, the plan defined the government's goals in promoting and protecting human rights as part of China's continuing development. It was obvious that the plan would not extend to those hoping for open political debate, such as Professor Liu, but it signalled China's relatively new approach of responding to international calls for improving human rights worldwide.

Other practices of the government and Party showed little change. The top tier of leaders in the government still held comparably high positions in the CCP, as was the practice during the period of Chairman Mao. The National People's Congress, which, in theory, is the highest power in China, still convened only once a year for approximately two weeks. The National Party Congress of the CCP continued to meet once every five years, with plenary sessions between those meetings to handle the nation's business. The Party's powerful standing committee of the CCP's Central Committee and the smaller Political Bureau (Politburo) meet regularly, with the Politburo sometimes convening daily, to discuss and decide policy. This small group of men thus continued to represent the core of power and decision-making for China.

Problems within the structure and membership of the government and Party also remained. The single most serious problem was corruption. At the provincial and county levels, charges of corruption became a common occurrence. In 2009, prosecutors investigated over 41,000 officials accused of a range of crimes including bribery, embezzlement and dereliction of duty. Despite these admirable efforts, anger and frustration continued, particularly over officials who added new taxes and levies seemingly at will. Rural residents believed that many such taxes served no purpose other than enriching their local officials. Corruption was also blamed for the low levels of compensation, or no compensation at all, for farmers whose land was expropriated, usually to businesses willing to pay well for the privilege. Although the 1998 Revised Land Administration Law was intended to protect farmers' rights in this key area, abuses still drove many farmers into the streets in spontaneous demonstrations over compensation issues. Land use rights transferred to industrialists or real estate companies brought new income to smaller cities and towns, but residents often suspected that such land deals also enriched local leaders. The taking of land for more lucrative purposes also displaced and impoverished farm families who could not live for long on the meagre compensation they were offered. Some observers believed that failure to resolve these and other forms of corruption could undermine China's economic advances. However, others suggest that as long as China continues to offer the majority of its people the opportunity to improve their lives step by step and generation by generation, the government and Party will retain the people's acquiescence if not full-hearted support.

Maintaining order and stability was an on-going concern for the Party, and in some instances the Chinese military was called upon to assist in keeping the peace. Usually, this role is assumed by the People's Armed Police Force (PAP) which grew from around 600,000 to 1 million in 2004. This force is linked directly to the Chinese military which is charged with protecting the country but also with upholding the principles and ideology of the Communist Party. Party control over the military is exercised by the Central Military Commission which is directly under the Political Bureau that appoints its members (Deng Xiaoping retained control over the Commission until his death, signifying his hold over the ultimate source of power throughout his final years in power).

Prior to the reform era, the military was beset with a host of problems such as out-of-date equipment and backward technology. This did not improve in the early years of the reform era when new problems emerged. In an effort to raise funds, for example, military units engaged in non-military production of various kinds, and the capabilities of some units were severely compromised by this practice, which was finally ended in 1999.

In 1997, China's military establishment of 3 million personnel was double that of the United States's 1.5 million but it remained technologically behind. Its 110 navy craft were not in good condition, and while it had numeric supremacy in terms of aircraft (5,224 to America's 4,971), quality of planes and pilots was an issue.

After 2000, Chinese spending on all branches of its military jumped dramatically while at the same time the number of military personnel dropped, from 4 million to 2.3 million in 2003. The shift to a more professional, better-trained and better-educated force was complemented with improved equipment and better technology. In 2006, China's military spending amounted to 4.3% of its GDP. While the military remains behind those of developed nations, these efforts point to a much more formidable military establishment in coming decades.

China also continued to build its space programme. By 2008, it had made 115 launches. It had already successfully sent its first man into space in 2003, only the third country to do so, after Russia and the United States. This was followed by further successful missions in 2005 and 2008. Like Russia, China has declared its support for a ban on all weapons in space.

THE ECONOMY

China's astonishing economic growth was both a validation of the policies of the reform era as well as a testament to the work ethic and entrepreneurial skills of China's people. Together, these led to China's GDP growing from US$1.2 trillion in 2000 to US$4.3 trillion in 2008, an increase of 261%. Its third place international ranking was behind only the United States (US$14.4 trillion) and Japan (US$5.1 trillion).

The history of this seismic economic event is also astonishingly brief. China's economy began to recover from Maoist policies in the 1980s and then grew at single-digit rates for much of the 1990s. Double-digit growth became the norm after 2000. In 2002, China joined the **World Trade Organization (WTO)**, giving it further access to markets while protecting China, which initially held the status of a developing economy. On-going government reforms, and particularly assurances over private property rights, added to the heated business climate. China drew corporations from around the globe eager to establish offices in its major coastal cities where life for international executives was of a global standard. Of the 'Fortune 500', over 400 had offices in China by 2009.

WTO: Acronym for the World Trade Organization. The WTO is a global agency that sets trade regulations and requires all members to conform to global standards for trade and commerce.

In late 2009, China became the world's largest exporter. The largest markets for Chinese-made goods were the European Union, the United States and

Hong Kong. In some categories of goods, such as machinery, electrical and electronic products, a large percentage of the exports were made by foreign or foreign-funded enterprises using inexpensive Chinese labour. Goods produced by state-owned enterprises fell as a percentage of exports, continuing a well-established trend.

Although economic growth brought great prosperity overall, it also magnified income disparity. In 2001, the richest 20% of the population held 50% of China's wealth; the poorest 20% of the people had only 4.7%. While the wealthy, urban elite lived the life of rich entrepreneurs, at the bottom millions of people remained in extreme poverty. Many of the poor were rural residents who accounted for some 50% of the population. Urban dwellers earned far more money, approaching four times that of their country cousins, although low-income families could also be found in every major city. In 2005, official Chinese statistics reported that the richest 10% of urban households owned 45% of urban wealth; the poorest 10% had less than 1.4%. Among urban families, 77% had an annual income of US$3,000, while wealthy families earned between US$165,000 and US$200,000. The gap was expected to increase, despite government efforts and the warnings of Chinese economists that the income gap would lead to ever greater social conflict (Lollar, 2009: 528–9).

Income disparity also occurred across regions. The coastal provinces did very well, earning them the nickname 'the Gold Coast', while those in the hinterland remained well behind, in terms of income and access to education, health care and amenities. Among the very poorest areas were minority regions where as many as 40% lived in poverty in 2000. Between these extremes, however, the majority of Chinese saw their lives improve dramatically. A new, growing, Chinese middle class enjoyed some of the pleasures of their counterparts elsewhere in Asia.

The new economy also led to the rapid rise of consumerism. A product now within range of the middle class was the automobile, and in 2010 high domestic demand made China the world's number one car market. Chinese car-makers produced millions of affordable cars each year, and foreign models also attracted buyers, with luxury brands such as Mercedes, BMW and Lexus doing well among the wealthy. Buying, displaying and/or wearing Western brands from clothing to household gadgets became popular and a sign of wealth, as did designer clothes, imported liquor and cigarettes, and meals at expensive restaurants. Living an urban lifestyle was the goal of many ambitious Chinese and helped fuel the growth of urban centres. In 2008, China had 92 cities with a population over 1 million, in comparison to 17 in the EU and 9 in the United States.

An example of the strength of China's economy, as well as the government's power to shape its continued growth, can be seen in the impact of the global recession that began at the end of 2007. Sparked by an investment bubble driven by American banks and Wall Street investors, the recession deeply affected the United States, where in 2008 a stimulus plan was hastily prepared and put in place to prevent what some described as a potential global collapse of the world economy. China's exports no longer found the mass market they had enjoyed abroad as spending by individuals and corporations fell, and China braced for a halt in its non-stop economic growth.

China's government moved quickly to put together its own economic stimulus plan. Formally announced on 12 November 2008, the package totalled 4 trillion *yuan* (US$586 billion), or 16% of China's GDP. Details, made public in March 2009, indicated that 70% of the money would come from local governments and private companies, with central government providing the rest. The largest amounts went to post-earthquake reconstruction in Sichuan (25%), technological advances and industry restructuring (nearly 10%), rural civilian projects (9.25%) and sustainable environment projects (5.25%). The largest share by far went to the development of infrastructure: 1.5 trillion *yuan* (37.5%). This included construction of new highways and affordable housing units as well as the provision of clean drinking water and public utilities for rural areas. By the spring of 2009, the government reported that much had been accomplished toward all of its goals.

As a result, China's economy was the least affected major world economy during the recession. Growth cooled from double digits, but it far exceeded the World Bank estimate which had predicted China's growth for 2009 would fall to 6.8% of its GDP. Instead, China recovered toward the end of the year and recorded an overall growth rate of 8.7% for the year. Growth for 2010 was again on track for double-digit growth.

China continued its economic sprint toward becoming the world's second largest economy. In 2009, its foreign currency reserves reached $US2.2 trillion, an increase of 1,273% over the year 2000. It also became the single largest lender to the United States; never before had any country loaned as much money to another or held as much foreign currency in reserve (*New York Times*, 15 November 2009, p. 4).

A question of greatest importance for the future is whether or not China's growth can be sustained. Certainly, the CCP's hold on power requires continued economic prosperity, but the problems that could derail that goal have yet to be effectively addressed [**Doc. 27, p. 165–6**]. Income disparity, the growing need for new energy sources, reliance on exports and the need for a sustainable environment all raise great concern and await solutions.

China's booming economy shaped the new China of the twenty-first century and brought enormous economic clout around the globe. China was now a major world power and, in keeping with its new status, it moved to reshape its global position with an eye on potential new trading partners, particularly those with oil and other essential commodities. The next chapter discusses the impact of China's new international role and its increasing involvement in world politics.

10

China and the world

Since 2000, China has greatly expanded its global connections, increasing its diplomatic and economic reach. China became the world's second largest economy in 2010 and the world's number one exporter. Chinese-made merchandise became nearly ubiquitous across the globe. Not only did well-established trade with the United States and EU grow, but China also greatly expanded its trade with countries in Africa and Latin America. Its economic clout in Asia also reshaped relations with contiguous states and throughout the entire Asian region. China had become a powerful new global force and, as discussion below indicates, this brought China a warm welcome in some regions but raised concerns in others, particularly over its perceived efforts to secure access to natural resources vital to its continued economic growth.

China's foreign policy statements stressed the country's desire for a 'peaceful rise' and the goal of shaping a 'harmonious world' [**Doc. 28, pp. 167–8**]. A major tenet of its policy was non-interference in other countries' domestic affairs, a principle that in part reflected China's own desire to deflect criticism of its human rights record. Chinese officials asserted that 'business was business' and each country had a right to pursue development in keeping with their own specific needs. In some instances this meant doing business with countries made internationally notorious for treatment of their own people, such as the crisis in Darfur precipitated by the government of Sudan, one of China's key African oil suppliers. In this and other instances, China clearly had the power to influence powerful national leaders. How it handles such cases in future will have an enormous impact on how it is regarded internationally.

CHINA, EUROPE AND THE UNITED STATES

The transformation of China from a struggling, third-world country to a leading economic power changed its relationships with the world's major powers.

This process began at the start of the reform era when, in 1979, the United States finally extended official recognition to the Chinese government. At the same time, American derecognition of Taiwan as the only legitimate government of China came on the heels of the unsuccessful American intervention in **Vietnam**, and signalled a shift in power relations in Asia. In the mid-1980s, the United Kingdom recognized China's changing status as an emerging power by signing the 1984 agreement to return Hong Kong which had been a British colony since 1842. Hong Kong returned to China in 1997 as a Special Administrative Region, and despite worries over the future, the city of over 7 million people thrived under the PRC. The reintegration of the former colony with China provided the CCP with an opportunity to show its ability to reunite peacefully the capitalist enclave of the south with its own increasingly diversified economic system. Hong Kong's strong economy and nascent democratic forms did not collapse, as some predicted, but instead the city remained an important component of south China's economic engine.

The return of Hong Kong was followed by the recovery of Macao, a colony of Portugal since 1557. The Portuguese had, in fact, sought to return the small Sino European town on the South China Sea in 1976, but at that time China had not been prepared to begin the negotiations for a settlement. It was thus in 1999, at the very end of the twentieth century, that Macao also reverted to Chinese control. The unique Macanese society quietly began its new existence as a Special Administrative Region which, like Hong Kong, was protected from inundation by Chinese from elsewhere in the PRC by rules that continued to restrict travel in and out of the two former colonies.

Although China's trade relations with countries around the globe expanded rapidly, Western states' concerns with human rights issues in China stirred controversy over granting China normal trading privileges and entrance into world trade organizations. In the United States and Great Britain, supporters of Tibetan independence, Christian activists and anti-abortion groups worked against the normalization of trade relations; in contrast, major corporations put increasing pressure on the American government for an end to the annual review of China's trading status.

In 2000, the United States' decision to grant China **'permanent normal trade relations' (PNTR)** status confirmed China's importance as a world economic power, and set the stage for an era of more equitable trade relations between the two states. This change ended the American practice of holding trade privileges hostage to human rights issues and the vagaries of American politics. It also opened the door for China's entry into the World Trade Organization in 2002. As a WTO member, China became subject to WTO regulations and practices. Since joining, it has filed complaints over trade issues and has been the subject of complaints in return. The WTO is thus

Vietnam War: Initially a local conflict between the Communist forces of North Vietnam and the US-backed Nguyen government of the South, the confrontation escalated with increased US involvement in the 1960s. The United States withdrew its troops in 1975, and in 1976 Vietnam was united under Ho Chi-min's Communist Party.

PNTR: Permanent normal trade relations; granted to China by the United States in 2000, paving the way for China's entry into the WTO.

doing what it was designed to do in assisting to resolve international trading issues peacefully.

The shifting nature of American relations with China came into focus early in the administration of President George W. Bush when an American surveillance plane made a forced landing on the island of Hainan, off China's southern coast, on 1 April 2001. Each side provided its own account of what appeared to be an accidental collision between the slow-moving American aeroplane and a Chinese fighter plane which crashed, killing its pilot, as a result of the encounter. After a series of talks and diplomatic manoeuvring on both sides, the American crew was allowed to return to the United States. The aeroplane was later dismantled and returned. For China, its ability to 'say no' was impressed upon the United States as well as its own citizenry, whose growing nationalism was fed by American reluctance to offer an apology or, initially, even condolences for the death of the Chinese pilot, who was the only casualty. Nonetheless, while the political posturing continued on both sides, business transactions also continued as usual, strengthening observers' belief that economics would ultimately outweigh any political issues that may arise between the two nations, at least in the immediate future [**Doc. 29, pp. 168–9**].

Under the Bush presidency, China's relations with the United States included both improvements and stalemates. On one hand, following the September 11 2001 terrorist attacks on New York, President Bush visited China and, as a result, China joined the 'war on terror'. Nonetheless, China continued to oppose American weapon sales to Taiwan and stationing of American troops in South Korea. American businessmen and government officials periodically demanded that China revalue its currency on the basis that it was greatly undervalued and thus gave China an unfair trade advantage. There were also periodic flare-ups in China over American statements on its human rights record and visits to Washington DC by the Dalai Lama.

It was also during the Bush administration that the United States' national debt mounted, first from the war in Iraq and Afghanistan and then from the bruising economic recession at the end of the Bush presidency. When the new Obama administration came to power in 2009, Chinese involvement in the American economy was of staggering size. In 2010, China held nearly US$1 trillion in US treasures and government agency debt, and the American trade imbalance with China had grown to US$227 billion. In the United States, the appetite for inexpensive Chinese-made goods seemed endless, although the recession cut into consumer spending. China's economy was affected by falling demand, because it relied on Western consumers to keep its millions of workers employed at home. But China's stimulus plan proved effective and the Chinese economy rebounded (see further discussion in Chapter 9). Regardless of complaints from each side regarding trade issues, the reality was that the two countries' economic interdependence meant each needed the other and would therefore need to move cautiously on the issues that divided them [**Doc 30, pp. 169–70**].

CHINA, LATIN AMERICA AND AFRICA

China's new and widening economic role in Latin America was clearly reflected in trade figures with the continent: in 2000, bilateral trade was valued at US$10 billion, but by 2010 it had grown to 10 times that amount, over US$100 billion. China became Brazil's biggest trading partner, supplanting the United States, which had occupied that role since the 1930s. Plans to expand China–Brazil trade took a further leap in 2010 when President Hu personally visited the country to sign a five-year strategic plan with South America's largest economy.

China's exchanges with Venezuela also grew. In 2004, the country's avowedly Maoist leader, Hugo Chavez, visited Beijing; the following year the two countries signed a series of agreements covering oil, technology and agriculture. As the world's fifth largest oil producer, Venezuela was selling 60% of its oil to the United States but, in 2008, relations deteriorated and the American Ambassador was expelled. Chavez saw the China market as an alternative to trade with the United States, and in 2010 Venezuela signed further agreements with China on oil exploration. China promised to provide US$20 billion for the project through the China Development Bank. Venezuela's future relations thus promised to benefit China at the expense of the United States.

In addition to relations with Brazil and Venezuela, exports to China grew increasingly important to Chile, Peru and Argentina, which sold China commodities and raw materials. Mexico, El Salvador and Costa Rica sent manufactured goods. Projections for overall growth in trade are that China may buy as much as 20% of Latin America's exports by 2020, compared with 7.6% in 2009. The region's expanding importance to China could also be seen in the growing number of visits by high-ranking Chinese officials to Latin America and the increasing size of Chinese embassies, particularly in Brasilia and Caracas.

African countries also built new relationships with China based on trade and financial assistance programmes. In 2000, China and Africa paved the way for improving relations by signing the China–Africa Cooperation Forum (CACF). In 1999, the volume of trade was US$5.6 billion, but grew steadily in the years that followed, to US$29.5 billion in 2004, and then leapt to US$73 billion in 2007. That same year the African economy grew 5.8%, mainly as a result of Chinese investments. In 2008, China became the continent's second largest trading partner, behind the United States but surpassing France and Great Britain. In addition to oil and other natural resources, Chinese firms imported timber, copper and diamonds; Zimbabwe and South Africa continued to be major suppliers of iron ore and platinum. Chinese traders also began to view Africa as a strong market for Chinese goods.

Oil provided a major motivation for China's expanding relations with Africa. About one-third of its oil supply came from Africa (and half from the Middle East). In 2004, the economic boom had made China the world's second largest oil consumer, and estimates of China's future oil needs provided a powerful motivator for China to invest in Africa, which has an estimated 9% of the world's oil supply. In addition to trade, China also invested in African infrastructure by building roads, bridges, railways and dams at relatively low cost. High-ranking Chinese leaders visited regularly and reiterated their policy of peaceful coexistence as well as non-interference in other countries' internal affairs. President Hu himself visited current and potential African trading partners in 2003, 2004 and 2007.

Some international agencies saw China's increasing involvement in Africa as a good way to build the African economy, but others saw China's willingness to work with some of the world's most dictatorial and inhumane rulers as ultimately harmful to Africa's vulnerable populations. Sudan was a case in point. China became Sudan's largest economic partner and held a 40% share in their oil. The profits from oil sales enabled Sudan to buy arms used in the Darfur region where thousands of non-Muslims were killed or driven from their homes, an act many observers termed genocide. China, however, asserted that this was an internal matter. It also abstained from supporting a UN resolution condemning Sudan's actions.

China also continued to trade with Zimbabwe's Robert Mugabe, whose policies nearly bankrupted his country. When Mugabe took power in 1980, the country was prosperous, but two decades later unemployment had reached 70% and people faced chronic food shortages. His forcible evictions of residents who had supported the political opposition added to the ongoing national tragedy. The EU and United States saw Mugabe as one of Africa's most despotic rulers and placed sanctions on Zimbabwean officials in an effort to curtail abuses while China maintained its adherence to its non-interference policy.

International concerns over China's growing role in Africa stemmed from Chinese support of regimes like those of Sudan and Zimbabwe. While its assistance with anti-piracy operations off the African coast was welcomed, its trading policies drew criticism. Its role in Africa may not be helped by its seemingly supportive attitude toward rulers who, when finally out of power, are likely to be vilified by their own people. As China gains experience in balancing trade needs and providing an economic development model for African, Latin American and other developing economies, it will need to weigh carefully its policy of dealing with officials who are widely regarded as brutal and corrupt by much of the global community.

CHINA AND ITS ASIAN NEIGHBOURS

China's new economic power has had a huge impact on all its Asian neighbours, to the north, south, east and west. Some relationships saw new tensions arising from China's muscle flexing and its determination to develop new sources of fresh water, as well as ambitions to drill offshore for oil and natural gas. China's trading economy was fuelled by energy, just as water provided the basic fuel for agriculture, and its drive to secure these and other resources complicated relations with some neighbours while it enhanced relations with others.

In Southeast Asia, Vietnam was one of the two Asian states still under Communist leadership in the early twenty first century. Its recovery from long years of warfare in the 1960s and 1970s was relatively rapid, and trade between China and Vietnam soon thrived. Increasingly, Vietnam followed China's lead, with a market-driven economy gradually replacing its Communist system. The two countries disagreed over access to natural resources in the South China Sea, but this eased somewhat after the 2002 Declaration on the Conduct of Parties in the South China Sea, which included Vietnam, Taiwan, Philippines, Brunei and other neighbouring states. However, ongoing concerns revolved around Chinese occupation of some of the Paracel Islands which are also claimed by Taiwan and Vietnam.

Vietnam, along with Thailand, Laos and Cambodia, also became deeply concerned over China's plans to build new dams on the upper reaches of the Mekong River. The river's waters are vital to some 60 million farmers who rely on the Mekong for water, transport and food. In 2010, the water level fell to its lowest in half a century. Although some experts believed that the new dams did not cause the diminished supply of water, the perception of China intentionally diverting water nonetheless fuelled resentments among China's neighbours to the south and stirred further opposition to Chinese plans for additional dam-building projects.

In 2010, south Asia's new economic powerhouse was India whose economy was growing at 9% a year prior to the global recession; economists predicted that higher growth rates would return after 2010–11. India's trade with China boomed, growing from US$2.9 billion in 2000 to US$51.8 billion in 2008. Trade was important to both sides, but in 2009 India's trade deficit with China rose to US$15.8 billion, an unwelcome development from the Indian perspective. That same year India charged China with dumping goods on its domestic market and asked for WTO invention. Other issues between the two Asian giants included long-standing border disputes and concerns over China's assistance to Pakistan, particularly with weapons sales and development of nuclear power. In 2010, India's Prime Minister, Manmohan Singh, met with President Hu in Brasilia, during Hu's visit to Brazil. The two announced their countries would go forward not as competitors but as cooperative trading partners. China agreed to ease market access for Indians doing business in China and to increase Chinese-funded projects in India.

Pakistan's relations with China had always been on a very different footing. After the two countries established diplomatic ties in 1951, China consistently supported Pakistan with military and economic aid. Enmity between Pakistan and India, which led to three wars and on-going disputes, found China firmly on Pakistan's side, a policy that persisted into the twenty-first century. Pakistan received substantial Chinese assistance, especially with greatly needed infrastructure projects. Of particular importance to both countries was the development of a major port at Gwadar for which China supplied some 80% of the funds as well as technical assistance. The port provides access to the Persian Gulf, which China will be able to use in return for its support of the project. The value of the two countries' trade was US$7 billion in 2009, far below that of rapidly growing India. Despite historically close ties between Pakistan and China in the past, it appeared probable that China would move to strengthen its relationship with India, not only for economic reasons, but also because of its concerns about the volatility of Pakistan's northwest frontier region and the possibility of Muslim extremism crossing the porous border into its own Muslim region of Xinjiang.

China's relations with poor, war-plagued Afghanistan (which shares a 90-mile long border with China high in the Pamir Mountains) saw an important development. In 2007, China became the single largest investor in the country with a US$3 billion contract to develop a copper mine.

Copper is also a key commodity in China's northern, land-locked neighbour, Mongolia. Following the fall of the USSR, Mongolia began its journey toward a democratic government and market-based economy. President Hu visited the country in 2003, and Mongolia's President Bagabandi travelled to Beijing in 2004, at which time China extended Mongolia observer status in the Shanghai Cooperative Organization (see discussion of the SCO, below). Mongolia's vast copper reserves are to be developed by Canadian and Australian companies, not by China, but China nonetheless remained the country's largest trade partner and provided the majority of its direct investments. Mongolian leaders have sought to balance Russian and Chinese influence in their country by forming alliances with Japan and the United States, both of which have provided assistance.

China also shares a long border in the northeast with Russia as a result of Russian expansion across Central Asia and into Siberia in the nineteenth century. The two nations have had differing policy objects elsewhere in the world and have disagreed on a variety of issues. For example, China was not supportive of Russian involvement in its conflict with Georgia, in keeping with China's policy of non-interference in other countries' internal affairs. The Sino-Russian border itself, however, remained quiet with trade moving across the border on a regular basis (see also comments on Russia and the SCO, below).

Quite a different situation existed along China's northeastern border with North Korea, which remained under Communist leadership and existed in self-imposed isolation. In the late 1990s, it suffered from severe famine, and North Koreans swarmed across the border in search of food. China sought to repatriate these and later refugees, who were termed economic migrants and sent back across the border. North Korea opened its doors far enough to admit aid from international relief organizations, but little changed in terms of its relations with the rest of the world, although it maintained relations with China. In 2000, a historic meeting took place between President Kim Dae Jung of South Korea and Kim Jong Il of North Korea. Visits by selected groups of South Koreans to the North followed, but North Korea's xenophobic leaders continued to limit contacts with either South Koreans or outsiders. President Kim also continued his practice of stopping and then restarting plans to develop nuclear weapons. This erratic behaviour constituted a headache for China which continued to wrestle with its unpredictable neighbour.

To the east, China's long-standing trade relations with Japan continued to grow, interrupted by the Asian crisis of 1997, which hurt Japan's economy far more than China's. After 2000, these two great economies of Asia, which together represent almost three-quarters of the region's economic activity, experienced strained relations over economic interests and cultural matters, as Japan stagnated and China charged ahead. Key among the issues was the on-going dispute over the Japanese characterization in history books of Japan's actions in China during the Second World War. In 2005, when Japanese Prime Minister Junichiro Koizumi visited a Shinto Shrine for the war dead, which also was a memorial to men convicted of war crimes against China, relations deteriorated further. Nonetheless, Japan was still China's fourth biggest market for exports, and Japan had invested over US$58 billion in its economy through 2006, making it a key regional trading partner. Despite a shadow cast over relations by historic events, trade, technological advice and a huge tourism industry catering to Japanese tourists meant that relations with Japan remained important to China.

Tensions eased considerably under the new Prime Minister, Yukio Hatoyama, who took office in 2009. He focused his China policy on co-operation, encouraging China's reforms and promoting bilateral dialogue.

Although concerns remained over Chinese exploration of the Sea of Japan and possible exploitation of oil and gas reserves, their relationship appeared on a firmer track.

China's neighbours far to the west included the newly independent states of the former USSR. In 1991, China had faced the issue of establishing diplomatic relations with new Central Asian countries. Abruptly independent from Russian dominance, the former Soviet republics of Kazakhstan, Kyrgyzstan and Tajikistan now shared China's long northwestern border. The PRC moved quickly to open talks with these governments, most of which were led by men who owed their positions of power to the former USSR. New agreements replaced the former Sino-Soviet arrangements and enhanced the amount of cross-border trade. China's concern over its own Muslim populations prompted additional agreements that were intended to limit agitation by representatives of China's Muslim communities for greater rights and political autonomy. Despite such assurances, however, the predominantly Muslim region of Xinjiang continued to experience considerable unrest, suggesting that China's internal problems with minorities could not be resolved simply through agreements with neighbouring states [**Doc. 31, pp. 171–2**].

In 1996, China helped form the 'Shanghai Five' which grew to become the Shanghai Cooperative Organization (SCO) in 2001. Members included China, Russia, Kazakhstan, Kyrgyzstan, Tajikistan and Uzbekistan. The group met periodically to discuss common interests and policy issues, including trade and security. In 2007, Russia proposed that SCO organize a regional energy group to promote the development of energy resources, but little headway had been made on such a group at the end of 2009.

Individually, the Central Eurasian states maintained relatively good relations with China, with Kazakhstan being most important in terms of trade and other forms of cooperation. Its leader since 1989, President Nursultan Nazarbayev, came to power before the fall of the USSR and was repeatedly re-elected until 2007 when term limits were eliminated, leaving Nazarbayev in office for life. Under his leadership, Kazakhstan signed an agreement with China to build an oil pipeline enabling China to access Kazakhstan oil from the Caspian Sea. Oil began to flow to coastal China in 2004.

Less stable were the small countries of Tajikistan and Kyrgyzstan. The former experienced a civil war from 1992 to 1997. Russia aided in bringing the competing sides together, and the country's President, Imomali Rakhmanov, remained in power. Following re-election to a third term in 2006, he cracked down on the opposition and continued to rule with little reference to the views or needs of his people. Kyrgyzstan also experienced instability; despite the much-praised 'Tulip Revolution' of 2005, President Kurmanbek Bakiyev was overthrown in early 2010. It was unclear whether the new leadership under Roza Otunbayeve would prove longer lasting.

CHINA AND TAIWAN

The situation with Taiwan was far different from any of the neighbours mentioned above as the island has always been viewed by China as a part of the PRC. Since 1949, Taiwan had remained separate from China politically and militarily, but economic ties increasingly bound the two together at the end of the twentieth century. Taiwan underwent dramatic changes after 2000, among them the shifting expectations of its own citizens and upsets in political leadership. In 2000, the Nationalist Party (Guomindang) lost its half-century-long hold on the presidency of Taiwan. Ever since their defeat in 1948–9 by the CCP, the Nationalists dominated Taiwan where the United States' Second World War ally Jiang Jieshi (Chiang Kai-shek) served as President from 1950 until his death in 1975, with American military support to buoy his claim to leadership of all China. His son, **Jiang Jingguo** (Chiang Ching-kuo) followed him, and successfully weathered the derecognition of Taiwan by the United States in 1979 as well as the emergence of an opposition political party, the **Democratic Progressive Party (DPP)**. The latter openly advocated the independence of the island. Reluctantly, the Nationalists extended recognition to the DPP in the 1990s but government control of Taiwan media limited the new party's impact. When Jiang Jingguo died, still in office in 1988, leadership passed to the Vice-President, Taiwan-born and American-educated **Li Denghui** (Lee Teng-hui), who continued the Nationalist policies he inherited.

However, Taiwan's strong economy and high standard of living were not enough to ensure a continued Nationalist hold on the presidency. In 2000, the Nationalist Party, weakened by internal divisions, lost to the DPP candidate, **Chen Shuibian**. The new President was sworn into office that May. Taiwan's election was not only ground-breaking in its defeat of the Nationalists, it also placed a woman in the second highest office in the land. The new Vice-President was Annette Lu, whose credentials included long years of opposition to the Nationalists. Although Chen's election was a remarkable event, the Nationalists retained control of Taiwan's legislature with 55% of the seats compared to the DPP's 31%.

China's opposition to Chen Shuibian was made clear prior to the March 2000 and 2004 elections [**Doc. 32, pp. 172–4** written by Vice-President Lu]. Because Chen was known as an advocate for Taiwan independence, China repeated its conviction that Taiwan was a Chinese province and that its future lay with China. Just as it had done prior to the 1996 elections, the CCP issued threatening warnings about what might happen in the future should Chen win. Despite the heated rhetoric, both sides defused the situation by moderating their tones after the election. Chen issued a call for friendly ties with China and spoke of future direct transport and communication links. China remained cool to Taiwan's overtures, but at the same time continued

Jiang Jingguo (1909–88): Son of Jiang Jieshi. In the 1940s, he held posts in the Nationalist-led government; after the move to Taiwan, he became head of the Nationalist secret police before assuming the presidency after his father's death in 1975.

DPP: Acronym for Taiwan's Democratic Progressive Party which, in 2000, gained the Taiwan government presidency.

Li Denghui (Lee Teng-hui) (b. 1929): President of the "Republic of China" on Taiwan (1988–2000). US-educated Li was a native of Taiwan and thus the first native to hold the top political office on the island.

Chen Shuibian (b. 1950): Born in Taiwan, Chen led Taiwan's opposition party, the DPP, to victory in the 2000 and 2004 presidential elections.

to welcome Taiwan businesses. Altogether, Taiwan businessmen had invested some US$30 billion in China since the 1980s.

The 2004 presidential elections nearly led to Chen's ousting as accusations of nepotism and corruption plagued his administration, but he managed to win by a slim margin. Popular perception had clearly shifted, however, and, in 2008, Chen lost to **Ma Yingjiu** (also spelled Ma Ying-jeou) of the Nationalist (Guomindang) Party. Ma's election reduced the threat of war over the Taiwan Straits substantially as his agenda put relations with China on a new footing. He sought closer ties to the mainland, and Taiwan's already substantial investment in China continued to grow as Taiwanese investors sought to maximize their profits in China's booming economy. The long-anticipated possibility of direct flights between Taiwan and the mainland was finally realized when charter passenger flights began between Taipei, Shanghai and other mainland cities in 2010. Proposals for new China–Taiwan cooperation promised to smooth relations even further.

Ma Yingjiu (b. 1950): Also spelled Ma Ying-jeou. Elected in 2008 as the 12th President of Taiwan; member of the Nationalist Party (GMD); his election eased relations with the PRC.

CHINA'S CONTINUING RISE

As the examples surveyed in this chapter have shown, China moved from its position as an isolated, marginal state preoccupied with domestic socialist change and defence of its immediate borders, to that of a powerful player in Asia's regional affairs and an increasingly important and assertive player in international politics. This rapid shift raised concerns among some who saw China as a new, emergent threat that could replace the USSR as the world's second great superpower. The integration of China into the WTO in 2002 offers an alternative path for China, one that does not necessarily lead to growing antagonism or confrontation between East and West or with China's immediate neighbours. Whether international affairs move toward greater cooperation and understanding will ultimately depend not only on China, the United States and the EU, but on the determination of all nations to use dialogue and diplomacy in resolving their differences.

Part 3

ASSESSING CHINA'S RISE

11

Conclusions

In an astonishingly brief period, China has risen to become an economic powerhouse. Its dominant position in the global marketplace and rapidly expanding influence in Latin America, Africa and Asia constitute a major shift in the world order that will shape the twenty-first century. The Chinese can take pride in all they have accomplished, and the Beijing Olympics of 2008 fittingly celebrated truly historic achievements.

Concerns over China's 'peaceful rise' emerged as its economic clout grew, with some viewing China as the next great superpower, ending the American and European dominance which marked the twentieth century. Chinese and Indian competition for world energy resources and the expanding consumer demand from each country's rising middle class means a continuing shift of the world economy toward Asia, which is set to become the world's largest market as well as the world's largest producer of goods. This new competition may prove to be a positive force but it could also become antagonistic and lead to a decrease in world stability. While India is the world's single largest democracy, Western democracies remain concerned about the role of the CCP and its control of China's government. A one-party system without open elections is viewed in the West as contrary to notions of good government and basic human rights. Developing countries view things somewhat differently, with China seen as a new, respectful partner who buys their products and assists with their economic development. Some have also seen China as a counterweight to American power and influence, both in terms of trade and in international relations. Whether China's growing involvement with these nations will ultimately be of equal benefit to both sides is difficult to predict. Certainly, some leaders, such as those in Zimbabwe and Sudan, have little apparent interest in the outcome as long as they continue to benefit personally from Chinese trade.

One way to understand China's new international role and its place in the world is to examine China's rise in broad terms and to compare the nearly three decades of Maoist policies (1949–78) with the several decades since the advent of the reforms. As the preceding chapters have shown, the CCP-led government faced enormous challenges in its early years and Maoist leaders failed to resolve issues within the Party's leadership or to provide stable economic development. After Mao's death, the CCP continued to lead China but in a radically different direction economically. The world has watched with enormous interest as a new experiment unfolded: the rise of an aggressive capitalist economy guided by the world's largest Communist party. In these most unlikely circumstances, what are the prospects for continuing change in China and for the CCP?

Whether China's socialist experiment under revolutionary leader Mao was more failure than success remains a topic of scholarly discussion. Most would agree that Mao led China out of an era of national division and toward an egalitarian society with a relatively narrow gap between the wealthiest and poorest groups of Chinese. But most would also agree that the promised new society, built on loyalty to the Party and its socialist ideals, not only never materialized but instead gave rise to a new bureaucratic elite that wielded unquestioned power and enjoyed prerogatives not available to the ordinary citizen. While the old landlord class was gone, the new elite followed in the time-worn footsteps of those who, for many centuries past, led the people but also cultivated personal and familial benefits in the process. The Maoist system was not able to prevent this, nor was it able to forestall the concentration of great power in the hands of a small gerontocracy which managed to maintain its hold over Chinese society.

Mao's stature as a leader of the Chinese people was also been marred by the ill-considered policies of the Great Leap Forward and the Cultural Revolution. Suffering inflicted through blind obedience to ideals that were poorly understood by either the rural cadres ordering foolish agricultural practices or by teenage Red Guards inflicting pain on their elders was ultimately the responsibility of Mao and his hand-picked supporters. Their responsibility for bringing disaster to millions of people cannot be forgotten in any assessment of either Mao or the CCP as a whole.

Following Mao's death in 1976, the CCP shifted course dramatically. The Dengist reform policies rejuvenated a stagnant economy and unleashed the energies of ordinary men and women who quickly embraced the new opportunities in rural and urban China. While the average incomes of Chinese people remained far below those of their counterparts in Hong Kong or Taiwan, the standard of living improved enormously. Overall economic growth slowed in the late 1990s, but it nonetheless averaged an annual growth rate of over 7%. In 2000, China's GDP reached US$1.08 trillion, for a per capita income of US$800.

In the first decade of the twenty-first century, international corporations once more saw China as a land of business opportunity. Although initial profits were not always as expected, corporate interest remained high. Skilled workers, without unions to represent their interests, became a key attraction as the workforces of other Asian countries became more expensive in comparison with workers in China. Foreign investment continued to climb, as did the amount provided to China in loans from international lenders such as the World Bank and the International Monetary Fund.

Overall, economic growth sky-rocketed. China's new wealth led to the rise of a new middle class and a small wealthy elite living in the country's rich coastal cities which showcase high-rise buildings for homes and businesses that rival those of the West. The glittering lights of Shanghai and its many attractions have been a magnet for Chinese and millions of foreign visitors. Leading world corporations have their headquarters in cities throughout China, and no major industry today is without its links to China. Growth rates soared, and by 2009, China's GDP had dramatically increased, reaching over US$4 trillion and an estimated per capita income of US$3,600.

However, the distribution of wealth has been far from universal. The rural–urban divide remains one of the most serious problems facing the government, and the vast majority of the population has yet to enjoy the fruits of China's new riches. This and other problems attending China's transformation into a modern economy are likely to remain a challenge for the country and its one-party system for some time to come. Younger Chinese may be increasingly patriotic, and ultra-nationalist views may appeal to some, but these trends also face a counter-current in the form of increasing discontent with the government's handling of unemployment, land compensation, corruption and the overall lack of government accountability. Year by year the number of large and small public demonstrations over land use, for example, has become a common occurrence; arrests and trials of officials accused of bribery and corruption have become almost as common.

Certainly, some groups feel the problems of reform more acutely than others. For China's women, there are special problems in this 'get-rich-quick' era. Today, most women work, but jobs for women are disproportionately found in the low-paid sectors of the economy. Urban women complain of the 'double burden' of housework and a job, as well as primary responsibility for their child. In rural areas, the tendency for farming families to rely on women and the elderly as the primary labour force, means that rural women are often left with the responsibility of both the farmwork and all family matters. While the level of education for girls has shown positive growth, they remain at a disadvantage in seeking employment. The return of prostitution and trafficking in women are further instances of the negative impact of the reforms on China's women. New laws have been enacted to address some of these issues, but enforcement remains a problem.

Among China's minority groups, there is also a mixed response to China's policies. On the one hand, the minority regions have seen their economies grow and facilities for health care and education improve. On the other hand, some areas have seen an increase in complaints over Chinese domination in economic and cultural affairs. In Xinjiang, local people have long complained that economic development benefits Han newcomers and the central government, but not them [Doc. 31, pp. 171–2]. This on-going grievance is aggravated by the arrival of Han Chinese migrant workers seeking new opportunities not only in Xinjiang but also in Tibet and other minority areas.

What, then, are the prospects for change, and for the current political system in coming decades? China's political life has already changed in some important ways when compared with earlier decades. Constitutional amendments and new laws recognize the socioeconomic changes that have occurred and represent an effort to move the country closer to rule of law rather than rule by the Party. Top leaders are increasingly seen in public, and not only on formal occasions. For example, Premier Wen presents a caring, human face when he promises greater assistance to poor and lower-middle-class Chinese and when he personally visits the sites of national disasters, as leaders of Western democracies do, or goes online for a public chat. Yet the CCP has continued to keep its highest-echelon activities shrouded in secrecy. Perhaps of more immediate importance to ordinary people is the Party's – and government's – control over economic matters. Here the lack of openness enables the forms of corruption that have brought well-connected men and women huge personal fortunes. Without a shift to greater transparency, political reform is likely to be slow. The CCP has not yet proven its ability to monitor its own members, despite the well-publicized cases of corrupt officials that make their way into the news. If corrupt practices continue, the Party may find it difficult to maintain its position as the legitimate ruling authority. As new generations of middle-class men and women make their way up the economic ladder, their expectations for a different kind of political system may provide the basis for yet another dramatic leap in China's political development.

In sum, China's historical record since 1949 reveals a pattern of dramatic changes and policy reversals as well as more gradual changes that have wrought important improvements for the majority of the population. The CCP's assignment of class background as a determiner of social status in the 1950s cut deeply into the traditional social fabric; the emergence of a new middle class has rendered those early Maoist categories irrelevant, to the dismay of some but to the delight and relief of many. China has also seen gradual changes for the better, particularly the improvement in overall health and longevity and in the climbing levels of education. But what do these mean for the future of the CCP?

The new middle class and the millions of Chinese aspiring to that status in the next decade suggest the possibility of a society that can accept the seemingly unworkable combination of a Communist political system and a capitalist economy. Even those who have yet to reap the real benefits of China's economic transformation nonetheless live in a world of greater opportunity, better access to information and entertainment, and improving legal protections. These are undoubtedly significant changes that, for some, make the system seem workable. As long as the CCP can sustain its break-neck speed toward a stronger economy, it may be able to maintain its hold on power. But it will also continue to bear full responsibility for any future economic reverses as well as growing income disparity which, thus far, shows no sign of decreasing.

In many ways the questions facing China today reflect the country's long struggle to find a political form that meets both the economic and social needs of all its people – urban and rural, minority and majority, male and female. Whether that future form includes only the CCP – or a Western-style multiparty system – will largely depend on the CCP's ability to resolve the country's major problems and, at the same time, ensure an acceptable standard of living for the majority of the population. As Taiwan's own long struggle toward a more accountable government has shown, the Chinese peoples' collective abilities are the single greatest asset China has as it moves through the twenty-first century.

Part 4

DOCUMENTS

Document 1   THE 1950 MARRIAGE LAW

One of the first laws passed by the new government was the Marriage Law which made women the legal equals of men. It was promulgated on 1 May 1950.

GENERAL PRINCIPLES

Article 1. The arbitrary and compulsory feudal marriage system, the supremacy of man over woman, and disregard of the interests of children is abolished.

The new democratic marriage system, which is based on the free choice of partners, on monogamy, on equal rights for both sexes, and on the protection of the lawful interests of women and children, is put into effect.

Article 2. Bigamy, concubinage, child betrothal, interference in the re-marriage of widows, and the exaction of money or gifts in connection with marriages, are prohibited.

THE MARRIAGE CONTRACT

Article 3. Marriage is based upon the complete willingness of the two parties. Neither party shall use compulsion and no third party is allowed to interfere.

Article 4. A marriage can be contracted only after the man reaches twenty years of age and the woman eighteen years of age . . .

RIGHTS AND DUTIES OF HUSBAND AND WIFE

Article 7. Husband and wife are companions living together and enjoy equal status in the home.

Article 8. Husband and wife are in duty bound to love, respect, assist and look after each other, to live in harmony, to engage in productive work, to care for their children, and to strive jointly for the welfare of the family and for the building up of the new society.

Article 9. Both husband and wife have the right to use free choice of occupation and free participation in work or in social activities . . .

DIVORCE

Article 17. Divorce is granted when the husband and wife both desire it. In the event of the husband or the wife alone insisting upon divorce, it may be granted only when mediation by the district people's government and the judicial organ has failed to bring about a reconciliation . . .

Article 18. The husband is not allowed to apply for a divorce when his wife is pregnant, and may apply for divorce only one year after the birth of the child. In the case of a woman applying for divorce, this restriction does not apply . . .

MAINTENANCE AND EDUCATION OF CHILDREN AFTER DIVORCE

Article 20. The blood ties between parents and children are not ended by the divorce of the parents. No matter whether the father or the mother has custody of the children, they remain the children of both parties.

After divorce, both parents continue to have the duty to support and educate their children.

After divorce, the guiding principle is to allow the mother to have the custody of a breast-fed infant. After the weaning of the child, if a dispute arises between the two parties over the guardianship and an agreement cannot be reached, the people's court should render a decision in accordance with the interests of the child.

Article 21. If, after the divorce, the mother is given custody of a child, the father is responsible for the whole or part of the necessary cost of maintenance and education of the child. Both parties should reach an agreement regarding the amount and the duration of such maintenance and education. Lacking such an agreement, the people's court should render a decision.

Source: Kay Ann Johnson (1983) *Women, the Family and Peasant Revolution in China* (Chicago, IL: University of Chicago Press), pp. 235–9. (From a 1950 Chinese government pamphlet issued in Beijing.)

THE 17-POINT AGREEMENT BETWEEN TIBET AND CHINA   **Document 2**

On 23 May 1951, representatives of the PRC and the Dalai Lama signed the 'Agreement on Measures for the Peaceful Liberation of Tibet', also known as the '17-Point Agreement'. This document set out the terms for the peaceful merging of Tibet with the new PRC. The following is a Chinese summary of the content of the agreement which was abrogated by both sides in 1959.

The important content [of the agreement] was as follows: expel imperialist aggressors from Tibet; assist the Chinese People's Liberation Army to enter Tibet [in order to] strengthen border defense; merge all of Tibet's local government departments with the central people's government departments; put into practice minority district governments or autonomous government under the united leadership of the CCP and the central people's government; reform Tibet's social system; change the Tibetan military step by step; expand Tibetan government, economy and culture; improve the people's livelihood; and so on.

In signing this agreement, Tibetans threw off forever imperialist aggression and returned to the motherland, thereby consolidating the unity of the motherland.

Source: Shi Zhengdyi (ed.) (1984) *Minzu Cidian* [*Dictionary of the Nationalities*] (Chengdu, Sichuan: Sichuan minzu chubanshe), p. 44. Translated by Linda Benson.

Document 3   THE TIBETAN VIEW OF THE 17-POINT AGREEMENT

In 1962, the Dalai Lama published his memoirs in which he recounted the cir-
cumstances and the content of the 17-Point Agreement. The following selection
is his summary of the content and what it meant to the Tibetans.

Neither I nor my government were told that an agreement had been signed.
We first came to know of it from a broadcast which Nagbo* made on Peking
Radio. It was a terrible shock when we heard the terms of it. We were
appalled at the mixture of Communist clichés, vainglorious assertions which
were completely false, and bold statements which were only partly true.
And the terms were far worse and more oppressive than anything we had
imagined.

The preamble said that 'over the last one hundred years or more', imperialist forces had penetrated into China and Tibet and 'carried out all kinds of
deceptions and provocations', and that 'under such conditions, the Tibetan
nationality and people were plunged into the depths of enslavement and
suffering'. This was pure nonsense. It admitted that the Chinese government
had ordered the 'People's Liberation Army' to march into Tibet. Among the
reasons given were that the influence of aggressive imperialist forces in Tibet
might be successfully eliminated and that the Tibetan people might be freed
and return to the 'big family' of the People's Republic of China.

That was also the subject of Clause One of the agreement: 'The Tibetan
people shall unite and drive out imperialist aggressive forces from Tibet. The
Tibetan people shall return to the big family of the Motherland – the People's
Republic of China.' Reading this, we reflected bitterly that there had been no
foreign forces whatever in Tibet since we drove out the last of the Chinese
forces in 1912. Clause Two provided that the 'local government of Tibet shall
actively assist the People's Liberation Army to enter Tibet and consolidate the
national defense'. This in itself went beyond the specific limits we had placed
on Nagbo's authority. Clause Eight provided for the absorption of the Tibetan
army into the Chinese army. Clause Fourteen deprived Tibet of all authority
in external affairs.

In between these clauses, which no Tibetan would ever willingly accept,
were others in which the Chinese made many promises: not to alter the existing political system in Tibet; not to alter the status, functions, and powers
of the Dalai Lama; to respect the religious beliefs, customs, and habits of
the Tibetan people and protect the monasteries; to develop agriculture and
improve the people's standard of living; and not to compel the people to
accept reforms. But these promises were small comfort beside the fact that
we were expected to hand ourselves and our country over to China and cease
to exist as a nation. Yet we were helpless. Without friends there was nothing
we could do but acquiesce, submit to the Chinese dictates in spite of our

strong opposition, and swallow our resentment. We could only hope that the Chinese would keep their side of this forced, one-sided bargain.

* Nagbo Ngawan Jigme was governor of eastern Tibet in 1950; he was appointed to open negotiations with the new PRC by the Dalai Lama.

Source: Dalai Lama (1962) *My Land and My People* (New York: McGraw Hill), pp. 88–9.

'SPEAK BITTERNESS' MEETINGS   **Document 4**

As part of the land redistribution process, poor peasants were encouraged to speak out publicly against those who had abused or exploited them. The following selection is a villager's description of how this process worked, as told to William Hinton, author and Sinologist. This particular meeting occurred before 1949, in an area already under CCP control, but it was to be duplicated many times all across China in the early 1950s.

When the final struggle began Ching-ho [a local landlord] was faced not only with those hundred accusations but with many many more. Old women who had never spoken in public before stood up to accuse him. Even Li Mao's wife – a woman so pitiable she hardly dared look anyone in the face – shook her fist before his nose and cried out, 'Once I went to glean wheat on your land. But you cursed me and drove me away. Why did you curse me and beat me? And why did you seize the wheat I had already gleaned?' Altogether over 180 opinions were raised. Ching-ho had no answer to any of them. He stood there with his head bowed. We asked him whether the accusations were false or true. He said they were all true. When the committee of our Association met to figure up what he owed, it came to 400 bags of milled grain, not coarse grain.

That evening all the people went to Ching-ho's courtyard to help take over his property. It was very cold that night so we built bonfires and the flames shot up toward the stars. It was very beautiful. We went in to register his grain and altogether found but 200 bags of unmilled millet – only a quarter of what he owed us. Right then and there we decided to call another meeting. People all said he must have a lot of silver dollars – they thought of the wine plant, and the pigs he raised on the distillers' grains, and the North Temple Society and the Confucius Association.

We called him out of the house and asked him what he intended to do since the grain was not nearly enough. He said, 'I have land and house.'

'But all this is not enough,' shouted the people. So then we began to beat him. Finally he said, 'I have 40 silver dollars under the *k'ang*.' We went in and dug it up. The money stirred up everyone. We beat him again. He told us where to find another hundred after that. But no one believed that this was the end of his hoard. We beat him again and several militiamen began to heat an iron bar in one of the fires. Then Ching-ho admitted that he had hid 110 silver dollars in militiaman Man-hsi's uncle's home. Man-hsi was very hot-headed. When he heard that his uncle had helped Sheng Ching-ho he got very angry. He ran home and began to beat his father's own brother. We stopped him. We told him, 'Your uncle didn't know it was a crime.' We asked the old man why he had hidden money for Ching-ho and he said, 'No one ever told me anything. I didn't know there was anything wrong in it.' You see, they were relatives and the money had been given to him for safe-keeping years before. So Man-hsi finally cooled down. It was a good thing for he was angry enough to beat his uncle to death and he was strong enough to do it.

Altogether we got $500 from Ching-ho that night. By that time the sun was already rising in the eastern sky. We were all tired and hungry, especially the militiamen who had called the people to the meeting, kept guard on Ching-ho's house, and taken an active part in beating Ching-ho and digging for the money. So we decided to eat all the things that Ching-ho had prepared to pass the New Year – a whole crock of dumplings stuffed with pork and peppers and other delicacies. He even had shrimp.

All said, 'In the past we never lived through a happy New Year because he always asked for his rent and interest then and cleaned our houses bare. This time we'll eat what we like,' and everyone ate his fill and didn't even notice the cold.

Source: William Hinton (1968) *Fanshen: A Documentary of Revolution in a Chinese Village* (New York: Random House), pp. 137–8.

Document 5   CHINA'S REGIONAL AUTONOMY SYSTEM

In order to give minority groups a voice in local government, the new Chinese government passed the Program for Enforcement of Nationality Regional Autonomy on 8 August 1952. The following are extracts from the Program.

CHAPTER I.   GENERAL PRINCIPLES
Article 1. This program is enacted on the basis of the provisions of Articles 9, 50, 51, 52 and 53 of the People's Political Consultative Conference's [PPCC's] Common Program.

Article 2. All national autonomous districts shall be an inseparable part of the territory of the People's Republic of China. All autonomous organs of the national autonomous districts shall be local state power organs under the unified leadership of the Central People's Government and subject to guidance by the people's governments of superior levels.

Article 3. The PPCC Common Program shall be the general direction for unity and struggle of all nationalities of the People's Republic of China at the present stage, and the people of all national autonomous districts shall proceed along this general path in administering the internal affairs of their own nationalities . . .

CHAPTER III.   AUTONOMOUS ORGANS

Article 12. The people's government organs of national autonomous districts shall be formed principally of personnel of national minorities carrying out regional autonomy and shall include an appropriate number of personnel of other national minorities and Han Chinese in the autonomous districts . . .

CHAPTER IV.   RIGHTS OF AUTONOMY

Article 15. The autonomous organs of national autonomous districts may adopt the national language commonly used in the autonomous districts as the principal instrument to exercise their authority but, in exercising authority among national minorities not using such language, should adopt the language of the national minorities in question at the same time.

Article 16. The autonomous organs of national autonomous districts may adopt their own national language, both spoken and written, for the development of the cultural and educational work of national minorities . . .

Article 18. Internal reform of national autonomous districts shall be carried out according to the will of the majority of people of national minorities and the leaders having close ties with the people.

Article 19. Under the unified financial system of the state, the autonomous organs of national autonomous districts may, according to the power concerning financial matters of the national autonomous districts as defined by the Central People's Government and governments of superior levels, administer the finance of their own districts . . .

Article 23. Within the scope defined by the laws of the Central People's Government and of governments of superior levels and according to their prescribed rights, the autonomous organs of national autonomous districts may enact their own independent laws and regulations and report them step-by-step to the people's governments of two levels above for approval . . .

CHAPTER VI.   GUIDING PRINCIPLES FOR PEOPLE'S GOVERNMENT OF SUPERIOR LEVELS

Article 33. The people's governments of superior levels shall introduce, by appropriate means, advanced experience and conditions of political, economic and cultural construction to the people of autonomous districts . . .

Article 35. The people's governments of superior levels shall educate and assist the people of all nationalities to establish the viewpoint of equality, fraternity, unity and mutual help among all nationalities and shall combat all tendencies of greater nationalism and narrow nationalism.

Source: New China News Agency (12 August 1952), translated in *Survey of China Mainland Press*, No. 394, pp. 12–16.

Document 6   POLITICAL CAMPAIGNS OF 1957–8

During the '100 Flowers' Campaign, criticism of the CCP emerged which then became the basis for attacking individuals who had dared to speak up. Some of the criticisms put forward in minority areas are mentioned in the following selection which dates from the end of the Anti-Rightist Campaign of 1957–8. The names are romanized in the Wade–Giles system, as in the original translation.

Vice Chairman Ts'ui K'e-nan of the Provincial Nationalities Affairs Commission [of Hunan] said at the meeting: These few years our province has established one autonomous *chou* [prefecture] and four autonomous *hsien* [counties] in areas where the Tuchia, the Miao, the Tung and the Yao nationalities live collectively . . . Great progress has been made in the various tasks of construction . . .

He pointed out: Rightists among the minority nationalities negated the achievement in the nationality work and exaggerated or even fabricated shortcomings and mistakes, thus basically disagreeing with us on the key issue[s] in the nationality work.

Ts'ui K'e-nan said: The Party's policy is, on the foundation of the socialist system, to consolidate the unity of the motherland and the unity of the various nationalities, so that they may together construct the big socialist family. We advocate the placing of national self-respect and national sentiments under the guidance of the socialist ideology, and their association with class sentiments and the interests of the state. While giving due consideration to national characteristics, we must associate them with the interests of the collective body. The rightists cherish the diametrically opposite view. They insist on placing national sentiments above class sentiments and the interest of the state, putting local interests above collective interests. . . . In the various reforms and constructive tasks carried out in minority nationality areas, the help of the Han cadres is essential. But the rightists say that the Han cadres and the Han Communists cannot stand for the interests of the minority nationalities, cannot serve the minority nationalities. They negate the fact that the Communist Party stands for the interests of all nationalities . . .

P'eng Tsu-kuei, deputy chief of the West Hunan Tuchia and Miao autonomous *chou*, said: Rightists P'an Kuang-tan and Hsiang Ta work in collaboration with P'eng P'e and other rightists of the Tuchia nationality. Wearing the cloak of 'attending to the interests of the nationalities' and waving the flag of 'fighting for regional autonomy for the nationalities,' they carry out activities in an organized and planned manner to create incidents on the issue of regional autonomy for the people of West Hunan, sow discord, and organize landlords, rich peasants, counter-revolutionaries, bad elements, rascals, ruffians and what not into a nuclear sub-committee to expand their reactionary anti-communist, anti-popular and anti-socialist force . . .

On the issue of the relations among the nationalities, the rightists claim that the Communist Party 'favors the Miao and discriminates against the Tuchia,' thereby intending to arouse the discontent of the Tuchia people against the Communist Party and excite mutual suspicions among, and split, the nationalities. . . . Thus they try by various means to sabotage the unity among our nationalities.

P'eng Tsu-kuei added: The rightist crimes, having been exposed, arouse the great indignation of all the nationalities in the *chou*. After several months' anti-rightist struggle, the rightists have been isolated from the masses of nationality people.

Source: New China News Agency (2 January 1958) 'Hunan Provincial People's Congress Criticizes Local Nationalism', translated in *Survey of China Mainland Press*, No. 1689, pp. 20–3.

RECOLLECTIONS OF THE GREAT LEAP FORWARD   **Document 7**

China's peasant-farmers at first supported the Great Leap Forward, but it soon became apparent that the new planting practices were a disaster. In interviews with villagers in south China, the following account was given by local farmers.

They pushed a system of planting called 'Sky Full of Stars' where a field would be so overplanted the seedlings starved each other out. . . . The peasants knew it was useless, but there was simply no way to oppose anything, because the orders came from so high above. And if one of our Chen Village cadres protested at commune meetings, he laid himself open to criticisms: 'a rightist, against the revolution.' . . . The peasants were ordered to smash their water jars to make them into fertilizer. They said it was stupid, that the jars were just sterile clay, but they had to smash the jars nonetheless. What a mess! Cut rice was left overnight in the fields [and mildewed] while exhausted villagers were ordered off to do other things. The period was called the 'Eat-It-All-Up Period' because people were eating five and six times daily – but there was no harvest that year. Everything had been given to the collective. Nothing was left in the houses. No grain had been stored. People were so hungry they had difficulty sleeping . . . some people became ill, and some of the elderly died. Our village became quiet, as if the people were dead.

Source: Anita Chen, Richard Madsen and Jonathan Unger (1992) *Chen Village under Mao and Deng* (Berkeley, CA: University of California Press), p. 25.

Document 8   A LETTER TO MAO ON THE GREAT LEAP FORWARD

This letter by Peng Dehuai pointed out the shortcomings of the Great Leap Forward; despite the truth of Peng's observations, he was removed from all positions of power after this letter was circulated, by Mao, among the top CCP leaders in 1959.

Dear Chairman:

This Lushan Meeting is important. In the discussions in the Northwest Group, I commented on other speakers' remarks several times. Now I am stating, specially for your reference, a number of my views that I have not expressed fully at the group meetings. I may be as straightforward as Zhang Fei, but I possess only his roughness without his tact. Therefore, please consider whether what I am about to write is worth your attention, point out whatever is wrong, and give me your instructions.

. . . The Great Leap Forward has basically proved the correctness of the General Line for building socialism with greater, quicker, better, and more economical results in a country like ours, hampered by a weak economic foundation and by backward technology and equipment. Not only is this a great success for China, it will also play a long-term positive role in the socialist camp.

But as we can see now, an excessive number of capital construction projects were hastily started in 1958. With part of the funds being dispersed, completion of some essential projects had to be postponed. This is a shortcoming, one caused mainly by lack of experience. Because we did not have a deep enough understanding, we came to be aware of it too late. So we continued with our Great Leap Forward in 1959 instead of putting on the brakes and slowing down our pace accordingly. As a result, imbalances were not corrected in time and new temporary difficulties cropped up . . .

In the nationwide campaign for the production of iron and steel, too many small blast furnaces were built with a waste of material, money, and manpower. This, of course, was a rather big loss. On the other hand, through the campaign we have been able to conduct a preliminary geological survey across the country, train many technicians, temper the vast numbers of cadres and raise their level. Though we paid a steep tuition (we spent over 2,000 million *yuan* to subsidize the effort), there were gains as well as losses in this endeavor.

Considering the above-mentioned points alone, we can say that our achievements have been really great, but we also have quite a few profound lessons to learn . . .

A number of problems that have developed merit attention in regard to our way of thinking and style of work. . . . The exaggeration trend has become so common in various areas and departments that reports of unbelievable miracles have appeared in newspapers and magazines to bring a great loss of prestige to the Party. According to what was reported, it seemed that communism was just around the corner, and this turned the heads of many comrades. Extravagance and waste grew in the wake of reports of extra-large grain and cotton harvests and a doubling of iron and steel output. As a result, the autumn harvest was done in a slipshod manner, and costs were not taken into consideration. Though we were poor, we lived as if we were rich.

Source: Reprinted with the permission of Free Press, a Division of Simon & Schuster, Inc., from CHINESE CIVILIZATION: A Sourcebook, Second Edition, Revised & Expanded by Patricia Buckley Ebrey. Copyright © 1993 by Patricia Buckley Ebrey. Copyright © 1981 by The Free Press. All rights reserved.

'THE LITTLE RED BOOK': QUOTATIONS FROM CHAIRMAN MAO   **Document 9**

The following quotations were among those studied diligently by soldiers of the PLA and then by millions of young people who joined the ranks of the Red Guards between 1966–9.

'The Chinese Communist Party is the core of leadership of the whole Chinese people. Without this core, the cause of socialism cannot be victorious.'

'A revolution is not a dinner party, or writing an essay, or painting a picture, or doing embroidery; it cannot be so refined, so leisurely and gentle, so temperate, kind, courteous, restrained and magnanimous. A revolution is an insurrection, an act of violence by which one class overthrows another.'

'It is an arduous task to ensure a better life for the several hundred million people of China and to build our economically and culturally backward country into a prosperous and powerful one with a high level of culture. And it is precisely in order to be able to shoulder this task more competently and work better together with all non-Party people who are actuated by high ideals and determined to institute reforms that we must conduct rectification movements both now and in the future, and constantly rid ourselves of whatever is wrong.'

'Every Communist must grasp the truth, "Political power grows out of the barrel of a gun."'

'Our principle is that the Party commands the gun, and the gun must never be allowed to command the Party.'

'The people and the people alone, are the motive force in the making of world history.'

'The wealth of society is created by the workers, peasants and working intellectuals. If they take their destiny into their own hands, follow a Marxist–Leninist line and take an active attitude in solving problems instead of evading them, there will be no difficulty in the world which they cannot overcome.'

'A Communist should have largeness of mind and he should be staunch and active, looking upon the interests of the revolution as his very life and subordinating his personal interests to those of the revolution; always and everywhere he should adhere to principle and wage a tireless struggle against all incorrect ideas and actions, so as to consolidate the collective life of the Party and strengthen the ties between the Party and the masses; he should be more concerned about the Party and the masses than about any individual, and more concerned about others than about himself. Only thus can he be considered a Communist.'

Source: Quotations from Chairman Mao Tse-tung (1967) (London and New York: Bantam Books), pp. 1, 3, 6, 33, 55, 65, 112 and 153.

Document 10   THE 16-POINT DIRECTIVE ON THE CULTURAL REVOLUTION

This document, officially adopted on 8 August 1966, became the basis for the Great Proletarian Cultural Revolution. The following extracts call on the Chinese people to wage a new kind of revolution, to reform totally all aspects of Chinese life.

1. *A New Stage in the Socialist Revolution*. The Great Proletarian Cultural Revolution now unfolding is a great revolution that touches people to their very souls and constitutes a new stage in the development of the socialist revolution in our country, a stage which is both broader and deeper . . .

Although the bourgeoisie has been overthrown, it is still trying to use the old ideas, culture, customs and habits of the exploiting classes to corrupt the masses, capture their minds and endeavor to stage a comeback. The proletariat must do the exact opposite: it must meet head-on every challenge of the bourgeoisie in the ideological field and use the new ideas, culture, customs and habits of the proletariat to change the mental outlook of the whole of society. At present, our objective is to struggle against and overthrow those persons in power taking the capitalist road, to criticize and repudiate the bourgeois reactionary academic 'authorities' and the ideology of the bourgeoisie and all other exploiting classes and to transform education, literature, and art and all other parts of the super-structure not in correspondence with the socialist economic base, so as to facilitate the consolidation and development of the socialist system.

2. *The Main Current and the Twists and Turns*. Since the Cultural Revolution is a revolution, it inevitably meets with resistance. This resistance comes chiefly from those persons in power taking the capitalist road who have wormed their way into the Party. It also comes from the force of habits from the old society. At present, this resistance is still fairly strong and stubborn. But after all, the Great Proletarian Cultural Revolution is an irresistible general trend. There is abundant evidence that such resistance will be quickly broken down once the masses become fully aroused . . .

4. *Let the Masses Educate Themselves in the Movement* . . . Trust the masses, rely on them and respect their initiative. Cast out fear. Don't be afraid of disturbances. Chairman Mao has often told us that revolution cannot be so very refined, so gentle, so temperate, kind, courteous, restrained and magnanimous. Let the masses educate themselves in this great revolutionary movement and learn to distinguish between right and wrong and between correct and incorrect ways of doing things . . .

Make the fullest use of big-character posters and great debates to argue matters out, so that the masses can clarify the correct views, criticize the wrong views and expose all ghosts and monsters. In this way, the masses will be able to raise their political consciousness in the course of the struggle, enhance their abilities and talents, distinguish right from wrong and draw a clear line between ourselves and the enemy.

Document 11   ACCOUNTS OF THE CULTURAL REVOLUTION

Yue Daiyun, a university professor, was witness to much of the violence that marked the early stages of the Cultural Revolution (CR). The following selection, from her account of events in August 1966, is part of China's 'scar literature' – books that detail individual experiences during the CR.

Violence, brutality, tragedy became commonplace at Beida* that August. Every day and night small groups of four or five would be picked up to be criticized in their departments and then paraded through the campus to 'accept struggle from the masses'. The targets of these 'mass ground struggle sessions' would always be forced to balance on one of the high, narrow dining hall benches and told to answer questions. If the answers were considered unsatisfactory, the person's head would be pushed down or he would be instructed to bend low or he would be held in the agonizing jet plane position, continually begging the people's pardon for his past offenses. Because I lived in the area of the student dormitories, I would see several groups of some twenty or thirty people conducting these struggle sessions every night when I went out after supper to read the latest wall posters by lamplight. Usually the abuse would last for about an hour, then the victim would be allowed to return home.

One evening I had gone out to read the new posters when I came upon a group of students surrounding a teacher from the math department, a woman who had graduated in the same class as I, standing on one of those benches, her hair disheveled and a big placard across her chest announcing that she was an active counter-revolutionary. She had once remarked that the Cultural Revolution was wrong, I learned, and when her comment was reported, she was taken into custody and held somewhere on campus, perhaps in a classroom building. Suddenly out of the crowd I heard her husband's voice declaring with icy piety that he could never live with her again, that their relationship was finished, that she was no longer the mother of their three children. Following his denunciation, the Red Guards commanded her again to admit her guilt. Provoked by her silence, they shoved her head down very low, knocking out all of her hairpins and causing her hair to fall forward and cover her face. I had seen such scenes of humiliation and abuse many times by then, but never had I heard such a heartless repudiation by a husband.

Witnessing such daily cruelty had a numbing effect. One evening when I returned home after doing my labor, I saw my neighbor's cook and lifetime friend sitting on the threshold weeping. The neighbor, the chairman of the physics department and an especially kind old man who had never married, had returned home that day after a particularly harsh struggle session. The cook had discovered him with a scarf tied around his neck, hanging from the ceiling. Hearing the news of this latest tragedy, I recalled how after I had been condemned as a rightist, when I was shunned by everyone, this professor would always smile warmly at me and say hello when he worked in his courtyard, and how he had tried to save his favorite student from being exiled to the countryside. I thought bitterly that it was better for him to be dead, as he was now over seventy and couldn't bear such harsh treatment. His body was quickly taken away to be cremated, and no one mentioned him again.

* 'Beida' is a contraction for 'Beijing Daxue' or Beijing University.

Source: Yue Daiyun and Carolyn Wakeman (1985) *To the Storm: The Odyssey of a Revolutionary Chinese Woman* (Berkeley, CA: University of California Press), pp. 180–2.

THE 'TEN LOST YEARS' OF THE CULTURAL REVOLUTION   **Document 12**

Following the Cultural Revolution, many Chinese felt that ten years of their lives had been wasted. The following selection is from a satirical short story, 'Ten Years Deducted', written by Shen Rong, a woman writer. Her collection of stories, At Middle Age, *was a Chinese bestseller in the late 1970s and included this story.*

Word wafted like a spring breeze through the whole office building. 'They say a directive will be coming down, deducting ten years from everybody's age!'

'Wishful thinking,' said a sceptic.

'Believe it or not,' was the indignant retort. 'The Chinese Age Research Association after two years' investigation and three months' discussion has drafted a proposal for the higher-ups. It's going to be ratified and issued any day now.'

The sceptic remained dubious.

'Really? If so, that's the best news I ever heard!'

His informant explained:

'The age researchers agreed that the ten years of the "cultural revolution" wasted ten years of everyone's precious time. This ten years debit should be canceled out . . .'

'Deduct ten years and instead of sixty-one I'll be fifty-one – splendid!'

'And I'll be forty-eight, not fifty-eight – fine!'

'This is wonderful news!'

'Brilliant, great!'

The gentle spring breeze swelled up into a whirlwind engulfing everyone.

'Have you heard? Ten years deducted!'

'Ten years off, no doubt about it.'

'Minus ten years!'

All dashed around to spread the news.

An hour before it was time to leave the whole building was deserted . . .

'Little Lin. There's a dance tomorrow at the Workers' Cultural Palace. Here's a ticket for you.' Big sister Li of the trade union beckoned to Lin Sufen.

Ignoring her, Sufen quickened her step and hurried out of the bureau.

Take off ten years and she was only nineteen. No one could call her an old maid any more. The trade union needn't worry about a slip of a girl. She didn't need help from the matchmakers' office either. Didn't need to attend dances organized to bring young people together. All that was done with!

Unmarried at twenty-nine she found it hard to bear the pitying, derisive, vigilant or suspicious glances that everyone cast at her. She was pitied for being single, all alone; scoffed at for missing the bus by being too choosey; guarded against as hyper-sensitive and easily hurt; suspected of being hysterical and warped. One noon when she went to the boiler room to poach herself two eggs in a bowl of instant noodles, she heard someone behind her comment:

'Knows how to cosset herself,'

'Neurotic.'

She swallowed back tears. If a girl of twenty-nine poached herself two eggs instead of having lunch in the canteen, did that make her neurotic? What theory of psychology was that?

Even her best friends kept urging her to find a man to share her life. As if to be single at twenty-nine were a crime, making her a target of public criticism, a natural object of gossip. The endless idle talk had destroyed her peace of mind. Was there nothing more important in the world, no more urgent business than finding yourself a husband? How wretched, hateful, maddening, and ridiculous!

Now she had been liberated. I'm a girl of nineteen, so all of you shut up! She looked up at the clear blue sky flecked with small white clouds like handkerchiefs to gag those officious gossips. Wonderful! Throwing out her chest, glancing neither to right or left, she hurried with a light step to the bicycle shed, found her 'Pigeon' bicycle and flew off like a pigeon herself through the main gate.

It was the rush hour; The crowded streets were lined with state stores, collectively run or private shops. Pop music sounded on all sides. 'I love you . . .' 'You don't love me . . .' 'I can't live without you . . .' 'You've no place in your heart for me . . .' To hell with that rubbish!

Love was no longer old stock to be sold off fast. At nineteen she had plenty of time, plenty of chances. She must give top priority now to studying and improving herself. Real knowledge and ability could benefit society and create happiness for the people, thereby earning her respect, enriching her life and making it more significant. Then love would naturally seek her out and of course she wouldn't refuse it. But it should be a quiet, deep, half-hidden love.

She must get into college. Nineteen was just the age to go to college. There was no time to be wasted . . .

Source: Shen Rong (1987) *At Middle Age* (Beijing: Chinese Literature Press), pp. 343–64.

FANG LIZHI ON MODERNIZATION AND DEMOCRACY IN CHINA   **Document 13**

The following paragraphs are taken from Dr Fang Lizhi's best-known speech, delivered in Shanghai on 18 November 1986.

Our goal at present is the thorough modernization of China. We all have a compelling sense of the need for modernization. There is a widespread demand for change among people in all walks of life; and very few find any reason for complacency. None feel this more strongly than those of us in science and academia. Modernization has been our national theme since the Gang of Four were overthrown ten years ago, but we are just beginning to understand what it really means. In the beginning we were mainly aware of the grave shortcomings in our production of goods, our economy, our science and technology, and that modernization was required in these areas. But now we understand our situation much better. We realize that grave shortcomings exist not only in our 'material civilization' but also in our spiritual civilization' – our culture, our ethical standards, our political institutions – and that these also require modernization.

Why is China so backward? To answer this question, we need to take a clear look at history. China has been undergoing revolutions for a century, but we are still very backward. This is all the more true since Liberation, these decades of the socialist revolution that we all know firsthand as students and workers. Speaking quite dispassionately, I have to judge this era a failure. This is not my opinion only, by any means; many of our leaders are also admitting as much, saying that socialism is in trouble everywhere. Since the end of World War II, socialist countries have by and large not been successful. There is no getting around this. As far as I'm concerned, the last thirty-odd years in China have been a failure in virtually every aspect of economic and political life.

We need to take a careful look at why socialism has failed. Socialist ideals are admirable. But we have to ask two questions about the way they have been put into practice: Are the things done in the name of socialism actually socialist? And, do they make any sense? We have to take a fresh look at these questions and the first step in that process is to free our minds from the narrow confines of orthodox Marxism.

We've talked about the need for modernization and reform, so now let's consider democracy. Our understanding of the concept of democracy is so inadequate that we can barely even discuss it. With our thinking so hobbled by old dogmas, it is no wonder we don't achieve democracy in practice. Not long ago it was constantly being said that calling for democracy was equivalent to requesting that things be 'loosened up'. In fact the word 'democracy' is quite clear, and it is poles apart in meaning from 'loosening up'. If you want to understand democracy, look at how people understand it in the developed countries, and compare that to how people understand it here, and then decide for yourself what's right and what's wrong.

Democracy is based on recognizing the rights of every single individual. Naturally, not everyone wants the same thing, and therefore the desires of different individuals have to be mediated through a democratic process, to form a society, a nation, a collectivity. But it is only on the foundation of recognizing the humanity and rights of each person that we can build democracy. However, when we talk about 'extending democracy' here, it refers to your superiors 'extending democracy' for you. This is a mistaken concept. This is not democracy.

In democratic countries, democracy begins with the individual. *I* am the master, and the government is responsible to *me*. Citizens of democracies believe that the people maintain the government, paying taxes in return for services – running schools and hospitals, administering the city, providing for the public welfare. . . . A government depends on the taxpayers for support and therefore *has to be* responsible to its citizens. This is what people think in a democratic society. But here in China, we think the opposite way. If the government does something commendable, people say, 'Oh, isn't the government great for providing us with public transportation.' But this is really something it *ought* to be doing in exchange for our tax money. . . . You have to be clear about who is supporting whom economically, because setting this straight leads to the kind of thinking that democracy requires. Yet China is so feudalistic that we always expect superiors to give orders and inferiors to follow them. What our 'spiritual civilization' lacks above all other things is the spirit of democracy. If you want reform – and there are more reforms needed in our political institutions than I have time to talk about –

the most crucial thing of all is to have a democratic mentality and a democratic spirit.

Source: From BRINGING DOWN THE GREAT WALL by Fang Lizhi, translated by J. Williams, copyright © 1991 by Fang Lizhi. Used by permission of Alfred A. Knopf, a division of Random House, Inc.

CCP STATEMENT ON THE EVENTS OF 4 JUNE 1989   **Document 14**

The following was broadcast by China's official Xinhua News Agency in Chinese on 9 June 1989, to provide the public with the 'facts' of the Tiananmen Square 'rebellion'.

A shocking counter-revolutionary rebellion took place in the capital of Beijing on the 3rd and 4th of June following more than a month of turmoil. Owing to the heroic struggle put up by the martial law enforcement officers and men of the People's Liberation Army [PLA], the Armed Police Force, and public security cadres and police, as well as the cooperation and support of large numbers of people, initial victory has been won in suppressing the rebellion. However, this counter-revolutionary rebellion has not yet been put down completely. A handful of rioters are still hatching plots, spreading rumors to confuse and poison people's minds, and launching counterattacks. They are firing in the dark with firearms and ammunition they have seized; they are burning motor vehicles, smashing police boxes, and storming stores and public places in an attempt to put up a last-ditch struggle. Many rumors are now being spread in society, and many members of the masses have yet to understand the truth of the facts; they still have some problems to solve ideologically and emotionally. Therefore, it is necessary to clearly tell the masses about the truth of this counter-revolutionary rebellion to enable them to understand the causes and effects of the rebellion and the necessity and urgency of suppressing it. In this way, the masses will throw themselves into the struggle and contribute to stabilizing the situation in the capital . . .

In the early morning hours of June 4, a group of rioters at a junction on Dongdan Road attacked fighters with bottles, bricks, and bicycles. The faces of the fighters were covered with blood. At Fuxing Gate a vehicle was intercepted. All 12 fighters, including the chief of the administrative department of a military unit, members of the department, and cooks, were dragged from the vehicle and forcefully searched. After that, they were beaten soundly. Many of them were seriously wounded. At Liubukou four fighters were surrounded and beaten. Some of them died on the spot. . . . At Huguo Temple after a military vehicle was intercepted, its fighters were dragged down, beaten soundly, and held hostage. A number of submachine guns were taken . . .

After dawn, the beating and killing of PLA fighters reached a degree that made one's blood boil. While an armed police detachment was carrying eight wounded fighters to a nearby hospital, it was intercepted by a group of rioters. After killing one of the fighters on the spot, the rioters threatened to kill the other seven . . .

Here are the facts. After the martial law enforcement units entered the square, the Beijing Municipal People's Government and the command of the martial law enforcement units issued an emergency notice at 0130 [1630 GMT]:

> 'A serious counter-revolutionary rebellion has occurred in the capital this evening. Rioters have savagely attacked PLA commanders and fighters, seized arms and munition, burned military vehicles, set up road barricades, and kidnapped PLA commanders and fighters in a vain attempt to subvert the People's Republic of China and overthrow the socialist system. The PLA has exercised utmost restraint for the past several days. Now it must resolutely strike back at the counter-revolutionary rebellion. Citizens in the capital must abide by the provisions of the martial law order and closely cooperate with the PLA in resolutely defending the constitution, the great socialist motherland, and the capital. Those who refuse to listen to our advice will have to be entirely responsible for the consequences because it will be impossible to ensure safety.'

At 0430, the notice of the Martial Law Command was broadcast in the square: 'Evacuation from the square will begin now. We agree to the students' appeal on evacuating from the square.'

Upon hearing the notice, the several thousand young students remaining in the square immediately assembled and deployed pickets who linked their hands. At around 0500, holding their banners, they began to move out of the square in an orderly way. The martial law troops left a wide opening in the southern entrance of the eastern side of the square, thereby ensuring the swift, smooth, and safe withdrawal of the students. At this time, there were still a small number of students who persistently refused to leave. In accordance with the demands of the 'circular', soldiers of the Armed Police Force forced them to leave the square. The square evacuation task was completely carried out by 0530. During the entire course of evacuation, which took less than 30 minutes, not a single one of the sit-in students in the square, including those who were forced to leave the square at the end, died. The claim that 'blood has formed a stream in Tiananmen' is sheer nonsense.

Source: Xinhua News Agency, translated in Foreign Broadcast Information Service (FBIS-CHI-89-111) 12 June 1989, pp. 62–6.

PRIVATIZATION OF STATE-OWNED ENTERPRISES   **Document 15**

This article highlights a woman entrepreneur who took over a failing govern-
ment-owned factory and turned it around in 1999.

'I argued with myself for two months,' recalls Hu Ying. 'One moment I'd
think, go ahead and buy it. The next moment I'd think, forget it. This is too
dangerous.'

Finally, in November 1997, Hu, a 40-year-old former local government
official, took the plunge. She put down 1.2 million *renminbi* (US$145,100)
to buy a 51% stake in the troubled state-owned leather factory the government had assigned her to run 18 months earlier.

With that move, Hu became part of the mass privatization of small and
medium-sized state-owned companies across China. To the consternation of
China's vocal but marginalized conservative Marxists, China's leaders say
they are committed to keeping a controlling interest only in large state
enterprises and in companies in select industries, such as public utilities and
communications.

Right in the forefront of the privatization movement is Hu's home town of
Leshan, a city of 3.4 million people located three hours drive southwest of
Chengdu, in western China. Over the past two years, Leshan has sold over
80% of its more than 400 small state manufacturing enterprises – those with
net assets of 20 million *renminbi* or less. It wanted to sell them all, but some
were in such bad shape that no one would have them . . .

Today, the renamed Leshan Lucky Dove Leather Co. is a busy place. It
exported 300,000 garments in 1998, earning nearly US$1 million. Hu credits
a strong emphasis on quality control, and the flexibility in setting salaries,
assigning tasks and hiring workers that she gained when the company ceased
to be state-owned.

Under state ownership, for example, the government Labour Bureau set
pay scales. Employees who worked hard earned the same as those who didn't.
Hu says she changed work attitudes by telling employees: 'If you don't work,
we won't pay you.' She says 77 employees quit, and she has signed fixed-
term contracts with the rest . . .

Like Leshan Mayor Liu, Hu believes Lucky Dove's privatization has been
good for the state. 'If the enterprise develops and pays taxes, the government
can still get a high return,' she says. In addition, Lucky Dove is now paying
the bank interest on its outstanding debts.

Source: Susan V. Lawrence (18 February 1999) 'Selling the Burden', *Far Eastern
Economic Review*, pp. 15–16.

Document 16   UNDERGROUND CHRISTIAN CHURCHES

Only those religious groups that register with the Chinese government are allowed to practise their religions. Those who refuse to comply are subject to arrest, as recounted in the following news release.

Beijing, Sept. 1, 2000. China has arrested a priest, 20 nuns and three others from an underground Catholic church in southern Fujian province, in an ongoing crackdown on religious groups refusing to adhere to Communist Party ideology, a rights group said Friday. Police arrested Father Lin Sho-zhang Wednesday and beat him severely, causing him to vomit blood, the US-based Cardinal Kung Foundation said in a statement sent to Beijing.

Also arrested were 20 nuns, one seminarian and two lay persons who belong to the same church, an underground Roman Catholic Church in Gongtou Village in Fujian's capital, Fuzhou, the Foundation said.

A police official on Friday told AFP [Agence France Presse] the group was arrested when police found them using a mushroom processing factory for church services. He said police confiscated religious articles from the group and turned them over to county police. County police declined to comment.

Two of the nuns were released Thursday after a group of parishioners paid a large sum of money to the police bureau, the Foundation said. They were ordered not to leave their house unless they received permission from the police.

The remaining 22 people are still detained and their whereabouts are unknown, the Foundation said.

The arrests come less than two weeks after another priest was detained in Fujian. Father Gao Yihua was detained on August 19 and released on August 29, the Foundation said. An archbishop in Fuzhou, Yang Shudao, who was arrested on February 10 and released shortly afterwards, remains under heavy surveillance with several guards staying in his house 24 hours a day, the Foundation said.

The Foundation said China has recently begun a new crackdown to force members of the underground Roman Catholic Church to register with the Chinese government and join the Patriotic Association, which was set up to monitor and force religious groups to conform to Communist Party ideology. Two Catholic churches co-exist in China. The official one pledging allegiance to the Communist Party and rejecting the authority of the pope has between four and five million members, according to Beijing. The other clandestine church is loyal to the pope and is said to count around 10 million followers . . .

Other religious groups have also come under pressure in recent weeks. Fifty underground Protestants have been detained in three provinces in the

Plate 1 Rural Shanxi province, China. Terraced fields make some of Shanxi's mountainous terrain productive, but local farmers' incomes remain well below the national average in this arid northern region.
Author's own photograph

Plate 2 Mao Zedong (1893–1976) Leader of the CCP's struggle with Japan and the Civil War with the Nationalist Party of Jiang Jieshi (Chiang Kai-shek), Mao and his policies brought hardship to many of his people after 1949. Despite his tarnished legacy, Mao remains the foremost Chinese political figure of the twentieth century.
© Corbis/Swim Ink

Plate 3 Liu Shaoqi (1898–1969) After becoming President of China in 1959, Liu was instrumental in helping China recover from the disastrous Great Leap Forward, but ran afoul of Chairman Mao. He died in prison, the highest-ranking victim of the Cultural Revolution.
© Getty Images/Agence France Presse/Archive Photos

Plate 4 Deng Xiaoping (1904–97) Deng directed the shift away from Mao's policies and inaugurated the reform era in which China's dramatic economic transformation began.
© Getty Images/Keystone/Hulton Archive

Plate 5 Hu Jintao (b. 1943) President of China, Chairman of the CCP and head of China's military, Hu represents a new generation of Chinese leaders intent on building the country's international economic role and enhancing its status within the global community.
© Corbis/XinHua/Xinhua Press

Plate 8 Olympic riders pass the Gate of Heavenly Peace, in the heart of Beijing, under the gaze of Chairman Mao. Mao's portrait still hangs over this entrance to the Forbidden City, once the residence of the Qing dynasty's emperors.

© Press Association Images/John Giles/PA Archive

Plate 9 Pingyao, a small town in Shanxi province, features traditional-style architecture in the city centre which is closed to motor vehicles. Hotels, shops and restaurants retain the traditional style, making it an appealing destination for Chinese and foreign visitors.
Author's own photograph

Plate 10 Shanghai, with a population of close to 20 million, is China's premier city for business and finance. The World Expo of 2010 offered the city an opportunity to showcase its dramatic transformation into a world-class city as it welcomed visitors from around the globe.
© Robert Harding World Imagery/Jochen Schlenker

past month and another 130 Protestants from an underground church in central Henan province were detained last week.

Source: 'China Arrests 24 Catholics from Underground Church' (1 September 2000) Agence France Presse.

ATHEISM IN CHINA   **Document 17**

Although religious practice is allowed in China, the government makes it clear that Party members are required to follow the official ideology which includes atheism. For minority cadres, this proved particularly difficult, as religion was seen as a part of their cultural identities. In this article from northwest China, Party members are reminded of their responsibility to serve as models for the area's largely Muslim population.

Urumqi *Xinjiang Ribao* [the Xinjiang Daily] 9 April 1997 – Considering the religious issue for party members as an important part of a party member's education, the Turpan prefectural party committee has carried out in-depth atheist education throughout the prefecture and brought about encouraging changes in the ideological and spiritual outlook of the broad masses of party members.

Turpan prefecture is an area where many ethnic groups, mostly Islamic, are concentrated. The number of believers is great and the religious belief is strong. Under the strong influence of religious belief, some party members' ideology has been corroded and they have begun to believe in religion or participate in religious activities in different degrees. Before the 4th plenary session of the 14th party central committee, 25% of the more than 18,000 party members in Turpan Prefecture were religious believers. In some villages, the percentage was over 40. A small number of party members even withdrew from the party because of their religious belief. Party members engaging in religious activities not only impair the image and authority of the party among the people and weaken the fighting force of party organizations but also encourage religious fanaticism and affect social stability. Through investigations and fact-finding, the Turpan prefectural party committee acquired a better understanding of the seriousness of the issue of religious party members and of the necessity and urgency of carrying out atheistic education. The prefectural party committee called a special meeting to include the education in atheism in the prefecture's general plan for education of party members and the objective control of party improvement, making this education a regular part of ideological and political work.

Atheistic education is based on a positive approach. They have conscientiously organized the broad masses of party members to study the basic concepts of Marxist dialectical materialism, Deng Xiaoping's theory of building Chinese-style socialism, the party's constitution, the party's religious policy, and scientific know-how. In accordance with the contents of education, the prefecture compiled, printed, and circulated 81,600 volumes (sets) of teaching materials about atheism to guarantee the learning needs of party members . . .

The prefecture has established a party member objective control system at different levels, constantly checked on the ideological condition of party members, and provided immediate education and assistance when any party member is found to have engaged in religious activities. Grassroots democratic evaluations at all levels have carried out annual democratic evaluation of party members which consider the religious status of a party member as an important element, thus subjecting party members to supervision inside and outside the party. Those party members who firmly believe in religion and who refuse to change their ways after education should be given a certain time period to make corrections, be persuaded to withdraw from the party, or dismissed from the party according to the seriousness of their case. In recent years, 98 religious party members have been dealt with. Of them, six have been dismissed from the party, 62 persuaded to withdraw from the party, and four have lost political and living privileges.

Source: Quan Deyi (9 April 1997) 'Education in Atheism for Xinjiang Party Members', in *Xinjiang Ribao* [*Xinjiang Daily*].

———————◄●►———————

Document 18   MEASURES OF CHINA'S MODERNIZATION

The following collection of comparative figures indicates China's improving standard of living, growing urbanization, and increasing access to forms of communication and transportation.

Gross national product, in US$

	1995	2008
China	728 billion	4.327 trillion
Germany	2.522 trillion	3.649 trillion
India	356 billion	1.159 trillion
Japan	5.247 trillion	4.910 trillion
Russia	395 billion	1.679 trillion
USA	7.342 trillion	14.326 trillion

Gross national product, per capita, in US$

	1995	2008
China	604	3,267
Germany	30,901	44,446
India	382	1,017
Japan	41,834	38,455
Russia	2,670	11,832
USA	27,574	46,350

Urban population as % of total

	1995	2008
China	31.4	43.1
Germany	73.3	73.6
India	26.6	29.5
Japan	64.6	66.5
Russia	73.4	72.8
USA	77.3	81.7

Passenger cars per 1,000 people

	1995	2008
China	8	22
Germany	541	566
India	7	(not available)
Japan	428	325
Russia	156	206
USA	(not available)	451

CO_2 emissions (metric tons per capita)

	1995	2008
China	2.7	4.7
Germany	11.0	9.8
India	1.0	1.4
Japan	10.1	10.1
Russia	10.5	11.0
USA	19.6	19.3

Mobile and fixed-line telephone subscribers (per 100 people)

	1995	2008
China	3.7	74.1
Germany	56.0	191.1
India	1.3	33.8
Japan	59.0	124.4
Russia	16.9	172.2
USA	72.6	139.8

Life expectancy at birth

	1995		2008	
	Males	Females	Males	Females
China	68	71	71	75
Germany	73	80	78	83
India	59	60	62	65
Japan	76	83	79	86
Russia	58	73	62	74
USA	73	79	76	81

Source: Based on World Bank; International Telecommunications Union. Both available at: www.data.worldbank.org.

Document 19   CHINA'S NEW CONSUMER CULTURE

The generational contrast between those who lived through the Cultural Revolution and those who have come of age in the reform era is illustrated in the following selection which also shows the influence of designer brands and a new pride in home ownership among those of the new middle class.

Qian Zhi Ying is the epitome of the stylish Shanghainese working mother. Dressed in her Dolce and Gabbana jeans and Mickey Mouse T-shirt, the 30-year-old greets American visitors in her sunny, lemon-colored living room in one of the city's average income neighborhoods. In the three-bedroom apartment, there's a modern sectional sofa, polished stone floors, Toshiba large-screen TV, recessed lighting and faux stainless steel in the kitchen.

Across the room sits her mother, Zhu Zhao Ling, separated by 26 years in age and a lifetime of change in China. Zhao Ling sits quietly, knitting and drinking tea, as her daughter talks about her new internet fashion business, which supplements the income from her customer service day job at an IT company.

The cruel ironies of modern China aren't lost on outsiders. The older woman, part of the country's lost generation, came of age during the Cultural Revolution when Mao's Communist revolution took aim at the very bourgeois lifestyle that is now the standard of social success. Denied the opportunity of a higher education (universities were closed from 1966 to 1976), Zhao Ling was instead sent to work on rural farms. It weas there that she met her husband, Qian Yu Sheng, 55, and they returned to Shanghai 10 years later. With their two children, Yu Sheng's parents and his two brothers, the couple squeezed eight people into a four-room, 900-square-foot home. At a time when wearing fashion was tantamount to political affront, they suppressed any sense of personal expression under their drab, tightly buttoned Mao suits. They survived the famine of the failed Great Leap Forward, but were nonetheless subjected to government-controlled consumption and rationed on staples like cooking oil and rice. The state owned all housing; for families like the Qians, bathrooms and kitchens were communal.

The now-retired couple – both former crane operators – scraped to save what they could. Their only indulgence was their two children, who not only represent the family's hopes for the future, but also serve as recompense for their parents' denied opportunities.

Zhi Ying and her husband, Jiang Bin, typify the ambition, optimism and national confidence of the emeerging capitalist class that is transforming the world's fastest-growing consumer society. Thanks to the economic reforms first introduced by Deng Xiaoping in 1978, this generation is living a lifestyle unimaginable as recently as 10 years ago. They own their own home and car, use credit, travel outside China and are fast adapters of the latest advances in personal technology and consumer electronics. They dine out and enjoy regular evenings on the town with friends, where premium brands like Chivas Regal and Heineken are the drinks of choice. In their living room, studio portraits of the family's much-adored only child show 6-year-old Jiang Ze Hao dressed in US stars and stripes, wearing a cowboy hat. Those preferences are proud badges of status as the new China opens up to the larger world.

Source: Noreen O'Leary (16 February 2007) 'The New Superpower: China's emerging Middle Class', *Adweek*, pp. 1–3, 5. *Adweek* article used with permission of e5 Global Media, LLC.

Document 20   REVISIONS TO THE 1980 MARRIAGE LAW

China's Marriage Law was revised in 2001 to reflect social changes, particularly increased incomes and material possessions. As this following selection shows, new laws detailed both responsibilities and penalties aassociated with divorce and also the new phenomenon of prenuptial agreements.

Article 13. Husband and wife shall have equal status in the family.

Article 14. Both husband and wife shall have the right to use his or her own surname and given name.

Article 15. Both husband and wife shall have the freedom to engage in production and other work, to study and to participate in social activities; neither party may restrict or interfere with the other party.

Article 16. Both husband and wife shall have the duty to practise family planning.

Article 17. The following items of property acquired by husband and wife during the period in which they are under contract of marriage shall be jointly possessed: 1. Pay and bonus; 2. Earnings from production and operation; 3. Earnings from intellectual property rights; 4. Property obtained from inheritance or gift except as provided for in article 1(3) of this law; and, 5. Any other items of property which shall be in his or her separate possession.

Article 19. So far as the property acquired during the period in which they are under contract of marriage and the prenuptial property are concerned, husband and wife may agree as to whether they should be in the separate possession, joint possession or partly separate possession and partly joint possession. The agreement shall be made in writing.

Article 31. Divorce shall be granted if husband and wife both desire it. Both parties shall apply to the marriage registration office for divorce. The marriage registration office, after clearly establishing that divorce is desired by both parties and that appropriate arrangements have been made for the care of any children and the disposition of property, shall issue the divorce certificates.

Article 32. When one party alone desires a divorce, the organizations concerned may carry out mediation, or the party may appeal directly to a people's court to start divorce proceedings. In dealing with a divorce case, the people's court should carry out mediation between the parties. Divorce shall be granted if mediation fails because mutual affection no longer exists. Divorce shall be granted if mediation fails under any of the following circumstances:

1   Bigamy or cohabitation of a married person with any third party;
2   Domestic violence or maltreatment and desertion of one family member by another;
3   Bad habits of gambling or drug addiction which remain incorrigible despite repeated admonition;

4   Separation caused by incompatibility which lasts two full years; and

5   Any other circumstances causing alienation of mutual affection.

Article 45. If bigamy, domestic violence to or maltreatment and desertion of family member(s) constitute a crime, the criminal responsibility of the wrongdoer shall be investigated according to law. The victim may institute a voluntary prosecution in a people's court in accordance with the relevant provisions of the criminal procedure law. The public security organ shall investigate the case according to law and the people's procuratorate shall initiate a public prosecution according to law.

Article 46. A no-fault party shall have the right to request for damage compensation under any of the following circumstances bringing about divorce: 1. Bigamy; 2. Cohabitation of a married person with any third party; 3. Domestic violence; and 5. Maltreatment and desertion of one family member by another.

Article 47. When the couple's joint property is divided, the party may get [a] smaller or no share of the property if he or she conceals, transfers, sells off, destroys the couple's joint property, or forges debts in an attempt to convert the other party's property at the time of divorce. After divorce, the other party, on finding the above-mentioned acts, may file an action in a people's court, and make a request for another division of the couple's joint property.

Source: All-China Women's Federation. Available at: www.womenofchina.cn/Policies_Laws/Laws_Regulations/1477.jsp.

CHINESE HISTORY TEXT   **Document 21**

This selection is taken from an introductory text on China's history, culture and civilization which appeared in Shanghai in 2004. Praising China's many past achievements in chapters with titles such as 'The Long and Brilliant History of China' and 'Unparalleled Achievements in Art and Literature' it provokes pride in the past while giving scant coverage to the twentieth century during which the CCP came to power. As seen in the passage below, it is a patriotic summary of the past that stresses the powerful cohesiveness of the Chinese people as well as the role of a centralized state. It also implies an historical unity of all ethnic groups, despite long periods of warfare between the ancestors of present-day minority groups and the Chinese. The extract below is taken from the English version of the text released in 2005.

The nation of China developed, one step after another, in a long-flowing succession of eras. Looking back on its history, one can discern several distinct characteristics, which are worthy of remembering.

First, the Chinese civilization is the only civilization in the world that has an unbroken history of development. It is ancient, and it is also modern. Its qualities underpin its vitality now, and in the future.

Ancient human civilizations were precursors of today's civilizations, but the ancient civilizations of Mesopotamia, Egypt, or India were all afflicted and disrupted by wars, and finally exterminated by the invasion of foreign nations. The rupture of these civilizations is one of the tragedies of human existence, and is an inevitable misfortune. It was precisely because of its own powerfulness that Chinese civilization was able to withstand the assaults and invasions by so many foreign elements even with their gunships and airplanes. China steadfastly held its position by, in the the process of defending the nation, absorbing the benefits of foreign civilizations to enrich the country.

Second, the history of China is a history of constant internal merging and fusing; and every member of the Chinese nation of whatever ethnicity, has made his own contribution to the whole of Chinese civilization.

During the country's long history, there were several important phases of internal adjustments to accommodate the various ethnic groups. This bringing together was an endless process and a good example of cross-fertilization and assimilation. It was this open and harmonious characteristic of the Chinese nation that ensured its continuous regeneration and development. China showed the same openness to foreign influences: Buddhism originated in India, but the centre of the religion finally became lodged in China, and Buddhist thought became one of the three pillars of Chinese traditional culture. This is a vivid example of China's willingness and ability to absorb the merits of other cultures to its own benefit and use – this is why Chinese civilization extended for thousands of years of unbroken history.

Third, in Chinese history, the central government, presiding over the unification of many ethnic groups, was the main force of the nation.

Since the Qin and Han Dynasties, unity was the mainstream, and separation was the tributaries. A unified country encompassing many ethnic groups was the basic and stable base of the Chinese state's regime. After the first emperor of Qin united China, the Chinese were united for far longer periods than they were being separated. Even in the periods of 'separation,' China never stopped its process of merging and assimilating. So for most of the country's history, all ethnic groups lived together in a unified country.

Fourth, though China's history is replete with accounts of war, turmoil, barbarism and cruelty, it never resorted to wars, oppression or force when dealing with the outside world. The external advances of the Chinese nation were carried out by peaceful means.

Fifth, the reason that the Chinese nation has a sturdy, cohesive constitution is because it has an enviable cultural tradition which is embraced by the whole nation. Solid values and moral standards are the spiritual Great Wall of the nation, accumulated, tested and refined during the centuries-long process of practice. Possessing these outstanding values and morals is one of the reasons why the Chinese nation has never been conquered or assimilated by another.

Source: Shuming Su (2005) *A Reader on China: An Introduction to China's History, Culture and Civilization* (Shanghai: Shanghai Press and Publishing Development Company), pp. 105–7.

CHINA AND CLIMATE CHANGE   **Document 22**

China's stance on the environment and climate change was evident in an address by President Hu Jintao at the UN in 2009. The selection below is taken from his remarks to the General Assembly.

Global climate change has a profound impact on the survival and development of mankind. It is a major challenge facing all countries.

I wish to highlight here a few principles that we need to follow in our common endeavor to tackle this issue of climate change. First, fulfilling our respective responsibilities should be at the core of our efforts. The principle of common, but differentiated, responsibilities embodies the consensus of the international community. Adherence to this principle is critical to keeping international cooperation on climate change on the right track . . .

Dear colleagues, out of a sense of responsibility to its own people and people across the world, China has taken and will continue to take determined and practical steps to tackle this challenge. China has adopted and is implementing its national climate change program. This includes mandatory national targets for reducing energy intensity and discharge of major pollutants and increasing forest coverage and the share of renewable energy for the period of 2005 through 2010.

In the years ahead, China will further integrate our actions on climate change into our economic and social development tasks and take the following forceful measures. First we will endeavor to cut carbon dioxide emissions . . . by a notable margin by 2020 from the 2005 level.

Second, we will vigorously develop renewable energy and nuclear energy. We will endeavor to increase the share of non-fossil fuels in primary energy consumption to around 15% by 2020. Third, we will energetically . . . endeavor to increase forest coverage by 40 million hectares and forest stock volume by 1.3 billion cubic meters by 2020 from the 2005 levels.

Fourth, we will step up our efforts to develop green economy, low carbon economy and . . . enhance research, development, and dissemination of climate-friendly technologies.

Source: 'Hu Jintao's Speech on Climate Change, September 2009', *Essential Documents, Council on Foreign Relations, 2010.* Transcript provided by the Federal News Service to the *New York Times.* Available at: www.cfr.org/publications/20262.

Document 23   CHINESE ARTISTS

As Chinese art began to find an international market and fame for its leading artists, the dilemmas of being Chinese with studios and admirers in both China and the West caused some artists to examine their place, not only in the art world, but also on the edges of Chinese political life. The extract below features artist Ji Yunfei whose work has appeared in galleries around the world.

The artist Yun-fei Ji was riding his electric bike through Beijing last October, snapping pictures of the elaborate parades honoring the 60th anniversary of the People's Republic of China. Suddenly, he said, among the white-uniformed soldiers holding bouquets of red flowers, and the rows of bright blue military tanks, 'everywhere I looked, I saw either a volunteer guard with a red armband or a policeman or a soldier.'

Feeling conflicted about what he considered to be an overzealous display of control by the Chinese authorities, Mr. Ji, 46, said he rode home to place an online order for 'The 120 Days of Sodom,' the scandalous 18th century French novel by the Marquis de Sade. 'For some reason,' explained Mr. Ji, who was born in Beijing but is now an American citizen, 'whenever I go to China, I feel the need to transgress.'

In the weeks that followed, Mr. Ji began to fill the walls of his temporary Beijing studio with sketches, and eventually paintings, of emaciated figures that appear by turns docile and domineering. These works, along with a 10-foot scroll, 'Migrants of the Three Gorges Dam,' critiquing the dam's social and environmental impact, are among the highlights of 'Mistaking Each Other for Ghosts,' a selection of Mr. Ji's recent work that opened Friday at the James Cohan Gallery in Chelsea.

Mr. Ji's subtle, subversive watercolors have appeared in important contemporary art round-ups like the 2002 Whitney Biennial, and last year in the 'Medals of Dishonour' show at the British Museum and in 'Chelsea Visits Havana' at the Museo Nacional de Bellas Artes in Cuba. The Contemporary Art Museum in St. Louis organized a 2004 solo exhibit of his work, 'The Empty City,' which traveled to the Rose Art Museum in Waltham, Mass., among other institutions. And in 2005 the American Academy in Rome awarded Mr. Ji a Prix de Rome. Although he is less known in China than in the West, a June show of his paintings at James Cohan's sister gallery in Shanghai, coinciding with the World's Fair there, may change that . . .

In 'Migrants of the Three Gorges Dam,' a project that Mr. Ji began several years ago under the auspices of MoMA, he once again uses traditional means to explore contemporary issues. Hand printed from 500 carved woodblocks made by the esteemed Rongbaozhai printing and publishing house, Mr. Ji's mounted scroll portrays flooded landscapes and dispossessed farmers along-side his calligraphic description of the flooding of the Yangtze River and reports on the displacement of inhabitants of the area based on his own inter-views, research and observations.

Yet Mr. Ji said he was less interested in criticizing the world's largest hydro-electric power plant – long a symbol of progress in China – than he was in revealing the interconnection between humans and their natural environment. 'The belief among ancient scholars,' he said, 'is that nature offers an ethical model that we should follow in human society. A horizontal line for example, in Chinese calligraphy, is like a cloud formation, or a natural, living form.'

Source: Dorothy Spears (21 February 2010) 'Part Traditionalist, Part Naturalist, Part Dissident', from *The New York Times*, © 21 February 2010, p 32. The *New York Times* All right reserved. Used by permission and protected by the Copyright Laws of the United States. The printing, copying, redistribution, or retransmission of the material without express written permission is prohibited.

AMENDMENTS TO THE PRC'S 1982 CONSTITUTION **Document 24**

Between 1988 and 2004 China added four amendments to its 1982 consti-tution. Some amendments revised the language of earlier articles and some added new material. In the examples below, changes to the preamble in 1988 indicate China's shift toward a market economy. Changes included in the fourth amendment, passed in 2004, went further, with the guarantee of the right to own and hold private property being foremost among them.

Amendments to the PRC Constitution of 1982

1   Amendment One (Approved April 12, 1988)
Article 11 of the Constitution shall include a new paragraph which reads: 'The State permits the private sector of the economy to exist and develop within the limits prescribed by law. The private sector of the economy is a complement to the socialist public economy. The State protects the lawful rights and interests of the private sector of the economy, and exercises guid-ance, supervision and control over the private sector of the economy.'

2   Amendment Two (Approved March 29, 1993)

The last two sentences of the seventh paragraph of the Preamble . . . shall be amended as: China is at the primary stage of socialism. The basic task of the nation is, according to theory of building socialism with Chinese character-istics, to concentrate its effort on socialist modernization.

Article 11 . . . is revised into: 'Individual, private and other non-public economies that exist within the limits prescribed by law are major compo-nents of the socialist market economy.' 'The State protects the lawful rights and interests of individual and private economies, and guides, supervises and administers individual and private economies.'

3   Amendment Four (Approved March 14, 2004)

Article 11, second paragraph, shall be revised to: 'The State protects the law-ful rights and interests of the non-public sectors of the economy such as the individual and private sectors of the economy. The State encourages, sup-ports and guides the development of the non-public sectors of the economy and, in accordance with law, exercises supervision and control over the non-public sectors of the economy.'

Article 13: 'The State protects the rights of citizens to own lawfully earned income, savings, houses and other lawful property.' And, 'The State protects according to the law the right of citizens to inherit private property.' Revised to: 'Citizens' lawful private property is inviolable' and 'The State may, in the public interest and in accordance with law, expropriate or requisition private property for its use and shall make compensation for the private property expropriated or requisitioned.'

Article 14 has a fourth paragraph added: 'The State establishes a sound social security system compatible with the level of economic development.'

Article 33 has a third paragraph added: 'The State respects and preserves human rights.'

Source: *People's Daily* (English) online; available at www.english.peopledaily.com. cn/constitution/constitution.html.

Document 25   NATIONALISM AND THE INTERNET

Among the groups allowed to organize and demonstrate with few limits were new nationalistic groups such as the Patriots Alliance. In the item below, a Western journalist offers his view of one group that uses the internet to organ-ize and arrange its meetings and activities.

A few years ago, Mr. Lu spent his weekends strumming his guitar and singing karaoke at Beijing nightclubs. Today, he spends all of his spare time – up to 50 hours a week – on his work with Patriots Alliance, a network of nationalist activists with close to 100 volunteer workers and 79,000 registered supporters on its website.

He has postponed his wedding to his fiancee three times in the past year because he is so busy with the alliance. He has helped organize more than 10 public protests in the past two years – a stunning number in a country where such gatherings are normally illegal.

The Nationalist mood seems to be gaining strength every year here. The schools are filled with 'patriotic education' classes. Young people are organizing boycotts of Japanese products. Web petitions against the Japanese government are attracting millions of supporters. The Japanese are routinely denounced as 'devils' and 'little Japs' in chat rooms on the Chinese Internet, and one bar in southern China went so far as to post a 'Japanese not welcome' sign.

A few years ago, optimists had hoped democracy would be nurtured by China's growing personal freedoms and its new Internet culture. But in reality, it is the nationalists, not the democrats, who have scored the biggest victories from the relaxed atmosphere . . .

The nationalism has become so virulent that it even questions China's economic reforms. Several recent Chinese books have denounced globalization as an evil US plot and an attempt to imprison China. Chinese trade negotiators were called 'traitors' for leading China into the World Trade Organization. . . . When liberal journalist Ma Licheng wrote an article in 2002 that criticized the anti-Japanese mood and called for rapprochement between China and Japan, he was immediately condemned as a 'traitor.' He suffered death threats and his home address and telephone number were posted on the Internet, along with a call to burn down his house. He was obliged to quit his job and move to Hong Kong.

Despite a strict ban on political activism in China, the patriots have been free to display their slogans on their chests. 'Nobody tells us not to wear such T-shirts,' Mr. Lu says. He sees the rise of China as a rightful return to its place as the dominant force in the world.

Source: Geoffrey York (24 October 2004) 'Nationalist Fervor Runs Amok,' *Globe and Mail*.

Document 26   THE CASE OF LIU XIAOBO

On 25 December 2009, Liu Xiaobo was convicted of crimes against the state, namely inciting others to subvert state power and the socialist system. He had been arrested before, first for his role in the Tiananmen Square pro-democracy movement in 1989 and later for his criticism of the CCP. In 2008 he was arrested again and at his trial, which concluded only at the end of 2009, he was sentenced to 11 years in prison. Prior to confinement, he wrote 'I Have No Enemies: My Final Statement' which he read in court at the time of his conviction. An extract appears below.

In the course of my life, for more than half a century, June 1989 was the major turning point. Up to that point, I was a member of the first class to enter university when college entrance examinations were reinstated following the Cultural Revolution (Class of '77). From BA to MA and on to PhD my academic career was all smooth sailing. Upon receiving my degrees, I stayed on to teach at Beijing Normal University. As a teacher, I was well received by the students. At the same time, I was a public intellectual, writing articles and books that created quite a stir during the 1980s, frequently receiving invitations to give talks around the country, and going abroad as a visiting scholar upon invitation from Europe and America. What I demanded of myself was this: whether as a person or as a writer, I would lead a life of honesty, responsibility, and dignity. After that, because I had returned from the US to take part in the 1989 movement, I was thrown into prison for 'the crime of counter-revolutionary propaganda and incitement.' I also lost my beloved lectern and could no longer publish essays or give talks in China. Merely for publishing different political views and taking part in a peaceful democracy movement, a teacher lost his lectern, a writer lost his right to publish, and a public intellectual lost the opportunity to give talks publicly. This is a tragedy, both for me personally and for a China that has already seen thirty years of Reform and Opening Up . . .

Twenty years have passed, but the ghosts of June Fourth have not yet been laid to rest. Upon release from Qincheng Prison in 1991, I, who had been led onto the path of political dissent by the psychological chains of June Fourth, lost the right to speak publicly in my own country and could only speak through the foreign media. Because of this, I was subjected to year-round monitoring, kept under surveillance (May 1996 to January 1996) and sent to Reeducation-Through-Labor (October 1996 to October 1999). And now I still want to say to this regime which is depriving me of my freedom, that I stand by the convictions I expressed in my 'June Second Hunger Strike Declaration' twenty years ago – I have no enemies and no hatred . . .

Hatred can rot away at a person's intelligence and conscience. Enemy mentality will poison the spirit of a nation, incite cruel mortal struggles, destroy a society's tolerance and humanity, and hinder a nation's progress toward freedom and democracy. That is why I hope to be able to transcend my personal experiences as I look upon our nation's development and social change, to counter the regime's hostility with utmost goodwill, and to dispel hatred with love.

Source: Liu Xiaobo (2010) 'I Have No Enemies: My Final Statement', *China Rights Forum*, No. 1, pp. 116–17.

CHINA'S ECONOMIC FUTURE   **Document 27**

Potential difficulties facing China as it seeks to maintain its phenomenal economic growth is of concern not only to China, but also to the international community. In 2008, Steven Dunaway, of the International Monetary Fund, offered his observations on China's economic future in the extract below.

In the past 20 years, China has added about $US2 trillion to world domestic product (GDP), created 120 million new jobs, and pulled 400 million of its people out of poverty. Over the past decade, output growth has averaged more than 10% annually, while inflation has averaged less than 3%. During this period, China has become one of the largest economies in the world and the third largest trading nation.

These are remarkable achievements, but there is nonetheless considerable unease about the state of China's economy and the economic well-being of its people. Income on a per capita basis is still very low in China relative to other major countries, the benefits of economic development have been unevenly distributed across the country and across sectors of the economy, and an estimated 150–200 million workers are still underemployed. To deal with these problems, there remains a critical need for China to sustain rapid economic growth. Up to now, that rapid growth has been primarily achieved by heavy reliance on investment and exports. But it is increasingly recognized that China cannot continue indefinitely to rely principally on these sources for economic growth.

This concern was prominently articulated at the National People's Congress in March 2007 when Premier Wen Jiabao cautioned that 'the biggest problem with China's economy is that the growth is unstable, unbalanced, uncoordinated, and unsustainable.' The key concern is that the imbalances in the economy could in time slow growth, perhaps significantly, putting China's economic miracle at substantial risk, unless the country shifts policies to foster reliance on domestic consumption.

As a result, the need for policy action has become more urgent. Over the past four years, continued rapid credit and investment growth has sowed the seeds of overcapacity in certain sectors, undermining the asset quality of the banking system, and could ultimately lead to a sharp growth deceleration. This final reckoning has been put off in recent years by the surge in exports and increased substitution of domestically produced goods for imports that has taken place, which has effectively absorbed much of the capacity put in place by rapid investment growth. However, the resulting substantial rise in China's external surplus coupled with its efforts to continue to tightly manage the exchange rate have led to rising international reserves and more liquidity pouring into the banking system, fueling further lending and investment and a push for more export growth and import substitution. Policy measures used thus far – especially heavy reliance on administrative measures and financial repression (moral suasion against lending) – have been ineffective in breaking this vicious cycle and reestablishing macroeconomic control. To make matters worse, inflation is a new concern that has now emerged. High food price increases have persisted in a few categories, creating the potential for a shift in inflationary expectation that could trigger a more generalized inflation process.

What is driving these imbalances? A combination of distortions in key prices – including the cost of capital, the exchange rate, energy, other utilities, land, and pollution costs – and other policies and the structure of the economy have served to favor investment over consumption. These are the principal factors that have contributed to the current economic situation. To resolve it, the basic macroeconomic policy actions needed to carry the economy ahead and sustain growth and development include further liberalization of prices, greater reliance on monetary policy (especially to deal with short-term problems of macroeconomic control), additional financial market reform and development, and changes in government expenditure policies.

Source: Steven Dunaway (May 2008) 'Meeting China's Macroeconomic Challenge', *Asia Program, Special Report*, Woodrow Wilson International Centre for Scholars, pp. 13–14.

CHINA'S 'HARMONIOUS WORLD'   **Document 28**

*In 2005, China's President Hu Jintao attended ceremonies for the 60th anniver-
sary of the founding of the UN, held in New York City. He delivered a speech
entitled 'Making Great Efforts to Build a Harmonious World with Long-
lasting Peace and Common Prosperity,' parts of which are extracted below
from a statement released by the Ministry of Foreign Affairs, Beijing, PRC.
Since China ia a permanent member of the UN Security Council, his sugges-
tion that there be greater representation on the Council by small or medium-
sized countries takes on special significance.*

Hu noted that the establishment of the UN [was] a historic event in human
history. Over the past 60 years, the organization has played an important role
of, and scored major achievements in, safeguarding world peace, pushing
forward common development and promoting human civilization.

He raised the following suggestions on building a harmonious world with
long-lasting peace and common prosperity:

First, we should set up the new security concept of mutual trust, mutual
benefit, equality and collaboration and establish a fair and effective collective
security mechanism. We should encourage and support the efforts to settle
international disputes or conflicts through peaceful means and strengthen
cooperation and fight resolutely against terrorism. As the core of the collective security mechanism, the role of the UN can only be strengthen and must
not be weakened.

Second, the UN should take tangible measures to implement the millennium development goals, especially accelerate the development of developing nations and make the 21st century 'the century of development for
everyone' in a real sense. We should actively push forward the establishment
of an open and fair multilateral trade mechanism without discrimination and
further improve the international financial system; reinforce global energy
dialogue and cooperation and jointly maintain energy security and stability
of the energy market; promote and guarantee human rights and enable
everyone to enjoy the equal opportunities and rights to seek comprehensive
development. Developed nations should take greater responsibilities for real-
izing universal, coordinated and balanced development in the world.

Third, we should respect the right of each country to independently
choosing [sic] its social system and development road and support the efforts
of countries to realize rejuvenation and growth according to their own
national conditions. We should maintain the diversification of civilizations in
the spirit of equality and openness, reinforce dialogue and exchanges among
different civilizations and join hands to build a harmonious world where
various civilizations coexist.

Fourth, we should safeguard the authority of the UN through reasonable and necessary reform, raise the efficiency of the organization and strengthen its capacity of coping with new threats and challenges. The UN reform is all-dimensional and multi-sectoral. The reform should focus on increasing UN's input in the development areas. The reform of the Security Council should give more consideration to the representation of the developing countries, especially the African nations so that more countries, especially the small and medium-sized countries, will have greater opportunities to participate in the decision making of the body.

Hu reiterated that China will firmly hold high the banner of peace, development and cooperation and follow the road of peaceful development. China will unswervingly combine its own development and the progress of humanity. China's development, instead of hurting or threatening anyone, can only serve peace, stability and common prosperity in the world.

At the end of his speech Hu stressed that in the long history of human progress, the fate of people all around the world has never been as close and interdependent as today. Our common goals unite us and common challenges combine us together. Let's join hands to make great efforts to build a harmonious world with long-lasting peace and common prosperity!

Source: Ministry of Foreign Affairs of the People's Republic of China. Available online at: www.bw.china-embassy.org/eng/xwdt/t212851.htm.

Document 29   UNITED STATES–CHINA RELATIONS

Despite the ups and downs of United States–China relations at the turn of the twenty-first century, some observers saw commerce as the key element bringing the two countries closer, suggesting that economic interdependence will override other issues.

It may have escaped most people's notice, but April was a busy month for China–United States business ties. United Airlines and United Parcel Service both opened new direct flights to China. A slew of new investments were announced – ranging from Ford Motor's $49 million bet on a Chongqing compact-car venture to Wisconsin-based CNH Global's $45 million plunge into a tractor factory in Shanghai. Meanwhile, the mayor of Denver was marching around China with 50 executives in tow in an effort to promote bilateral trade. All this while the two countries were engaged in their most serious military confrontation since ties were established in 1979.

The collision between an American spy plane and a Chinese fighter off the south China coast on April 1 set off a war of words that recalled the darkest days of the Cold War. Bilateral ties were also strained over Taiwan. US President George W. Bush promised new submarines, destroyers, and aircraft to Taiwan on April 24, and pledged the next day to do 'whatever it took' to help the island defend itself against a mainland invasion. Washington also gave a transit visa to former Taiwan President Lee Teng-hui. Beijing protested loudly.

But while diplomats on both sides managed to steal the media limelight from businessmen for most of the month, it is the businessmen who are increasingly driving the relationship between the US and China. As a result, the impact of the diplomatic confrontation is likely to remain muted.

As the US economy slips close to recession and Western markets flounder, China is offering one of the few big markets and investment opportunities for US companies. At the same time, China's leaders are desperate to maintain rapid growth – targeted at 8% this year – in order to stave off social unrest and undertake much-needed reforms . . .

Consider how business ties between the two nations have grown since 1995, the last time bilateral military tensions peaked following Chinese missile tests off Taiwan. From 1995 to last year, US annual investment in China rose 50% to $4.5 billion, making it the largest source of foreign investment in the mainland after Hong Kong. Over the same period, bilateral trade doubled to $116 billion. The US now buys a third of China's exports, many of them made by US companies in China. Entry to the World Trade Organization is expected to make China a bigger buyer, too.

Source: Bruce Gilley and Murray Hiebert (10 May 2001) 'Diplomacy of the Dollar', *Far Eastern Economic Review*, pp. 16–17.

AN ASSESSMENT OF PRESIDENT HU   **Document 30**

President Hu made numerous trips abroad and innumerable speeches in China, yet few have a strong sense of the man's personality. Drawing on what is known of his background and his public policy statements, two journalists well-versed in Chinese affairs offered the following discussion of their impressions of Hu and his future place in history.

When President Hu arrived in Washington this week to attend the Nuclear Security Summit, it was his second visit to the United States. To many in this country, Mr. Hu was still a mystery.

In fact, many in China still haven't figured him out eight years after he has taken power. Has Hu really commanded the political power to rule according to his own will? Is he a true conservative or a closet liberal?

Hu always keeps an image of being a cautious leader – often he's cast as being boring and humorless. However, his cautious appearance can also be misleading, masking his true political instincts and aspirations.

One cannot overlook his uncanny ability to navigate the many political intrigues and maneuverings. Restraint is his ultimate virtue. In the past, this self-discipline has enabled him to rise from a humble technician to a well-behaved and well-loved head of the Communist Youth League, the party secretary of a poverty-stricken province, a controversial emissary to Tibet, and then the No. 1 of China. He has manifested humility, patience and industriousness, all of which are deemed to be virtues in Chinese culture.

During his reign, Hu has quietly promoted his own people to various important government posts. In the name of eliminating corruption, he has purged outspoken political rivals. He has also initiated many populist programs to alleviate social and economic inequality. Hu's survival instinct means that he is neither a liberal nor a conservative. He's a pragmatist.

While Deng proposed 'The Four Cardinal Principles' and Jiang Zeming came up with 'Three Represents', which legitimized the inclusion of capitalists and private entrepreneurs in the Communist Party, Hu advocates building a 'harmonious society.' He understands that the days are gone when the party can maintain political stability with the muzzle of a gun.

He needs a softer approach to resolving social conflicts. In addition, he also knows that overly ambitious political reforms could disrupt the power balance, offending the political elite. If not prudent, he could trigger an implosion of all pent-up conflicts. The party and the country could easily slip away from him . . .

Politically, Hu expresses no intention of being a historical giant who aspires to save the world. All he apparently wants is to complete his tenure peacefully and smoothly. He doesn't crave for [sic] posthumous fame. He pursues stability in the present, even though it means cracking down on free speech and worsening China's human rights record. He might occasionally sway to the left or the right, but his real aim is the middle, which makes him feel safe. His political inertia disarms and appeases Jiang [Zemin] and his loyalists . . .

Following the demise of Mao Zedong, whose sole obsession in life was revolution, all future generations of Communist leaders made economic development an irrevocable priority. At present, no other political party in the world has devoted more of its energy to generating wealth than the Chinese Communist Party . . .

Source: Pin Ho and Wen Huang (15 April 2010) 'Hu Jintao: The Mysterious Man behind China's "Harmonious Society"', *Christian Science Monitor*.

CHINA AND CENTRAL ASIA   **Document 31**

In the 1990s, China moved quickly to establish good relations with its new Central Asian neighbours who gained their independence with the collapse of the USSR. A major issue was the stability of Muslim Xinjiang where disaffected groups had staged demonstrations that led to violent confrontations with Chinese authorities. In 1997, new assurances were given to China by its immediate neighbours, as seen in the following selection.

Hong Kong AFP 18 June 1997 – Uighur exile groups seeking independence in northwestern China said on Wednesday that they can no longer count on help from neighboring Kyrgyzstan and Kazakhstan, following a visit there by the Chinese Defense Minister.

'We are not counting anymore on Kyrgyzstan and Kazakhstan to help us in the fight for the independence of Xinjiang,' Mukhidin Mukhlissi, spokesman for the United Revolutionary Front, the separatist Uighur group based in Kazakhstan, told AFP.

The shift came as Chinese Defense Minister Chi Haotian visited Kyrgyzstan, following a similar trip to Kazakhstan. He was to return to Beijing on Friday.

Both ex-Soviet republics border China and are home to about 300,000 ethnic Uighurs, a Moslem people who form the majority in Xinjiang. Chi has won support for his aim of cracking down on Uighur nationalist exile groups.

A Kyrgyz Defense Ministry spokesman said this week that 'the positions of Kyrgyzstan and China against separatism and religious extremism are identical.'

Over the past few weeks, security services in Kazakhstan have stepped up surveillance of several Uighur separatist groups in the republic. 'We are disappointed by the Central Asian governments' statements during Chi Haotian's visit,' said Kakhrama Khodzhaberdiyev, head of the Association of Uighur people, which is legally registered in Kazakhstan. 'Only the United States can help us. We are going to New York and Washington in July to meet with the State Department officials,' one Uighur leader in the Kazakh capital Almaty said.

Xinjiang, which borders Kazakhstan, has been plagued by violence in recent years as ethnic Uighurs fight for independence from Beijing. Up to 100 people died after clashes on February 5–6 between Uighurs and Chinese in the Xinjiang frontier town of Yining, according to witness reports.

China rarely admits to any violence in the region but Uighur nationalist groups there claim that 57,000 Uighurs have been arrested by the Chinese authorities in Xinjiang since April 1996.

Although Kazakhstan has said it opposes the Uighurs' separatist bid, it has also blamed China for human rights abuses in Beijing's dealings with the activists.

Source: 'Uighur Separatist Exiles See End to Central Asian Help' (18 June 1997) Agence France Presse report from Hong Kong.

Document 32   CHINA AND TAIWAN

The political positions of China and Taiwan following the 2004 Taiwan elections are evident in the following two documents. The first is from a statement by the Office for Taiwan Affairs of the Chinese Communist Party, dated May 17, 2004. The second is taken from Taiwan President Chen Shui-bian's inaugural address, delivered three days later, on May 20, 2004.

PRC Statement (extract):

At present, the relations across the Taiwan Straits are severely tested. To put a resolute check on the 'Taiwan independence' activities aimed at dismembering China and safeguarding peace and stability in the Taiwan Straits is the most pressing task before the compatriots on both sides of the Straits.

Four years ago, Chen Shui-bian pledged himself to the so-called 'five no's' policy. His track record, however, was one of the broken promises and bad faith. M He said he would not declare 'independence,' but he has mustered together all kinds of separatists for 'Taiwan independence' activities. He said he would not change Taiwan's so-called 'national title,' but he has incessantly clamored for 'rectification of Taiwan's name' and 'disunification' in Taiwan. He said he would not push for the incursion of the so-called 'state-to-state' description in the 'constitution,' but he has dished out a separatists proposition of 'one country on each side.' He said he would not promote 'referendum to change the status quo in regard to the question of independence or unification,' but he has tried every possible means to promote 'Taiwan independence' by way of referendum. He said there was no question of abolishing the 'National Unification Council' and the 'National Unification Guidelines,' but he has long since shelved them, letting them exist only in name. What's more, Chen Shui-bian has left Taiwan society deeply torn with his vicious mischaracterization of the popular will of Taiwan people, his unbridled instigation of hostility and animosity towards the mainland, and his frenzied provocation to the status quo that both the mainland and Taiwan belong to the one and same China. He has even put out a timetable to move the island to independence through the making of a new constitution, thus pushing the cross-straits relations to the brink of danger.

'Taiwan independence' does not lead to peace, nor national dismemberment to stability. We will never compromise on the one-China principle, never give up our efforts for peace negotiations, never falter in our sincere pursuit of peace and development on both sides of the Straits with our Taiwan compatriots, never waver in our resolve to safeguard China's sovereignty and territorial integrity, and never put up with 'Taiwan independence.'

No matter who holds power in Taiwan in the next four years, as long as they recognize that there is only one Chia in the world and both the mainland and Taiwan belong to that one and same China, abandon the 'Taiwan independence' stance and stop the separatist activities, then, cross-straits relations can hold out a bright prospect of peace, stability and development . . .

Taiwan Statement (extract):

The people on both sides [of the Straits] share a common ancestral, cultural, and historical heritage. In the past century, both have endured the repression of foreign powers and the domination of authoritarian rule. Both our peoples now share an indomitable resolve to stand up and be the masters of their own destiny, a sentiment that is worthy of our full, mutual understanding.

We can understand why the government on the other side of the Strait, in light of historical complexities and ethnic sentiments, cannot relinquish its insistence on the 'One China Principle.' By the same token the Beijing authorities must understand the deep conviction held by the people of Taiwan to strive for democracy, to love peace, to pursue their dreams free from the threat, and, to embrace progress. But if the other side is unable to comprehend that this honest and simple wish represents the aspirations of Taiwan's 23 million people, if it continues to threaten Taiwan with military force, if it persists in isolating Taiwan diplomatically, if it keeps up irrational efforts to block Taiwan's rightful participation in the international areas, this will only serve to drive the hearts of the Taiwanese people further away and widen the divide in the Strait.

History has given rise to the development of two very different political systems as well as two dissimilar ways of life on either side of the Taiwan Strait. However, if we make a concerted effort to find some positive aspect of our differences and commonalities, perhaps we shall discover a wonderful opportunity, a catalyst for building a cooperative and mutually beneficial relationship. Taiwan is a completely free and democratic society. Neither single individual nor a political party can make the ultimate choice for the people. If both sides are willing, on the basis of goodwill, to create an environment engendered upon 'peaceful development and freedom of choice,' then in the future, the Republic of China and the People's Republic of China – or Taiwan and China – can seek to establish relations in any form whatsoever. We would not exclude any possibility, as long as there is the consent of the 23 million people of Taiwan.

Source: Copyright 2004 from 'The Taiwan Factor in U.S.–China Relations: An Interpretation' by Chai, Winberg, in *Asian Affairs: An American Review*. Reproduced by permission of Taylor & Francis Group, LLC., http://www.taylorandfrancis.com

Further reading

Primary sources

There are a number of compilations that provide important documents, in translation, on the People's Republic of China as well as a wealth of modern literature that vividly depicts contemporary life. Among the collections of primary documents most readily available, the following are highly recommended: Pei-kai Cheng and Michael Lestz, with Jonathan Spence *The Search for Modern China: A Documentary Collection* (New York: W.W. Norton, 1999) and, on the reform era, Orville Schell and David Shambaugh (eds) *The China Reader: The Reform Era* (New York: Random House, 1999). For a day-by-day view of events in China, see the reports from FBIS (Foreign Broadcast Information Service) which are available from the US State Department in both hard copy and electronic form.

To understand the views of ordinary Chinese people on such events as the Cultural Revolution and the changes that followed, see the interviews provided in Zhang Xinxin and Sang Ye *Chinese Lives: An Oral History of Contemporary China* (New York: Pantheon Press, 1987). Also of great interest are the frank interviews with men and women – on the Cultural Revolution and also everyday life in the 1990s – transcribed in Yarong Jiang and David Ashley *Mao's Children in the New China: Voices from the Red Guard Generation* (New York: Routledge, 2000). For a view from the perspective of women participants in the Cultural Revolution sent to labour in rural areas, Xueping Zhong, Wang Zheng and Bai Di (eds) *Some of Us: Chinese Women Growing up in the Mao Era* (New Brunswick, NJ: Rutgers University Press, 2001) provides a thoughtful account of personal experiences that are remembered as a time of personal growth rather than misery.

For a lively set of essays by one of China's leading dissidents, see Fang Lizhi *Bringing down the Great Wall: Writings on Science, Culture, and Democracy in China* translated by James H. Williams (New York: Knopf, 1991). The outspoken Fang articulated the views of thousands of Chinese college students in the years leading up to 1989.

On the Tiananmen Square Massacre, see the documents compiled in Michael Oksenberg, Lawrence R. Sullivan and Marc Lambert (eds) *Beijing Spring 1989: Confrontation and Conflict – The Basic Documents* (Armonk, NY: M.E. Sharpe, 1990). For an assessment of the events by a Chinese dissident journalist, see Liu Binyan *Tell the World: What Happened in China and Why* translated by Henry Epstein (New York: Pantheon Books, 1989). Additional government documents on the events of 'Beijing Spring' that are widely accepted as authentic outside China are available in Andrew J. Nathan and Perry Link (eds) and Liang Zhang (compiler) *The Tiananmen Papers: Chinese Leadership's Decision to Use Force Against Their Own People – In Their Own Words* (New York: Public Affairs, 2001). A re-examination of key events by an eyewitness is Philip J. Cunningham's *Tiananmen Moon: Inside the Chinese Student Uprising of 1989* (Boulder, CO: Rowman & Littlefield, 2009).

Secondary sources

In addition to the primary sources listed above, many secondary sources document the recent history of the PRC and socio-political changes at various levels. For an account of change at the village level, see the interview-based account of Anita Chan, Richard Madsen and Jonathan Unger *Chen Village under Mao and Deng* (Los Angeles, CA: University of California Press, 1992). An anthropological study of changes in rural areas is provided in a classic study by Sulamith Heins Potter and Jack M. Potter *China's Peasants: The Anthropology of a Revolution* (New York and Cambridge: Cambridge University Press, 1990). For discussion of the government and politics, see the important early study by Franz Schurmann *Ideology and Organization in Communist China* (Berkeley, CA: University of California Press, 1966) on the early years and, for more recent political organization, see the authoritative work of Kenneth Lieberthal *Governing China: From Revolution through Reform* (New York: W.W. Norton & Co, 1995). On changes in the twenty-first century, see the excellent chapters in Peter Hays Gries and Stanley Rosen (eds) *State and Society in 21st Century China: Crisis, Contention, and Legitimation* (New York: Routledge Curzon, 2004) and in Lionel M. Jensen and Timothy Weston (eds) *China's Transformation: The Stories Beyond the Headlines* (New York: Rowman & Littlefield Publishers, 2007)

Biographies of leading figures in the PRC include a range of books, from the popular to the scholarly. On Mao, there are Jonathan Spence *Mao Zedong* (New York and London: Penguin, 1999); Ross Terrill *Mao: A Biography* (New York: Simon and Schuster, 1980; reissued 1993); and Philip Short *Mao: A*

Life (New York: Henry Holt and Co., 1999). Extremely critical and highly personal books on Mao are Li Zhisui *The Private Life of Chairman Mao* (New York: Random House, 1994), and Jung Chang and Jon Halliday *Mao: The Unknown Story* (New York: Anchor Books, 2006). A critique of the latter work is Gregor Benton and Lin Chun (eds) *Was Mao Really a Monster: The Academic Response to Chang and Halliday's 'Mao: The Unknown Story'* (New York: Routledge, 2009). On the life of reformer Deng Xiaoping, see Richard Evans *Deng Xiaoping and the Making of Modern China* (London: Penguin Books, 1995) and Benjamin Yang *Deng: A Political Biography* (Armonk, NY: M.E. Sharpe, 1998). The only English-language biography of President Jiang Zemin is the highly readable account by Bruce Gilley *Tiger on the Brink: Jiang Zemin and China's New Elite* (Berkeley, CA: University of California Press, 1998).

China's relations with the United States are the focus of Michael Schaller's excellent study *The United States and China* which has gone through three editions (New York: Oxford University Press, 2002). A detailed discussion of the Nixon visit is available in Margaret McMillan *Nixon and Mao* (New York: Random House, 2008). China's role as a regional power is analysed in the excellent essays compiled by Shiping Tang, Mingjiang Li and Amitav Acharya (eds) *Living with China: Regional States and China through Crises and Turning Points* (New York: Palgrave Macmillan, 2009).

There are numerous studies of the Cultural Revolution. Two that are particularly interesting include Lynn White III *Policies of Chaos: The Organizational Causes of Violence in China's Cultural Revolution* (Princeton, NJ: Princeton University Press, 1989) and Anne Thurston *Enemies of the People: The Ordeal of the Intellectuals in China's Great Cultural Revolution* (Cambridge, MA: Harvard University Press, 1988). On the role of Mao's wife, see Roxanne Witke *Comrade Chiang Ch'ing* (Boston, MA: Little Brown, 1977). A re-examination of the Cultural Revolution is the excellent study by Roderick MacFarquhar and Michael Schoenhals *Mao's Last Revolution* (New York: Belknap Press, 2008).

'Scar literature' detailing Chinese lives during this difficult time include Liang Heng and Judith Shapiro *Son of the Revolution* (New York: Vintage Books, 1983); Yue Daiyun, with Carolyn Wakeman *To the Storm: The Odyssey of a Revolutionary Chinese Woman* (Berkeley, CA: University of California Press, 1985); and Rae Yang *Spider Eaters* (Berkeley, CA: University of California Press, 1997). The gritty coming-of-age books by Da Chen include *Colors of the Mountain* (New York: Anchor, 2001) and *Sounds of the River: A Young Man's University Days in Beijing* (New York: HarperCollins, 2002), both of which provide fascinating accounts of life in a small town during the Cultural Revolution and in the years immediately following Mao's death.

On population issues, useful volumes include Judith Banister *China's Changing Population* (Stanford, CA: Stanford University Press, 1987) and Penny Kane *The Second Billion: Population and Family Planning in China* (New York: Penguin Books, 1987).

In the past two decades, a wealth of material has appeared on women's status. These include biographical works, such as Chang Jung *Wild Swans: Three Daughters of China* (New York: Doubleday/Anchor Books, 1991), which provides an account of women's lives from the early twentieth century through the Cultural Revolution. The readable memoirs of Anchee Min *Red Azalea* (New York: Pantheon Books, 1994) became an international best-seller as did her personal reflections on Mao's wife *Becoming Madame Mao* (New York: Mariner Books, 2000). Canadian-Chinese journalist Jan Wong also wrote of her personal experiences in her tale of life in the 1970s and 1980s, in *Red China Blues* (Toronto: Doubleday/Anchor Books, 1997).

Western and Chinese scholars have examined many aspects of women's lives; trail-blazing studies include Gail Hershatter and Emily Honig *Personal Voices: Chinese Women in the 1980s* (Stanford, CA: Stanford University Press, 1988). Surveying changes for women since 1949 is Harriet Evans who wrote *Women and Sexuality in China* (New York: Continuum Press, 1997); her detailed examination of urban women's lives in the new millennium is *The Subject of Gender: Daughters and Mothers in Urban China* (Boulder, CO: Rowman & Littlefield, 2009). Rural women are the focus of Tamara Jacka *Women's Work in Rural China* (Cambridge: Cambridge University Press, 1997) and rural women's lives as factory workers are explored in the interview-based exploration by Leslie Chang *Factory Girls: From Village to City in a Changing China* (New York: Random House, 2008). The lives of women living on the social edge are explored in Tiantian Zheng's *Red Lights: The Lives of Sex Workers in Postsocialist China* (Minneapolis, MN: University of Minnesota Press, 2009).

Broader discussion of changes in women's lives can be found in the various chapters of Barbara Entwisle and Gail E. Henderson (eds) *Re-drawing Boundaries: Work, Households, and Gender in China* (Berkeley, CA: University of California Press, 2000). A study covering over half a century of change in one province, Laurel Bossen's study, *Chinese Women and Rural Development* (Boulder, CO: Rowman & Littlefield, 2002) offers a fascinating discussion based on fieldwork between 1989 and 1997. Sara L. Friedman explores marriage patterns outside the usual Han norms in her study *Intimate Politics: Marriage, the Market, and State Power in Southeastern China* (Cambridge, MA: Harvard University Asia Centre, 2006).

On the family and private life, see Liu Dalin, Man Lun Ng, Li Ping Zhou and Edwin J. Haeberle *Sexual Behavior in Modern China* (New York: Continuum Press, 1997) and for details on changes within the Chinese family, see Deborah Davis and Stevan Harrell (eds) *Chinese Families in the Post-Mao Era* (Berkeley, CA: University of California Press, 1993).

China's new consumerism is surveyed in Deborah S. Davis (ed) *The Consumer Revolution in Urban China* (Berkeley, CA: University of California Press, 2000) and in Jing Wang *Brand New China: Advertising, Media, and Commercial Culture* (Cambridge, MA: Harvard University Press, 2008).

Related to consumerism and changes in popular culture during the 1990s, see the provocative account by Jianying Zha *China Pop: How Soap Operas, Tabloids, and Bestsellers Are Transforming a Culture* (New York: W.W. Norton, 1995). A study of popular culture and ethnic minorities is offered in Nimrod Baranovitch *China's New Voices: Popular Music, Ethnicity, Gender, and Politics, 1978–1997* (Berkeley, CA. University of California Press, 2003).

A number of works focus on minority populations in China. Among these are Linda Benson and Ingvar Svanberg *China's Last Nomads: The History and Culture of China's Kazaks* (Armonk, NY: M.E. Sharpe, 1998) and Dru C. Gladney *Muslim Chinese* (Cambridge, MA: Harvard University Press, 1991). On Tibet, the Dalai Lama's memoirs and other writings view events from his perspective, while Melvyn C. Goldstein *The Snow Lion and the Dragon* (Berkeley, CA: University of California Press, 1997) presents a concise and carefully balanced account of Tibet's relations with China. On the Xinjiang region, see Frederick F. Starr (ed) *Xinjiang: China's Muslim Borderland* (Armonk, NY: M.E. Sharpe, 2004) and James Millward *Eurasian Crossroads: A History of Xinjiang* (New York: Columbia University Press, 2007). For a survey of minorities and issues related to their role in Chinese society, an excellent overview is provided by Colin Mackerras *China's Minority Cultures: Identities and Integration Since 1912* (New York and London: Longman, 1995).

Religion in China is the subject of books such as the study of Catholicism in Richard Madsen *China's Catholics: Tragedy and Hope in an Emerging Civil Society* (Berkeley, CA: University of California Press, 1998). On Protestant belief and comparison with other religious traditions in China, see Alan Hunter and Kim-kwong Chan *Protestantism in Contemporary China* (Cambridge: Cambridge University Press, 1993). The *Falungong*, a religious movement banned in China in 1999, is the subject of books by practitioners and the founder, Master Li Hongzhi. His works may be downloaded from the internet free of charge. An assessment of religion through the early twenty-first century is in Adam Yuet Chau (ed) *Religion in Contemporary China* (Boulder, CO: Rowman & Littlefield, 2009). Among new studies of Buddhism is Francesca Tarocco *The Cultural Practices of Modern Chinese Buddhism* (New York: Routledge, 2006).

The many changes that mark the decades of the reform era are treated in a number of informative, insightful accounts. Among those from the 1980s documenting the first decade of reforms is the highly readable account by Orville Schell *Discos and Democracy: China in the Throes of Reform* (New York: Pantheon, 1988) and Harry Harding's *China's Second Revolution: Reform after Mao* (Washington, DC: Brookings Institute, 1987). Among the most valuable studies from the 1990s is Merle Goldman and Roderick MacFarquhar (eds) *The Paradox of China's Post-Mao Reforms* (Cambridge, MA: Harvard University Press, 1999). Important publications since 2000 include Elizabeth Perry and Mark Seldon (eds) *Chinese Society: Change, Conflict and Resistance* (New York: Routledge, 2000) and Lowell Dittmer and Guoli Liu *China's Deep Reform: Domestic Politics in Transition* (Boulder, CO: Rowman & Littlefield, 2006). A short, well-informed account of reforms since 1989 can be found in Timothy Cheek *Living with Reform: China Since 1989* (London: Zed Books, 2006). Public demonstrations and protests are examined in Kevin J. O'Brien (ed) *Popular Protest in China* (Cambridge, MA: Harvard University Press, 2008), and other dilemmas of change are assessed in Guoguang Wu and Helen Lansdowne *Socialist China, Capitalist China: Social Tension and Political Adaptation Under Economic Globalization* (New York: Routledge, 2009).

Change in China's military is treated in David Shambaugh and Richard H. Yang (eds) *China's Military in Transition* (Oxford: Oxford University Press, 1997).

An examination of the legal system is offered in Stanley B. Lubman *Bird in a Cage: Legal Reform after Mao* (Stanford, CA: Stanford University Press, 1999) and Jerome Cohen's now classic study *The Criminal Process in the People's Republic of China 1949–1963: An Introduction* (Cambridge: Cambridge University Press, 1968). A historical overview with a well-researched section on major revisions to the legal system in the reform era is provided by Klaus Muhlhahn *Criminal Justice in China* (Cambridge, MA: Harvard University Press, 2009).

Interest in China's use of the internet and new electronic media may be satisfied by reading studies such as Xiaoling Zhang and Yongnian Zheng (eds) *China's Information and Communications Technology Revolution* (New York: Routledge, 2009) and Haiqing Yu *Media and Cultural Transformation in China* (New York: Routledge, 2009). Among studies dealing with China's new consumer culture is Jing Wang *Brand New China: Advertising, Media, and Commercial Culture* (Cambridge, MA: Harvard University Press, 2008).

China's many pressing environmental issues are of international concern. For a discussion of many of the major issues, see Michael B. McElroy, Christopher P. Nielsen and Peter Lyndon (eds) *Energizing China:*

Reconciling Environmental Protection and Economic Growth (Cambridge, MA: Harvard University Press, 1998). Regarding the new dam on the Yangzi River in western China, see the critical book by Chinese writer Dai Qing *Yangtze! Yangtze!* (Toronto, ON: Probe International, 1994). On water pollution in particular, see Elizabeth Economy's excellent study *The River Runs Black: The Environmental Challenge to China's Future* (Ithaca, NY: Cornell University Press, 2004).

Literature on Hong Kong and Taiwan offers the opportunity to assess changes in China in comparison with Chinese areas with very different political and economic histories. On Taiwan, interesting studies of the past and contemporary issues include A-Chin Hsiao *Contemporary Taiwanese Cultural Nationalism* (London: Routledge, 2000); Murray Rubenstein (ed) *The Other Taiwan: 1945 to the Present* (Armonk, NY: M.E. Sharpe, 1994); and Robert M. Marsh *The Great Transformation: Social Change in Taipei, Taiwan, Since the 1960s* (Armonk, NY: M.E. Sharpe, 1996). Hong Kong's return to the PRC was the focus of various studies, among them the essays in Ming K. Chan (ed) *Precarious Balance: Hong Kong between China and Britain, 1982–1992* (Armonk, NY: M.E. Sharpe, 1994). For a discussion of the impact of Chinese sovereignty, see the articles in Gungwu Wang and John Wong (eds) *Hong Kong in China: The Challenges of Transition* (Singapore: Times Academic Press, 1999).

References

Becker, Jasper (1996) *Hungry Ghosts: China's Secret Famine*, London: John Murray.

Chang, Leslie (2008) *Factory Girls: From Village to City in a Changing China*, New York: Random House.

Cheek, Timothy (2006) *Living with Reform: China Since 1989*, London: Zed Books.

Dickson, Bruce J. (2004) 'Dilemmas of Party Adaptation: The CCP's Strategies for Survival', in Peter Hays Gries and Stanley Rosen (eds) *State and Society in 21st Century China: Crisis, Contention, and Legitimation*, New York: Routledge Curzon.

Economy, Elizabeth (2004) *The River Runs Black: The Environmental Challenge to China's Future*, Ithaca, NY: Cornell University Press.

Fang Lizhi (1991) *Bringing Down the Great Wall: Writings on Science, Culture and Democracy in China*, translated by James H. Williams, New York: Knopf.

Gao Yuan (1987) *Born Red: A Chronicle of the Cultural Revolution*, Stanford, CA: Stanford University Press.

Gilley, Bruce (1999) 'Jiang Zemin: On the Right side of History?', *Current History*, September, pp. 249–53.

Gladney, Dru C. (1998) *Ethnic Identity in China*, New York: Harcourt Brace & Company, pp. 12–13.

Goldman, Merle and MacFarquhar, Roderick (eds) (1999) *The Paradox of China's Post-Mao Reforms*, Cambridge, MA: Harvard University Press.

Goldstein, Melvyn C. (1997) *The Snow Lion and the Dragon: China, Tibet, and the Dalai Lama*, Berkeley, CA: University of California Press.

Greenhalgh, Susan (1994) 'Conrolling Births and Bodies in Village China', *American Ethnologist*, 21 (February), pp. 3–30.

Jacka, Tamara (1997) *Women's Work in Rural China*, Cambridge: Cambridge University Press.

Jiang Yurong and Ashley, David (2000) *Mao's Children in the New China: Voices from the Red Guard Generation*, New York: Routledge.

Lee, Ching Kwan (1998) *Gender and the South China Miracle: Two Worlds of Factory Women*, Berkeley, CA: University of California Press.

Li, Cheng (2001) *China's Leaders: The New Generation*, Boulder, CO: Rowman & Littlefield

Liang Heng and Shapiro, Judith (1983) *Son of the Revolution*, New York: Vintage Books.

Lollar, Xi Li (2009) 'The Impact of Government Corruption and Monopolized Industries on Poverty and Income Disparity in Urban China', *Asian Politics and Policy*, 1, 5 (July/September 2009), pp. 526–42.

Ma Bo (1996) *Blood Red Sunset: A Memoir of the Chinese Cultural Revolution*, translated by Howard Goldblatt, New York: Penguin Books.

MacFarquhar, Roderick (ed) (1997) *The Politics of China: The Eras of Mao and Deng*, New York: Cambridge University Press.

Mackerras, Colin (1998) *China in Transformation 1900–1949*, New York and London: Longman.

Meisner, Maurice (1999) 'China's Communist Revolution: A Half-century Perspective', *Current History*, 98, 629 (September), pp. 243–8.

Muhlhahn, Klaus (2009) *Criminal Justice in China*, Cambridge: Harvard University Press.

Parris, Kristen (1999) 'The Rise of Private Business Interests', in Merle Goldman and Roderick MacFarquhar (eds) *The Paradox of China's Post-Mao Reforms*, Cambridge, MA: Harvard University Press, pp. 262–82.

Pearson, Margaret M. (1997) *China's New Business Elite: The Political Consequences of Reform*, Berkeley, CA: University of California Press.

Selden, Mark (ed) (1979) *The People's Republic of China: A Documentary History of Revolutionary Change*, New York: Monthly Press Review, pp. 187–93.

Seymour, James (1999) 'Human Rights, Repression, and "Stability"', *Current History*, 98, 629 (September), pp. 281–5.

Short, Philip (1999) *Mao: A Life*, New York: Henry Holt and Co.

Spence, Jonathan (1999) *Mao Zedong*, New York: Penguin.

Terrill, Ross (1993) *Mao: A Biography*, New York: Simon and Schuster (first published in 1980).

Uhalley, Stephen Jr (1988) *A History of the Chinese Communist Party*, Stanford, CA: Stanford University Press.

Wright, Teresa (2004) 'Contesting State Legitimacy in the 1990s: The China Democracy Party and the China Labor Bulletin', in Peter Hays Gries and Stanley Rosen (eds) *State and Society in 21st Century China*, New York: Routledge Curzon.

Yang, W., Lu, J., Jia, W. *et al.* (2010) 'Prevalence of Diabetes among Men and Women in China', *New England Journal of Medicine*, 362, pp. 1090–101.

Yue Daiyun, with Carolyn Wakeman (1985) *To the Storm: The Odyssey of a Chinese Woman Revolutionary*, Berkeley, CA: University of California Press.

Zheng, Tiantian (2009) *Red Lights: The Lives of Sex Workers in Postsocialist China*, Minneapolis, MN: University of Minnesota Press.

Index